NO ONE SAID IT WOULD BE EASY

A YOUTHFUL FOLLY ACROSS THE AMERICAS ON OLD BIKES

DES MOLLOY

Kahuku
Publishing Collective

Publishing Collective

No One Said it Would Be Easy
A youthful folly across The Americas on old bikes

© **Des Molloy 2019**

Text design by The Design Dept.
Cover design by The Design Dept.
www.thedesigndept.com.au

Editing by Diarmuid Brazendale

First published in 2019 by
Kahuku Publishing
PO Box 149 Takaka
Tasman 7142, New Zealand
www.kahukupublishing.com

All rights reserved.
This book or any portion thereof may not be reproduced or used in any manner whatsoever without the express written permission of the author except for the use of brief quotations in a book review. All inquiries should be made to the author.

ISBN: 978-1-7386002-3-6

To my crew, the best that could be imagined for our adventure of a lifetime and a special big thanks to Steph (Best Pillion in the World) for the 40+ years that have followed

'The older we get, the better we were', is an oft-repeated refrain muttered by rheumy-eyed old duffers, amber ale in hand, as they drag back wondrous memories from their youth ... and accordingly pontificate dully. However, in the case of this account of a youthful adventure of some substance, it must be admitted that we were naïve, inept and blunderingly lucky. There is not a lot to glorify or revere in awe. Commenting on my proposed plans to write the book of the saga, fellow participant Roly said: "We must have been delusional!"

It is true that you can't put old (wise?) heads on young shoulders and in many ways that is a good thing. Don't, shouldn't, and can't, were not words that were ever associated with our youthful aspirations, which may be why they became a reality. My family assert that I suffer from 'terminal optimism' and I happily wear that mantle ... it served me quite well on the rugby field as a captain of semi-social sides and has seen me through numerous exploits since.

Time does dull our memories and when mixed with decades of dreams, it is no surprise that recollections can be inaccurate. It is also often said that the truth shouldn't get in the way of a good story. I hope that I haven't strayed too far from the reality of our ride. Although the diary of the trip has been lost in the mayhem of 10 or more house-shifts, a contemporary account was serialised in the Panther Owners' Club magazine *Sloper*. Also to hand are the letters written home at the time, and along with a collective sharing of memories by the 'crew', the full tale will be told, best as I can. The Sloper pieces are at times exciting but by necessity, they were a once-over-lightly scribble, dispatched every month from the road. Our emotions are rarely exposed and often kept completely out of the account.

Over the years we have shared our anecdotes with friends and family, we've given slide shows and Powerpoint presentations showing the trials and tribulations to like-minded groups. It is now finally time to 'spill my guts' to the world and tell the whole tale for posterity ... something I hope our descendants will read with interest.

It may be 40 years ago but in many instances, the memories are still graphically vivid and I only hope I can give them a suitable portrayal and 'life'.

Trust in dreams, for in them is hidden the gate to eternity.

KHALIL GIBRAN (1883-1931)

CONTENTS

Gestation 2

Tilbury Plus 24

Mexico 42

Belize and Guatemala 60

El Salvador, Honduras, Nicaragua, Costa Rica, Panama 74

Panama 88

Panama to Peru 104

Puerto Pizzaro to Lima 122

Lima to Cusco 138

Machu Picchu to La Paz 158

La Paz to Asunción 176

Asunción to Buenos Aires 202

Operation Rescue 218

The Cast 229

The world is a book and those who do not travel read only one page
ST. AUGUSTINE (354-430)

CHAPTER 1

GESTATION

I knew I had only about two or three k's to go but I couldn't make it up a small hill. I was crying from frustration and exhaustion and from the silence behind me I knew I was alone. The others were probably bogged and unable to follow me. Twice Penelope made a chuffing noise and died on me with no compression, but both times she started on cooling down a little. I was parched and scarcely able to breathe but I pushed and shoved and swore, screamed, yelled and cried and somehow I got Penelope up that bloody hill and struggled on until I could see the brick outpost over a sand dune. In the last 20 yards I bogged down again, and so leaving Penelope upright in the sand I staggered in, to the amazement of the soldiers. I beg for water. The soldiers helped me to get Penelope and then I set out on foot to look for the others. While walking along I felt proud of Penelope because despite everything she got me to safety. Panthers rule, Ok!

So I wrote in 1977 and the memory stays with me, like something from a French Foreign Legion movie … Penelope, my trusty old Panther motorcycle abandoned, sunk to her rear axle in a picture-perfect, tawny sand dune, overlooked by a harsh blue sky. And yes, like a Hollywood character, complete with torn clothes, I did stagger down the dune and in to Fortin Garay, an army outpost in the Chaco Desert of Paraguay. A grimy, sweat-ingrained face with long red hair and a large dust-matted auburn beard formed my presenting visage. Possibly I looked a little scary, certainly a little unusual. It was the end of the day and the troops were all assembled into a square formation. The Major was about to review and presumably dismiss. I knew I was intruding into a performance of importance, even if it was one of routine … a bit like walking onto the stage of an opera at The Royal Albert and asking for directions or some-such. I could see the soldiers all trying to look without looking, all smartly at attention, heads straight but eyes swivelling. Through the soft sand I struggled, stumbling a little, taking the decision that the man at the front was 'my man'.

"Aqua, por favor!"

The Major hesitated, then without smiling, snaps his fingers, and a minion trots off accordingly, returning with a glass of water. This disappears down my gullet almost instantly, not slaking my thirst in the slightest.

"Mas, por favor!"

Seven times this little interplay was repeated before I was no longer parched and aching for fluids.

… but this is mid-August 1977 and we had left London on Nov 27th 1976, a thousand memories back.

Not everyone travels, or has a youthful OE (Overseas Experience) … but it can be argued that those with any spark in their persona do. It is for many Antipodeans, a right-of-passage, a throwing-off of family-imposed conventions and influences. It usually also corresponds with the end of tertiary education or the attaining of trade qualifications. It was like being set free. For nearly 20 years there had been an over-arching purpose to your life. You went to kindy, school and then polytech or university and constantly a figure of authority told you things. Finally, you were deemed to know enough to be let loose on life. Of course, for some, there would be no escape, but simply a seamless transition into marriage, home-ownership, indebtedness, parenthood etc. It is a wonderful generalisation but dullards seldom travel and travellers are seldom dullards. To the contrary, they are often interesting, inquisitive, full-of-life figures in the full bloom of youthful vigour … in their prime, physically and mentally.

My OE (with two mates) started with a wonderful 6 weeks aboard the SS Australis with 2,250 other young escapees. From New Year's Eve 1971, my real life as an adult began, free to live, learn and love … I was least accomplished at the last.

By 1975 a pattern had established itself — play rugby in London during the winters and travel the summers. We were footloose and fancy-free, bound by no constraints or parameters other than financial ones. In 1972, the ubiquitous VW Combi had taken five of us through Central Europe's communist-bloc to the Black Sea, down to Istanbul and home up the old Yugoslavian coast. In 1973/74, *Ernie the*

ES2 Norton had taken flatmate Anne and me from London to Norway (to near the Arctic Circle) and onwards to the Persian Gulf via more of the communist-bloc in a five-month saga of much drama and adventure. 1975 had incorporated a Russian Ural sidecar jaunt with my mate Brown Dog down to Spain to participate in the Running of the Bulls in Pamplona, as well as a pilgrimage to the Isle of Man for the annual Tourist Trophy motorcycle races.

So what was I planning for 1976? My ride on *Ernie* had reaffirmed my attraction to simple, single-cylinder old British motorcycles. I'd loved my 1957 500cc Norton … but weren't there bigger singles? I'd heard of but never laid eyes on the obscure, long-stroke 650cc Panther motorcycles from Yorkshire. As with a lot of things in life, a whimsical dream sometimes slowly moves along from the "I'd like …" over a period of time to "I must have!" And so it was that by mid-1975 I had the makings of a 1961 Panther Model 120, complete with a factory sidecar chassis. An outsider would have been a little bemused at my fleet of vehicles, seeing as I was not really in permanent accommodation, had no storage facility, garage or workshop. I had an old London Taxi, the Ural and sidecar that I used on a daily basis, a 1937 BSA Empire Star which I had thought I could go vintage racing on, and now I was the owner of a collection of Panther bits. Dreams are free and can give a huge amount of joy even if nothing eventuates. Already I could feel the evocative thumping of the 106mm long-stroke Panther transporting me along in exotic, faraway locales, the sun shining and a huge smile on my face.

Say it quickly, and it never seems too hard or unachievable. What about a ride from New York to Rio? I must admit that my default reaction to a suggestion like that (even if it is my own) is always "that's sounds great … it'll be awesome!" It is possibly a small character flaw that I don't ever temper the thought with some balancing imagery, maybe some rain and cold, deprivation and misery? Gradually that wee burr under the saddle became something that had to be addressed. All I needed to do, was sell the dream to people I liked and wanted on the ride … competent mates, enjoyable and resilient. This often needs a bit of planning. You don't just go off blurting "Do you want to come to South America on a motorbike?" over the first pint. Of course candidates have to also have their shackles pretty loose and ready to be shaken free. They had to appear to like me and not be too dominating or domineering, they also had to be prepared to waste a significant amount of money doing this. How much? Dunno, never did a budget, that would probably have sunk the ship before it was even launched.

Lawrie in some ways is the archetypal Aussie — tall, broad and bronzed. I've always described Lawrie as a chameleon because of his amazing ability to adapt to his surroundings. He would have been a great undercover cop. If a situation called for a gentle caring soul, Lawrie would be the most earnest thoughtful person that could be imagined. He was new age before new age was even thought of. If a boorish yobbo was needed, his depravity would be of paramount substance. Being at the opera with the chinless-wonders of English society was as much Lawrie's environment as a rugby club trip with semi-neanderthal drunks. Largely self-educated, his adaptability was awesome to watch. He is an honest and fun-to-be-with companion who must count hundreds as close friends. Lawrie makes friends as easily and often as most people breathe.

Lawrie had been travelling for six or more years by this stage and seemed like an ideal candidate for position in the team. I believe I'd spent some quality time with him in the bars of Pamplona but neither of us could recall this with any clarity. He was a good loyal man in my rugby team, always supportive, always fun and amusing in a self-deprecating way. Never ridden a motorbike … well neither had I before I rode one. There is always the first time for everything.

I didn't want a big 'gang' but thought maybe two or three others along would make for group fun without the difficulties of large numbers. The earlier ride on Ernie with Anne had often been just a little too solitary. We'd had some amazing times but also squabbled a lot without any others along to diffuse tensions and minor irritations.

Around this time an American from my rugby team had asked "What are you doing next summer?" and when told, he'd said "Hell, I'd be keen!" I didn't know him very well outside of our weekend interactions but he met my criteria … so we had a crew. This meant three bikes and it didn't take long for me to decide that Bessie, the old BSA could be diverted away from a dream of vintage racing, into a reliable old road-warrior ready for the hard yards of a trans-continental adventure. Samantha, the 1961 Panther was soon joined by Penelope, a sibling from the same Cleckheaton factory but of 1965 vintage – one of the last made. It was all falling into place. There was a dream, there were three keen riders and three not-so-suitable bikes.

Again say it quickly and it isn't hard … just a bit of prep, and we'll be good to go! Simplicity is key … old bikes with uncomplicated low-compression engines, running the same magnetos, and all with same-size inter-changeable tyres. Such a great formula - couldn't possibly go wrong.

Well it would help if there was stability in the lives of the intended crew and a nice warm workshop to prepare the bikes in. Lawrie lived completely the other side of town and had no mechanical skills. I didn't even know where the American lived or what he did ... and can no longer recall his name. A lot of the friends from our early London days had now wandered off home and as each flat was disestablished, a new place would need to be found. For a while I was a 'guest' of 603 High Rd, Leyton, a flat originally of six Kiwi and Aussie teachers. This had been an all-girl flat but at different times quite a few of us of the wrong-gender had bunked down in the lounge or temporarily taken over a bed while someone was away. During these years there were always openings in flats because often occupants were temporarily 'going off to do Scandi' or 'driving across America' or having a 'Top-deck tour of Morocco', 'debauching at the wine festival in Fucina', etc. Some would even go off to Aussie for a couple of months of outback work to top-up the coffers, thus enabling more travel. Our lives were ones of low-level hedonism, with work always taking a back-step. Careers were not advanced, there was too much living to do.

While at 603 the bikes had an unpowered, unlit, falling-down shed to live in. The sidecar frame was randomly deposited in the next-door backyard that was shared. Vandals subsequently set fire to the yard area and later a rag-and-bone man made a raid and removed everything. It is only decades later that I can mourn the loss as at the time it solved a problem. Preparation for the big trip was glacial in its pace.

For the summer of 1975 I'd had a construction company and had won a contract to replace a district heating scheme in a housing estate. This involved getting a great suntan, a lot of workers and heaps of fun, but towards the end, when I had my hand out for legitimate contract extras, the money flow slowed to a trickle and delaying tactics from the client were very obvious. I seemed powerless to get my due. The timing of this crisis was corresponding with the disestablishment of 603. I needed to move and for the first time in 4 years there wasn't an obvious place to relocate to. After warning the client several times, I resorted to direct action and removed everything from site and went AWOL. I took an advertised room in West Hendon which I called The Box. It was tiny. I could almost touch the walls on either side with my finger-tips, and to put the light off I just swished away with my squash racket till I got the switch. For the first time I was not in an Antipodean enclave. It was just about OK and despite my reservations regarding a 30s+ male flat-mate being an avid *Come Dancing* fan, and a reclusive ascetic woman of similar age being an author of Mills and Boon 'Penny-dreadfuls', I got by and Lawrie engaged me in a work scam he had inherited.

We worked … or rather attended a double-glazing company of some substance. We were contractors and worked under the direct control of the accountant, so the woman who looked after all the clerical workers in accounts knew nothing of what we did, other than that it was an important analysis project of some sort. All day we copied out figures and made summaries of sales. Just occasionally we would gather up our findings and take the ream of paper into the accountant and he would ceremonially put it through the shredder and tell us to start again. The work was deemed so important that we also needed to work over-time. Often we would surreptitiously follow the last of the bosses out the door and be only one gear-change behind him going up the road. This scam had been passed on from hand to hand for some years, Lawrie getting it from some South Africans a year or so earlier. Each week we'd submit our invoices and accordingly get paid. During the day Lawrie often slipped in toll calls to home in Australia or to the US where he was planning to relocate to prior to our ride. The sweet old dear who looked after the office never seemed to suspect a thing.

Around this time, I got news that my mum and dad were going to visit the UK and some of Europe. There was also the exciting possibility that my brother Roly was thinking of coming for a look around with a couple of mates. Roly is less than two years younger than me and had served his time as a motor mechanic. I was seen as the academic and he was the tradesman … a good mix. We'd shared a love of old motorbikes and cars from our schooldays. The kitchen floor at home often was a depository for large work-in-progress lumps of old Brit Iron. We'd always been close even though I was seen at times as a Svengali figure with undue influence, likely to sweep him along on a path that might not be ideal for either of us. The pending visits were great news and I told Roly to definitely come and to bring his tools. Presumptuously, I also hit him with the thought that he'd be able to work on the three bikes I was planning to go off adventuring on. Bessie had a clear lineage to the post-war BSA models he was very familiar with and I was sure he would be keen as mustard to get into the Panthers, being as they were exotic and totally unknown to him.

Life is not always linear, and on reflection, it is often the zig-zags that are the most interesting. I hadn't really been living in The Box for all that long when I got a ring from one of the girls from another big well-known Anzac flat — 46 Alexandra Grove, North Finchley. A couple of my rugby team (and work crew) lived there, on and off. I'd partied there, so knew who Little Steph was when she introduced herself. She was the one that wasn't Big Steph. Big Steph was a tall, rubenesque red-head who another of my rugby team Kiwis quietly lusted after. It seemed that Big Steph was going home and there was going to be a vacancy in the flat ... was I interested?

My heart pounded, I didn't want to appear too keen ... but man oh man, this could be an escape from the solitary purgatory that was The Box. I desperately missed the shared meals and the group-fun I was used to as part of London's itinerant young colonials ... the vibrancy, the feeling of belonging! I expressed some reservation, noting that I had to extricate myself from the current situation, but I could be interested. Of course once off the phone I fist-pumped and did a little jig.

And the rest as they say is history. During my notice period I popped around with a friend one week-night for a reconnaissance visit. The flat was a familiar happy throng, some folk I knew well, others not so well. I recall as we left and were getting into the car my mate saying "That Little Steph's got a nice arse!" This was not something I would have articulated aloud ... well not before five or six pints of beer ... but he was so accurately observant, even if a little boorish. The raven-haired Little Steph was petite and full of energy. She was also gregarious and thoughtfully welcoming.

46 Alexandra Grove was a two storey semi-detached villa set back a little from the road with off-street parking and a driveway leading to a small garage and a substantial backyard. I was able to relocate the black cab and the motorbikes. The Ural and sidecar was stowed at the rugby club in Hounslow. Alexandra Grove was also only a bicycle ride distance to the double-glazing work ... so an old treadlie was bought and put into action.

It wasn't long before I was completely in thrall of Little Steph, who was now just Steph with the departure of her bigger namesake. She worked as an agency nurse and in her off-hours she barmaided at *The Cricketers*, the local tavern. It was clear that she was a popular part of the pub's community. She'd sweep in near closing-time after a nursing shift and greet most of the clientele by name before asking all with half-empty glasses what their tipple was. I couldn't see how she would ever get a return from this but was impressed by her selfless generosity. I learned later that she also topped up the flat's pantry when it ran low between the flatters' pay-in periods. She preferred food on the shelves to the groans of the flatmates when asked for more money. Small-breasted and liberated, Steph never saw the need to own a bra and in the wonderful and long 'Summer of 76', was in my eyes as exhilaratingly stunning as anything on the big or little screen. A visual treat in flimsy summer clothes, she was high on life and it was a pleasure to be in her realm, especially as she was beginning to demonstrate a fondness towards me.

It could never be said that I was a lothario in my youth. Apart from being a bit shy around young women, my Catholic upbringing had left me overly inhibited. I was often worried about getting out of a relationship, before I had even got in. The Exit Strategy always concerned me. Those bloody priests had indoctrinated us with a mantra of 'copulation is for making new life' and of course the act was not to happen outside of the sanctity of marriage … and marriage was forever. Over-arching this was the knowledge that straying from the true path and the many doctrines and dogma of Rome would lead to hellfire and damnation. The only redeeming part of the equation was the church having confessionals where, upon giving a salacious account of your failings, the slate would be wiped clean and both you and the priest would walk forth with a smile on your face, free to start over. So casual sex was not something I had achieved expert status in … I was still a stumbling amateur, willing to learn though.

One Friday night I awoke to Steph, *sans vêtement*, slipping in beside me in my narrow single bed. 'The Pope says it is OK' she whispered. This made the Summer of 76 even more wonderful. Thenceforth, during the day I walked three foot off the ground, and in the night embraced liberating mores. Often we all slept outside in the backyard under the stars, the evenings being so warm. Mum and dad's visit came and went, Steph charming them with her honest friendship. Roly came … and stayed, taking work in a local garage. Progress on the bikes began to be real. The glacier was on the move.

Pre-season rugby gatherings brought the realisation that I had lost my American. Of course this was in the days long before cell phones or the internet. With no way of finding him again, I needed a replacement, as we were now preparing three bikes. The obvious choice was Roly. The perfect wing-man, he just needed convincing that a gentle introduction into foreign travel was not necessary after all. I recall assuring

Steph and my ex-London taxi.

him that the food would always be great ... and edible, the weather would be benign, the adventure wonderful. A letter home from him to The Olds thanking them for a monetary gift (It was late Sep 1976 ... birthday time) advises them that it has enabled him to commit to going with me. He included the comment "I think I know what you will think of that !"

Things were falling into place, Lawrie had gone off to Terre Haute, Indiana and hopefully was earning lots of money. There was not really much of a plan, no real itinerary ... too restrictive. We would wander as we felt fit. There was no end date, no return point. We would work that out later ... you never know, we might find work. Quite clearly Steph and I could see a future together and whilst she would love to be a part with the adventure she was broke. Even taking a third job as a car cleaner wasn't filling her coffers quickly enough but we were loving the now. I got mail from Anne who'd shared the earlier moto adventure out to Iran. She was teaching Indians in Northern Saskatchewan but wanted in. She said she would meet us in Mexico City in her VW Combi, now repaired after an exploit in which she had managed to let it run backwards into a lake. She is a tough and intrepid Aussie who would be a good addition to the gang. She'd just ridden the freight trains of Canada for 1,100 kms, so clearly her sense of adventure had not lessened in the couple of years since I had seen her.

To get around, Roly bought a 1956 500cc BSA B33 from a Kiwi who was going home. Russell was an interesting, likeable character who had contacts in the motorcycle world and he sourced some cheap tyres for us. I had worked out that we should start off with road tyres and only switch to the chunky Trials Universals when we got to the unsealed roads of South America. Each bike would carry two spare tyres. Probably on some spectrum, Russell could remember all the number plates of every vehicle he'd had. Becoming friends, we shared a lot of tales as motorcyclists do … but he topped everything we could throw in the pot with one from earlier in the year. His daily ride was a snorting Norton Atlas, almost as powerful a bike as existed at the time. He'd had an occasion to park the bike near a biscuit factory and when he returned to the bike he found all the factory girls lined up at the bus stop opposite. As young men do … he strutted over to his steed, went through the pre-starting rituals, then fired her up with a mighty lunge. A 750cc four-stroke, tuned, twin-cylinder motor truly stirs the soul and Russell could imagine the collective hearts all a-flutter at his masculinity and derring-do. Spotting a gap in the traffic he dropped the clutch to smoke away in great style. The panache that he hoped would impress, was somewhat negated by the act of forgetting to remove the large chain from through his back wheel to the neighbouring lampost. The result was spectacular with all the spokes being torn from the hub and the bike collapsing to the ground in a shower of sparks. He reckoned the guffawing could be heard for miles and his humiliation rendered him speechless and lolly-pink with embarrassment.

I chuckle when recalling our lack of professionalism and the almost third-world conditions that were available to us for our bike preparation. Not always allowed to work inside the flat, and mainly having to work at night it meant adapting to what was available. The London Taxi had a large passenger area interior with two fold-down seats facing the rear where the main full-width bench seat was. Rebuilding Bessie's engine was done in the back of the taxi, on the street outside No 46 with the inside light on, occasionally augmented by the use of torches. We sat on the fold-down seats with the engine on the sturdy back seat. To our surprise, when easing the barrel off the piston, a bronze locating-button fell from the assembly, narrowly missing going into the gaping crankcase opening. This was not something we had encountered before. Instead of having circlips holding the gudgeon pin in place, pre-war BSAs had a pair of bronze buttons. This was a very simple and fail-safe solution. Ultimately Bessie's engine was fully fettled and re-inserted into the frame.

Bessie was the first bike adjudged ready for action and an autumn sortie into the New Forest for an overnight camp was our first significant jaunt. Steph and I were on Bessie and Roly on his B33. Although designated as an M23, Bessie was the first of what, post-war became the B series of the Birmingham factory's line-up, lasting

Penelope slowly growing on the front path of 46 Alexandra Grove.

GESTATION

Roly in action in the al fresco workshop in front of the flat.

right through to 1963. The two BSAs looked magnificent together, with their lineage so clearly displayed, they looked like a mother and daughter on an outing. I am not quite sure why we didn't consider the B33 for the big adventure being as she was newer, had a more developed engine and far superior suspension … but we didn't.

The New Forest episode sits in family folklore as 'what might have been'. It started well enough with a pretty mundane ride in the sun from North London to Southampton and beyond. It started to unravel when we attempted to check into a camp in the forest. I'd experienced the oddities of British campsites on a previous south coast adventure in the black cab, with another iteration of mates. We'd been turned away from numerous camps because we didn't have children. "We're a family camp" was the oft-repeated refrain. When finally a paddock for the infertile was found, a quiet night followed with the proprietor telling us she'd never, ever had any trouble and laughed at the main-stream paranoia of the resort areas.

This time, an even more bizarre scenario played out.

"Have you got your own toilet?"

We looked around in mock amazement, patting the meagre luggage whilst uttering suitable inanities.

"Oh, we seem to have forgotten it!"

"We don't need to go at the moment, thanks."

"I thought you were going to pack it!"

However, like their coastal counterparts they had decided on a demographic deemed suitable for their establishment and toilet-less motorcyclists weren't on the list. They were inflexible and not even pleading constipation was going to change their mind.

This meant free-camping in the forest itself, and that could have been ok. *All good things must come to an end* is a pretty obvious homily. It is often attributed to Chaucer but understood by all of us. Some prepare for it better than others. The 'Summer of 76' had set records and seemed to go on forever. However, lurking in the greenery of the New Forest was the trigger for change. The forces of yin and yang came into play immediately we had found a suitably remote and discreet place to establish a camp ... although camping seems to allude to some sort of temporary shelter, like a tent. For some reason we either didn't have one, or my optimism and confidence in the wonderful weather of the time persuaded the others that under the stars would be great. So it rained and it rained. The trees seemed pretty dense and initially we thought they might give us shelter but once the foliage got saturated, so did we. Not wise enough to cut and run, we toughed it out lying under the trees, all but floating away in the deluge. Steph still asserts that she nearly drowned. The night seemed endless. As a testament to resilience, this was right up there with anything I had been through. We became half-submerged islands in a lake of ground-water. The saving grace was that it wasn't cold. It stopped raining in the morning but being under the sodden tree canopy it continued to fall on us for quite some time before we wised up.

Quite clearly we survived to ineptly live many other days, but Steph often proclaims that it was a close-run thing. She only just gave me the benefit of the doubt that this was a one-off, and life with me wouldn't be a series of near-disasters and escapades of dubious viability. The wonders of youthful love and lust saved the day, and preparations continued.

As well as the obvious physical bike preparation to be done, there were paperwork hoops to be jumped through. The dream of riding a motorbike across the world is often scuttled at the first hurdle ... the right to do it. Because each country has their own regime of import duties, taxes, levies etc., it means that the value of the said vehicle will vary from country to country. Unchecked, sharp entrepreneurs would soon work out where a given model was cheap and take it to one where it was expensive and sell. To control this, most of the world's nations require you to have a document that ensures you keep on going. This is a Carnet de Passages en Douane, a document that is signed when you enter a country and signed when you leave. The muscle behind making you comply with this is quite simple ... you are required to lodge a significant bond which you don't get back until you return to where you set off from. Some countries require this bond to be as high as twice the new value of the vehicle, so when planning a trip, you need to find out the highest bond required and get an appropriate Carnet. With none of our bikes still being in production, our bacon was saved ... there was no 'new value'. This meant we were able to value the bikes ourselves and as you can imagine we valued 'the worthless old shitters' pretty low and as an added bonus found an insurance company to lodge the money, with us just paying a premium. Travellers we met on the road had either lodged huge cash bonds or in one case the parents had a significant mortgage taken over their house.

The next hurdle ... visas. Of course being 'Working-Joes' meant that getting our paperwork in place was a laborious chore necessitating taking time off and intermittently dashing into the madness of Central London. Getting the US Visa proved to be a real hurdle. If travelling from NZ, it is quite normal for you to pass through the US and as you might be going to do the same on the way home, the Embassy in Wellington typically issues you a multiple-entry visa for five years. The US Embassy in Grosvenor Square has no such largesse. The first visit was a complete fizzer as the queue stretched for several blocks and we didn't reach the front in the allotted time. It was an interesting process and once inside the actual building you could observe the 'culling process'. A row of front people reviewed your application and it seemed rejected it as a default position. It looked like only about one in ten were being ushered off to other small interview rooms. Our second visit at least got us to the rejection stage. For the third visit, we prepared quite thoroughly ... we thought. We pooled as much money as we could find from friends and got bank statements showing fat balances. We also worked our way through several of the Central American countries' embassies, getting visas.

So back into battle. We arrived, not quite in the middle of the night, but certainly at an hour when we should have still been somnolently dreaming of the wonderful ride to come. Getting to the front and trying not to look guilty of anything, we presented our applications along with evidence of funds to support ourselves.

"Why do you want to go to the US?"

"Well, we don't want to go to the US as such, we just need a transit visa to pass through!"

"Why should I believe that?"

"Because we have all these visas showing we are going to travel through these subsequent countries."

"But since 1949 tens of millions of people have entered on transit visas, then stayed illegally. I see no reason to issue you one"

Struggling to keep my cool and not tell the woman I didn't care about her dumb country, I tried again to explain about our motorbike adventure and how we were aiming to ride all the way to Rio. Fortunately, the official in the next booth overheard and pricked up his ears.

"Are you guys really going to try and ride all the way to Brazil from New York?"

Thankfully we had struck a fellow motorcyclist and in no time we were sharing stories and adventures, as is always the way with the two-wheeled brotherhood. The hefty thud of the US Visa being stamped into our passports was a welcoming end to a process that had been fraught and which had almost got us to our 'last resort'. Word on the street was that the US Embassy in Edinburgh was an easier hurdle. Already we had been working on a back-story to cover the lack of local address … phew, not needed.

Bessie was ridden to Liverpool and on 6th Oct dispatched to New Orleans as deck cargo. Things were now moving along at a frantic pace. Roly and I, along with Penelope and Samantha were booked to sail from Tilbury Docks to New York on 17th Oct. Along with these exciting developments it was a wonderful time to be young and in love. Even with Steph working at her three jobs and Roly and I putting in the hours to get the two old Panthers ready, there was still time for the joys of the besotted. There was no need to fret about an exit strategy, I knew I was in for the long-haul. The clarity was wonderful. We ventured out when we could and even managed to take in Leonard Cohen's last concert of a European tour. This was the one where after many encores, he came back out onto the stage and said "What the fuck … I've got nowhere to go! Let's party!" And so he did, telling us stories and performing with his backing singers until 1.00am. Luckily we had our own transport because in those days the last tube went before midnight and the night buses were pretty limited. For those few hours, we were his mates.

We also got across to Chelsea one Saturday so I could look in a pet shop window at snakes. Like many Kiwis (NZ and Ireland are reportedly the only snake-free countries in the world) I reckoned I suffered from herpetophobia. Aussie Ann had cracked up at my over-reaction to a grass snake encounter in Yugoslavia a couple of years back. Even looking through the glass brought on a shudder. By now I had The South American Handbook, a brick-like tome which detailed everywhere relating to where we were going and what we should know. It was a serious guide aimed at travelers, not tourists … not like the Fodor publications of the time. I'd read the bit about snakes and how it is vital you catch the snake that has bitten you, or can identify it accurately. My new knowledge allowed me to pontificate to all at-large how snake venom kills you either by over-exciting your nervous system or by slowing it down till life is precarious … or not at all. If the wrong antidote is taken it will certainly be the end of you … you'll either over-excite to death or just fade away.

I'd also seen the display in a posh Rover dealership of the British Army's 1972 expedition led by Sir John Blashford-Snell, detailing how they had gone the whole length of the Pan American Highway, including getting across the Darien Gap between Panama and Columbia. They had rafts, ladders, ramps, winches and all sorts of paraphernalia. Their Darian Gap team consisted of more 60 army engineers and civilian scientists. It took them over 100 days to get the two Range Rovers through the 66-mile swamp. Until viewing this I must admit I didn't know much about the Darian Gap and was unaware that the Pan American Highway hadn't made it through. I'd read in the early 1970s that the US was sponsoring an effort to build a road through and that it should be finished by 1975. Oh well, we'll cross that (non) bridge when we come to it!

My Latin education finished when I was 16, but I knew that tempus was bloody fugiting and it was not looking like there would be much time for sea trials or shake-downs. Penelope was up and running but Samantha still needed work. One small episode unnecessarily delayed us and it probably was down to me helping. Roly is not the world's fastest mechanic but he is thorough and meticulous, not one to make mistakes. On the other hand, I am neither thorough nor meticulous … and also not a mechanic. At best I am ok at holding things and passing over spanners.

Samantha was finally adjudged ready for her maiden voyage. I slopped in fuel from a four-gallon tin I had and she was tickled … a near-technical term relating to evidencing that fuel has reached the right part of the carburetor … and she was kicked, and kicked, and kicked again. For an engine to run it needs only air, fuel and a spark. These do need to be in the right volumes at the right time … but that is what Roly was for. Our efforts were rewarded by silence, graveyard-like silence. There was no sign of life in the corpse. Too late at night to do anything more we both went to bed grumpy and disappointed.

Next evening, still no life could be coaxed from her, despite there appearing to be a nice fat, blue spark. In frustration, Samantha was pushed out into the road in front of No 46 and then launched down the hill. This was an exercise we'd done dozens of times at home with numerous recalcitrant bikes, but never with one that seemed to be throwing out great gobs of electricity. She chuffed quietly down the hill with the engine spinning over but with no reward what so ever. Optimistically we kept pushing and trying a variety of throttle openings and gears … until we were right at the bottom of the hill. Of course, this meant a laborious joint-effort to push her back up to home-base and once again we went to bed pretty grumpy and disappointed.

Fuel flow was checked, the magneto was checked, valve timing and ignition timing were both confirmed as being what the book said. We were flummoxed. Roly was confused as a single cylinder engine with a magneto is as simple as mechanical things get. No battery is needed, as a magnetic field is 'broken' by points opening and closing as the armature spins around creating a spark. Even I could understand that … but why wasn't she showing any signs of life? You can have instances of a spark being able to be evidenced when 'outside' but once under compression in the combustion chamber being insufficient to ignite the mixture. Surely not! Not with the big, fat blue spark we were getting, irrespective of spark plug.

It wasn't until most of the week had been wasted before Roly twigged that the fuel I had tipped in from my 'petrol' tin was in fact 'red diesel'. It came back to me. I'd acquired some 'not for public road use' red diesel from my building site the winter before as spare for the London taxi. Roly felt that he should have smelt it or noticed the oiliness of the diesel and I had been a pillock presuming that if it was in a petrol tin, it must be petrol.

The count-down was stressing us a little. It is wonderful to be able to revel in the 'only seven more sleeps till … ' when you are ready and waiting, but nerve-wracking when you are not sure if the quantum of work left to do, will fit in the time available. I was having to miss out on a few social outings now that the adventure was looming large, including a festival headlined by 10cc and The Rolling Stones. Steph attended and blamed the sun and tiredness for her not making it through to the end in an upright position.

Pommie Jim made wooden pannier boxes for us, just as he had for my '*Ernie the ES2*' ride a couple of years earlier. The pending departure and the final completion of the bikes were converging and it was looking like it was going to be a close-run race. Sadly, the nice B33 BSA was taken to the nearest tube station and left outside in the car park after removing the magneto as a spare for the trip.

After many years, the flat at 46 was going to be abandoned with no replacement tenants lined up by any of the residents. This meant quite a big clear up and in the absence of any knowledge of how to get stuff to the dump … (we didn't actually know where there was a dump!) … we came up with a cunning plan. Some of the girls from the past including Steph had co-owned a VW Beetle which now seemed surplus. Steph could have the London taxi. The other owners were gone but the VW hadn't, so we filled it with the detritus of many years of itinerant young lives. We then drove to a posh neighbouring suburb, looked for a smart street and parked it outside the flashest, pleased-and-proud house we could find. We then locked it and walked away. This gave us immature pleasure for many weeks, wondering how long it would take for the home-owners to mobilise the council to remove the eyesore that was our legacy.

Our leave-taking was programmed for Sunday afternoon following the final farewell party for the flat. This would have been ok if we were ready. We weren't and spent half the party night working on the bikes, still trying to sort out primary chains of the correct lengths and getting luggage sorted. Half-heartedly we partied too, trying to be part of something that truly was the 'end of an era'. These last few days had been full to the point of over-flowing and I was neglecting Steph a bit, but I also knew that the ship wouldn't wait, whereas I was confident our relationship was not something that would wither and die because of such a trifle.

A myriad of last-minute things were attended to on the Sunday morning when we finally arose. All around us, there was activity as the flat was abandoned, farewells flying everywhere. There would be a skeleton crew only there that night. Around lunchtime, we had our maiden voyages, fully laden. They were a nightmare, the bikes were almost unrideable, with the loads not being distributed well enough. Frantically changes were made and way too late we were off, for better or for worse, clinging to the notion that we would put it right on 'the other side'.

For a lot of years, my building jobs had been all over London including south of the river, whilst the flats I'd lived in had all been north of the Thames. Transiting from the south to the north often took me past an arrowed sign which said Tilbury Docks, so at least I knew where we needed to get to.

Thinking "Shit, this will be close!" we wobbled our way through the stop-start suburbs towards the docks. Down the High St, we crossed the North Circular and achingly slowly passed through East Finchley and Highgate, onto the Archway Road and into the old City of London and finally to the turn-off to Tilbury Docks. Almost majestically we swept around the curving exit to what I hoped would be the wharves and a relieved welcome from eager stevedores awaiting our belated arrival. The sight and sensation of that moment lives with me to this day. The road led onto The Embankment and under a bridge and there before us, was a large two-posted road sign proclaiming TILBURY 34 Miles. My heart sank as I knew this was down to me ... I was the local expert ... I knew where Tilbury was. Bugger, bugger, bugger! There was no option but to carry on, clinging to the hope that for some reason the departure was delayed.

In life, not everything goes your way all of the time ... and this was one of those times. My emotions included pending-humiliation. I knew what my robust rugby club mates would soon be articulating.

"What Plonkers, couldn't even get to the boat on time!"

"Typical half-arse Molloy!"

I knew that many of the young guys at the rugby club envied our laid-back, cruisy lifestyle. We'd invite some to come along on summer adventures, but they would always say that they couldn't because they had jobs. We'd always opine that they could get another one when they got back and the hesitation indicated what they would like to do, not aligning with what they would do. Our friendships, however, didn't mean that they didn't secretly hope that we would fall on our faces occasionally. I know they enjoyed the vitality the colonials brought to the previously staid 'old boy' world of London rugger. The Aussies, Kiwis and South Africans brought a different dynamic and we could always be relied upon to bring a coterie of stunning young women to social events.

But back to the now, our ride takes us out into the country and includes a minor breakdown when one of the bike's magneto points' securing screw loosened off, disrupting the spark. Roly recalls this break-down quite clearly and the pull-off area where we attended to the problem. There were two derelicts lying about the place, one with his penis hanging out. We find the place quite unsavoury, and hastily make the requisite adjustment and we surge on. Unfortunately, there was no glorious skin-of-our-teeth reward awaiting us at Tilbury. Our ship had indeed sailed ... and not with us on it. Knowing it was making a quick stop in France the next morning, I did for a moment wonder about trying to get there overnight but it all became too hard ... and we didn't seem to have lights that worked. We hung about in Tilbury for a while and I found a phone and rang Steph giving her the news. She was sympathetic but also quite excited. We'd not really had time for a good farewell.

Telling Roly that we would worry tomorrow about what to do next, we headed back towards North Finchley. Of course riding that far on bikes without lights is never going to be uneventful and naturally enough an officer of the law intervened.

"Good evening lads, what is going on here? You are aware you are riding without lights!"

I could only think of bunging on my broadest colonial Aussie-type accent.

"Awwh yeah, gidday mate, yeaah the lights don't work and we have to get back to North Finchley."

"Right sir, but this is a public road and lights are a necessary piece of motoring equipment. What are your names and your addresses please?" He reached for his notebook, obviously about to issue us with a ticket.

"Well sorry officer, but we don't have an address, we were leaving the country, but we missed the boat."

"So where are you going now?"

"To my girlfriend's place."

"So what is that address?"

I gave out the information but added the info that no one would be living there from tomorrow.

"So where can I send an Infringement Notice?"

"Dunno mate ... maybe our folks' address in New Zealand."

"And when will you be there?"

"Dunno that either mate, maybe a year ... we're going to South America!"

"You're not going to pay this are you?"

"No, probably not!"

He ended our little inter-play with mutterings about bloody colonials and an earnest warning about taking care.

At 2.00am I slid in beside Steph in the make-shift bed on the lounge floor at No 46 ... shattered. It seemed that my head had hardly hit the rolled-up clothes that made do as a pillow, when the shrill ring of the phone in the corner, brought me to a blurred awakening. I crawled over and uttered a husky, sleep-deprived salutation.

"Mr Molloy ... you are not on the boat!"

"... I know, we missed it, we'll go on the next one."

A short silence followed.

"Mr Molloy, there is no next one!

Penelope in a state of nearly-readiness

The gladdest moment in human life, me thinks, is a departure into unknown lands.

SIR RICHARD BURTON (1821-1890)

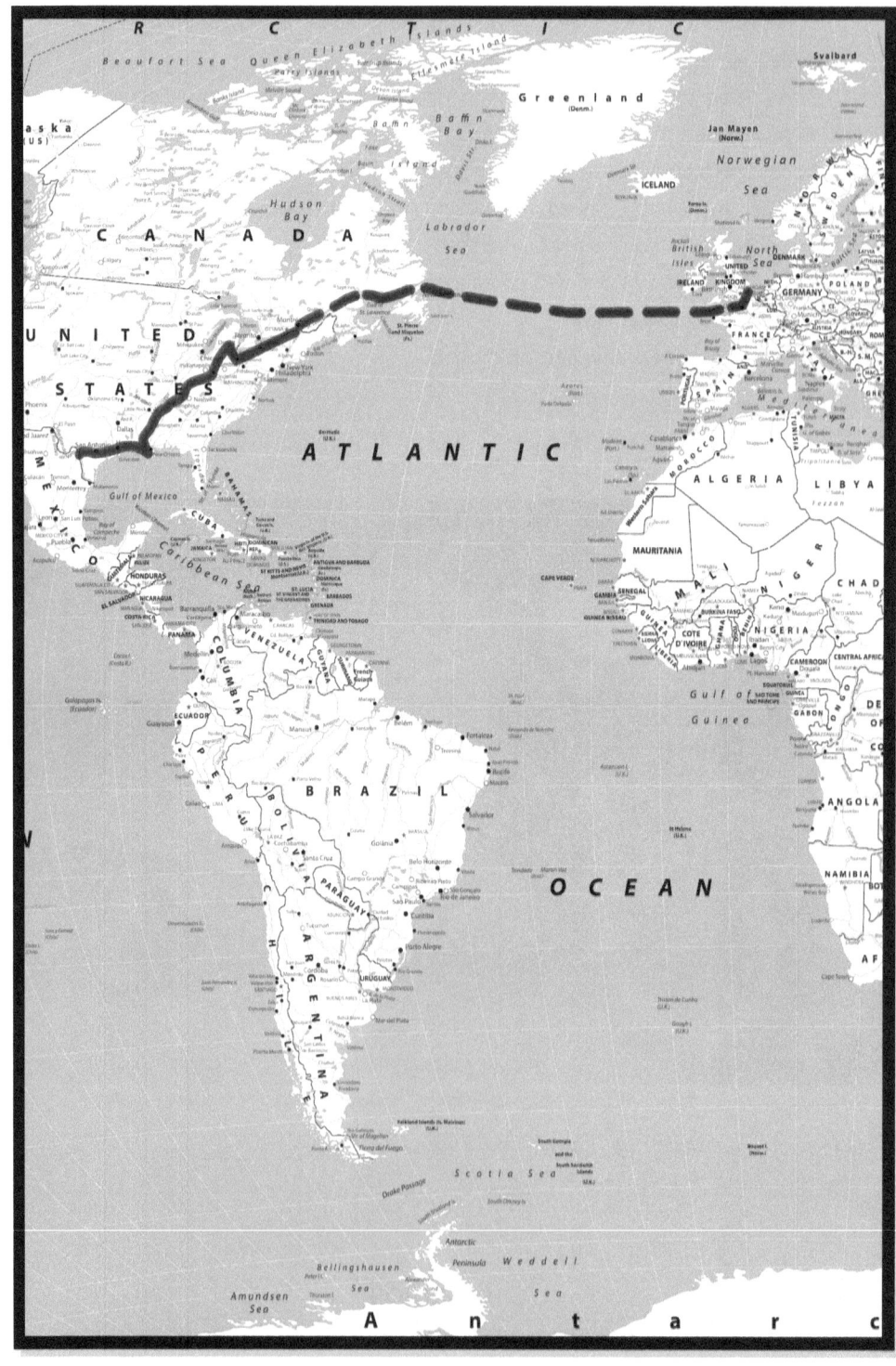

CHAPTER 2

TILBURY PLUS

The Tilbury cock-up had left us all dressed up and nowhere to go, so to speak. As well as being embarrassed, we were now homeless, jobless and down the gurglar for quite a bit of dosh. On the upside I was back in the arms of my beloved and we had the opportunity to do improvements on the bikes. Life goes on, the sun comes up (or not!), there'd been no loss of life or serious injury, just a little humiliation ... so fairly good result overall. It could be viewed as just being a pretty extreme measure to get a few laughs from the boys at the rugby club ... and beyond our pride taking a bit of a hammering, it was situation normal. Solutions to our mired state needed to be found. There were no more sailings for the season on ships that would take both passengers and freight but I did find that there was one last pre-winter sailing to Montreal with a Polish passenger line that could take us in economy, and the bikes could go to New Orleans just like Bessie did. Phew, the expedition might yet grow legs and run, albeit after a five-week delay to the UK departure.

Norman and Edna, the caretakers of the rugby club grounds and facilities let us use the clubrooms as a base for getting the bikes further fettled. They even provided us with a bit of work that we could do for pocket money. Other club members provided us with temporary lodgings and chores as well, so life was great ... if you disregarded the parlous state of our funds. Steph took a live-in job with an Arab family looking after a new baby which seemed to go well. She noted with irony that when they returned to Saudi, she started the day flashed-up in a shiny black Daimler limousine, transitioned into the First-class Lounge at Heathrow and ended it soaking wet and grease-covered after a recovery-mission involving both the old taxi and one of 'the girls'. Roly and I had somehow inveigled our way into mainly staying

Roly at the rugby club carpark, adjusting Penelope's clutch.

at Lawrie's girlfriend Mo's place. Mo was the archetypal English Rose, stunningly beautiful in an almost fragile way. She was vivacious, well-read and unexpectedly generous with her small flat, out in Twickenham. I'd been over-awed by Mo in years gone by, as her poise and style had always marked her out as being way out of our league. Posh and beautiful, scared most of us unsophisticated colonials. She even let us stay when she away in North America with work. Such an angel.

I've always been of the opinion that the hardest step in any venture is the first one. Coming up with the dream, and deciding that the sacrifices to expedite the dream will be repaid a thousand-fold, is the biggie that most stumble over ... that step out of the shadows and committing to do it is often a trepidatious one. Finding the money is a completely different exercise, just one of finding solutions to problems etc., planning, managing. If the lack of money is the reason for not doing the adventure, then you just haven't wanted to do it enough. It also helps if you are blindingly optimistic and unhearing of nay-sayer's wisdoms. It was now the second

Samantha trial-fitted with water bottles and two tyres.

step that we were struggling a bit with. Deep down I knew that if someone had said "How much is the trip going to cost?" and insisted on a clear viability analysis I'd be exposed as a charlatan. I had followers who were keen … and hopefully that would be enough, and besides maybe Lawrie would come through with a big cash injection. After all, he was working in the generous land of Uncle Sam.

Penelope and Samantha were uneventfully ridden to Liverpool and dispatched. Well, almost uneventfully. Spectacularly, one of the spares-filled army-surplus ammunition boxes came adrift from Samantha and bounced down the M40, throwing its contents into every lane. There was no way that the myriad of important bits and pieces could be gathered up safely or even unsafely, so we had to just abandon and ride away. With the bikes on the briny, there was lot more tranquillity to our lives. We tinkered about and prepared to say farewell. I'd been in the UK for five years and was wondering about a life back in New Zealand after South America. Steph was determined that she would somehow earn enough money to join us along the way, so we greeted each day with a smile on our faces. Mo was now back in residence and I can still taste the spaghetti bolognaise she introduced us to. I'd first tasted pizza at age 22 and now at 27 was a spag-bol fan. It could be said that sophistication came to me slowly.

A cabal of the rugby club stalwarts was summonsed to a farewell party at the Firsts' captain's house on the night before departure. This seemed a great idea … nothing could go wrong this time! Roy and Barbara were a smidgeon older than us and had a lovely place ideally suited for the occasion. This was not to be a raucous knees-up, rather a recognition that I had been part of the club for five years and now I was leaving. A couple of years earlier the club had hosted a team from Yugoslavia and the well-heeled like Roy and Barbara had taken them in as billets. The visit was memorable for the physical hardness of their players and their ability to drink copious amounts of slivovitz which they had brought with them in seemingly vast quantities. Apparently, it is a type of plum brandy but I would describe it as a beverage with the oiliness of kerosene and the pungent metallic tang of aftershave … in other words hideous. It is possible that it is just a kero-shave … no distilling needed, just a 50:50 blend. Those who had taken in billets, had each been bestowed with a bottle of this rocket-fuel. Roy and Barbara had been generous hosts and taken in two players so had been gifted two bottles of Yugoslavia's finest, which is a bit like being punished for coming first.

After two years of foisting the slivovitz on every new guest that visited, Roy and Barbara still had one and three-quarter bottles of the dreaded stuff. Being a newbie, Roly was the obvious next victim. It would never be said that Roly is a big drinker, but this was a big occasion and maybe it was with a bit of false bravado that he made the ominous uttering *"This isn't too bad!"*

Roly is not a naturally gregarious person and here he was in a social situation where he only knew a few of the attendees … so it would be expected that his shyness would prevail. To the contrary, fuelled by slivovitz he became more outgoing and relaxed. The three-quarter bottle was soon finished and the unopened one broached. This was an unbelievable performance. There was very little assistance from any of the rugby club. We all knew what it tasted like and suspected it led on to worse things. I think Roly achieved semi-legend status that night, being as he appeared to be able to tame that awful Slavic liquor whilst still being seemingly lucid and half-pie charming.

Of course, tamed is a relative term because although he kept it all together during the social intercourse that was my farewell, the journey back to Mo's place in Twickers was not as successful. It required an urgent stop, fortunately on a semi-country back road. Here Roly attempted to turn himself inside out, clearly an impossibility but give him his due, he tried … man did he try. The mighty had fallen.

There was a sadness at leaving Mo the next day, not knowing if I would ever see her again, seing as there was no commitment to returning to the UK. I gave her a Kiwi hongi which is the rubbing of nose and forehead together. The breath of the two hongi-ing mix, and it is a ceremony of accepting friendship, however, it would be some years before I would be aware enough of Maori protocols to know it is always only used as a greeting, not as a farewell. Still, the physical contact was emotional and strong. Interestingly I recall no such emotion in leaving Steph because I had such confidence that it was only a temporary separation and already there was an intention to meet in Mexico City at the Poste Restante on 15th Jan 1977 at Noon … only seven weeks hence. However, she clearly felt differently and wrote to my parents saying 'It was the worst goodbye I have experienced and I made a complete fool of myself by sobbing all over the place which embarrassed Roly terribly and even Des found it hard to handle'. Personally, I think Roly was too ill and hung-over to notice or feel anything. He was a very subdued and contrite boy who took to his bed immediately when we were on board, not to arise for several days.

The TSS Stefan Batory was built in Holland in the early 1950s but had been operated by the Polish Ocean Lines since 1969 after a refit in Gdansk. Although by 1976 air travel had largely superseded the common use of ocean liners for passenger travel, the news didn't seem to have filtered through to the communist-bloc. This was the cheapest way I could find to get to the North American continent. Of course, being that it was being run by the 'Commies', I'd taken a bit of ribbing and suffered many Skoda and Lada jokes. Everyone seemed to know a shocking anecdote about travelling by Aeroflot or had a neighbour who'd endured Moscovich or Trabant ownership. Pointing out that these were not Polish or ships didn't seem to make a difference. Of course, the food was Eastern European … it would be, it was a Polish ship. I found that OK and Roly didn't eat much. He came aboard in a pretty precarious state and we sailed out into the Atlantic before he could get any sea-legs. The head-on, Force-Eight high seas, and relentless motion kept him cabin-bound and queasy. I told table-mates I was travelling with my brother, but for a long time, I think it was doubted because of the lack of evidence. Roly's sea-sick period morphed into tonsillitis and we really were on the homeward straight before he was sighted.

My six-week voyage from NZ to the UK five years earlier had been a young person's delight, tropical skies, duty-free beers and non-stop partying. This voyage was the polar opposite and polar is quite apt because soon we were into such cold weather (-10C) that the ship's rails and guy ropes were swollen with ice making them a full hand-span thick. The removal of this ice was a full-time job for the crew. Once Roly was on deck (not really on deck as that was way too cold) we filled in the hours with endless games of Battleships and quite a few games of table tennis, which wasn't fully fair as I had been a regional representative player through the age-group years and up to A Reserve … when I retired and went to the UK. The other passengers were a much older lot but friendly enough. My recent research showed that Lee Harvey Oswald, President Kennedy's assassin, had travelled with his family from the USSR to the USA on an earlier branding of the Stefan Batory. Maybe we stayed in the same cabin.

After ten days or so, we sailed into the calm of the St Lawrence Seaway and for the first time, we observed Canadian life, even if distantly. We could see the distinctive orange school buses collecting kids, fully swaddled against the cold. Initially, these were almost lilliputian in scale, as the entry gulf is so wide but once into the 400-mile channel itself, the seaway narrowed somewhat and our views became more magnified. The snow-covered landscape captivated us but the cold would invariably send us back indoors pretty quickly. Montreal in early December was very cold and notable for the dented and derelict state of the taxi fleet. The roads were filled with brown-coloured, icy slush and driving a cab was probably like a spell on fairground dodgems. Maybe they repaired them every Spring.

As quickly as we could manage, the Greyhound Bus Station was located, and a bus to Terre Haute found and boarded. The distance between the two cities is about 1,000 miles or so, but we have no clear recollection of the exact route or how long it took … it seemed like a lifetime. Two options are listed currently, one taking 28 hours and the other 40 hours. Certainly, we rode through the day across endless prairies and through more than one night. By 1976 the Greyhound Bus service had lost its romance and attraction. The 99 days for $99 (1972) was no longer bringing in tourists and international travellers wanting to see the US from the ground. It was now simply for the poor and disadvantaged … with a few nutters thrown in for good measure. We saw the dregs of the greatest nation on earth. We also saw what seemed like mums fleeing bad home situations in the middle of the night, dragging sad little kids with them. I do recall an interesting interplay with a fellow traveller early on in the ride. The guy behind tapped me on the shoulder and said: "How far is it from London to Windsor?" Musing on this odd question, I thought for a while and said "About 30 or 40 miles, I think". My geographical ignorance only came to light a bit later when I realised that he probably meant in Canada as we drove through London. Windsor duly was reached about 120 miles later. How was I to know they had their own London and Windsor?

Pretty shattered, we finally reached Terre Haute, Indiana, in the middle of our second night at maybe 4.00 am. It was bitterly cold outside but cosily warm in the small terminal waiting-room. Way too early to look for Lawrie, we settled in for the remainder of the night. With no one else there except the night clerk, we stretched out on the empty seating. Almost immediately he was on us. "You can't lie down Bud … you gotta sit!" Every time we slumped to the side and fell into an exhausted sleep, he would poke us awake. This seemed irrational and didn't endear him to us or us to him. Even if Head-office rules did preclude sleeping in the public areas, we felt he could have demonstrated some leniency. It was almost like it was a crusade … if he had to be awake, so did we! Ultimately dawn finally rescued us and we could escape this tyrant and stagger off into the sub-zero murk that is a mid-west winter. I recall neon signs proclaiming it to be 15° Fahrenheit and 7.45 am.

Lawrie was looking good and it was great to have the brotherhood finally together. He and Roly hadn't previously met. Now we could get started and have our adventure. The pleasure of seeing my good mate was tempered slightly by the news that he hadn't a whole sack-load of money to tip into the coffers. This was a trifle that we could address later. Apart from a few hours in Miami I had never been to the US and had nothing to judge Terre Haute by, but my observations of the time record disappointment that for a city of about 70,000 it seemed soul-less. I was astonished to learn that most people ate out at least once a day and that the Central Business District was dominated by franchised eateries. This was something I hadn't encountered before and would be decades before this blight would also be endemic in New Zealand. McDonalds, Burger King, KFC, Pizza Hut, Taco Bell etc. all fought to capture your trade with lurid neon signs and tempting offers. There were very few independent cafes and restaurants, except for a small number of places for breakfast, which I quickly decided was the best meal of the day. It was almost ritualistic … you met a couple of mates, ordered anything you liked incorporating bacon, eggs, hash-browns etc and chewed the fat, all the while being regularly attended to by a roaming coffee girl who topped you up without cost. Subsequent mid-sized towns all showed the same dull formula of a couple of burger joints, a couple of chicken places, a couple of pizza parlours and maybe a couple of Mexican eateries … all being the big names we now recognise but back in the 1970s had not yet spread their invasive tentacles worldwide.

We only stayed a couple of days as we were eager to get going. We were also eager to get warm as we didn't really have clothes suitable for the often sub-zero temperatures. Lawrie's low-key farewell was held in a bar and was a friendly, inclusive evening. It seemed that not many of his acquaintances knew of his plans and the word was being spread with some incredulity. "Hey Mac, Lawrie's going to Mexico!" It was interesting that none of the group could grasp that we were not going to Mexico … we were going through Mexico to far, far beyond. Even when we would say we were going to ride through Central and South America, it would come back to Mexico. "Woah, you need a lot of spare tyres for Mexico! How many you got?" I remember telling an earnest, seemingly competent, blue-collar worker who appeared to be their resident Mexico expert, that we each had two spare tyres and all the bikes ran the same size front and back, so in effect, we had six spares. "Might be enough, but'll be touch and go … Mexico is hard on tyres!" With some emotion, one of the guys gave Lawrie a family heirloom, a US Treasury Sherriff's badge from the days of prohibition. Lawrie promised to look after it and wrapped it in a plastic covering and put it at the bottom of the leather pouch he always wore on his hip. Months later it would cause an interesting interlude.

For reasons lost in the mists of time, we decided that it was too expensive to use the Greyhound service down to New Orleans. It was deemed unlikely that three of us hitch-hiking together would be successful, so a split was proposed. Roly would take the bus and Lawrie and I would hit the road with our thumbs out. On reflection this seems a strange and flawed decision as Roly had no experience of this sort of independent travelling. He was more or less straight out of New Zealand and his natural reticence would make it a big challenge for him. A better mix would have been for me to go ahead by bus and Roly and Lawrie do the hitching thing.

As it happened it wasn't great for either party. Lawrie and I struggled with rides and Roly had a pretty nightmarish ride to New Orleans then a daunting stay in the bus terminus. We'd told him to just wait and we'd turn up sooner or later. If this meant sleeping there, so be it. I seem to recall Lawrie and I arrived a day or so after Roly who was naturally a very relieved and happy boy, seeing as we didn't really have any backup plans or instructions for him should we not appear. He recalls he'd had to adopt a tough streetwise persona so as to not appear vulnerable. He'd done well for a scrawny little boy from Berhampore. A ranting 'shell-shocked' fellow passenger had kept him on edge for most of the 24 hr ride.

We had quite a few days to wait before we could uplift Bessie so we settled into life living in the New Orleans Greyhound Bus Station. It was a busy and vibrant place with buses coming and going at all times which meant that we could merge with the people waiting for connections. There were always passengers in transit, as well as people awaiting arriving kin etc, an ever-changing throng of humanity. We soon realised that we were also part of a community of the lower-levels of society or itinerants who were using the station as somewhere to live. Nights were times to be wary, as the police would often do a sweep. Word would spread quickly and quite a number a people would discreetly as possible, arise and make their way to the toilets. Here we would cram into a cubicle and have only one pair of legs showing under the door. This took some gymnastic ability for the non-feet showers, involving standing on the seat, crouching to keep your heads from showing over the top of the partitions. We didn't quite manage a week there before we decided we were beginning to stand out, so we moved a few streets over to the Continental Trailways' terminal, amusingly finding some familiar faces there. We'd investigated cheap and skody hotels but in our price range even Lawrie was daunted and he was my arbiter for this sort of thing. The fear-factor was adjudged to be too high, especially as we witnessed what looked to be a knife-standoff outside the one we were considering.

One night the police arrived catching us unawares and woke the black guy next to me. *"Ticket!"*

The guy convincingly mumbled in a slumberous fashion and fished out a ticket. *"Hey, this is for Toosday!"*

The purported rider didn't open his eyes but again mumbled under his breath. *"Hang on, this is for last Toosday ... no, it is not, it's for last year! On your feet!"*

Whilst the supposed felon was being awoken and escorted from the concourse, I made my way to the toilets as nonchalantly as I could.

Once we had Bessie, we moved out of town to the Fontainebleau State Park on the other side of Lake Ponchartrain. The ride took us over The Causeway which is two parallel bridges, recognized as the longest bridges over water in the world. The slightly longer of the two is about 24 miles long. They both have a scary section of steel web-grating near the middle where the draw-bridges are. Web-grating causes motorbike tyres to squirm alarmingly and there is always the feeling that a pending disaster is about to befall you. Needless to say, this section of the bridge was dreaded on every crossing. With only one bike but three people, this had meant quite a bit of riding before we were together, tent-up in the park. Although Lousiana was going through an unseasonal cold-snap, we felt better out here than precariously living in a bus station constantly on edge, guarding against pick-pockets and police. Here there were people to openly talk to and we soon were learning all about the Appalachian Trail that a couple of guys had just abandoned because of the weather. This was new to us and we were a bit in awe that people would walk two thousand miles across 14 States. Another motorcyclist pausing a ride because of the cold introduced us to Mad Dog 20/20. This is colloquially known as 'bum wine' or 'brown bag vino'. It is a fortified wine that is high in alcohol content but low in price. Available in several ersatz-fruit flavours and fetching colours, this was pretty grim stuff but several notches above slivovitz. The community back in the bus station would have approved.

Lawrie and I were able to start an exercise regime of running and doing shoulder-loaded squats and more. The park was also where we taught him how to ride a motorbike. Because Bessie was the smallest and easiest to ride it was decided that she would be Lawrie's to ride, at least until we reached Panama. He took to it pretty well, although it was just around a flat, semi-empty park. A good start though. He'd hone his skills on the road, just as Roly and I had done a decade earlier. You can only gain experience from experience.

We'd not wanted to waste our meagre funds on doing touristy things in New Orleans but we did have to have one night in the French Quarter, exploring Bourbon St and making a pilgrimage to Preservation Hall, the home of traditional New Orleans jazz. I'd promised a blues and jazz lover from the rugby club that I would search it out and go. We enjoyed walking down the main thoroughfares, amazed

Relaxing in Fontainebleau State Park near Lake Ponchatrain

at how many 'name' entertainers were available for us to go and watch. Being used to just infrequent visits from famous artists back home, it seemed quite surreal. In awe we stood outside the glittering lights of a semi-seedy place advertising Clarence 'Frogman' Henry, a legendary blues singer from the 1950s. Later, in a back-street, we found the low-profile Preservation Hall, and enjoyed a wonderful night. The main singer for the evening was an elderly black woman who was partially-paralysed as a result of a stroke. Her voice was a whisper and she could only play the piano with one hand but the emotion she inspired that night was wonderful. It would have been nice to spend some money and let our hair down a bit but we knew that would have to wait, and we had to make do vicariously.

In due time Penelope and Samantha were also extricated from the docks and relocated out to the park. Again this took a bit of to-ing and fro-ing to get three riders on to three bikes as the park was way too far out for buses or taxis. It might be nearly Christmas, but we were finally ready to go. After a heavy frost on 24th December, we left our State park and hit the road, a bit late but happy that the wheels were turning. Almost the first surprise ... and learning, was that Baton Rouge was the first town west of New Orleans. The words of Kris Kristofferson's song 'Me and Bobby McGee' opens with -

'Busted flat in Baton Rouge, waiting for a train

When I was feeling nearly faded as my jeans Bobby thumbed a diesel down, just before it rained And rode us all the way to New Orleans'

Because the US is humungous, I had always pictured this ride being days long, as that 'all the way to New Orleans' is so evocative. Maybe 'just down the way to New Orleans' didn't fit but I couldn't help but be disappointed. The driver would have barely got into top gear before hauling up and saying *"Here you are then, I hope the rest of your life goes well!"*

We made an easy 130 miles before camping out, pretty pleased with ourselves. I don't know why but our tent was a single-skin one with negligible water resistance which was demonstrated to us immediately we put it up, as a torrential rain commenced which lasted for nigh-on 24 hours. This resulted in everything we owned being absolutely sodden, so when the deluge finally eased on Christmas afternoon we relocated to the Sam Houston State Park not much further along our way to Texas. We did this because we knew that toilet blocks in the State Parks usually had heaters. Luckily this was true of Sam Houston and this became our new

Watery sunshine livened up Christmas Day in Sam Houston State Park

TILBURY PLUS

New Year's Eve 1976 saw us all under plastic enduring a wet and cold night.

NO ONE SAID IT WOULD BE EASY

home. In a letter home we contrasted our misery with the other holidaymakers who we knew were feasting on turkey, cranberry sauce, pumpkin pie etc., in their warm and dry caravans. I note our Christmas Dinner as being Stodge Special of rice, split peas, and egg noodles. I indicate things are on the up as we've been loaned a sleeping bag and that coffee and ham and eggs have been promised by another camper for the morning. After the final evening ablution by the other campers, we finally settle down on the concrete floor, the three of us in the one sleeping bag, pretty happy that things will get better. We are in the dry, have a heater blasting away and tomorrow's forecast is for a much better day.

We are seen as a bit of a novelty and treated very kindly and generously the next day by the other campers. It was sunny and whilst not warm, photos show us looking pretty happy and amused by the tame squirrels. Clearly, we have to get better at handling the conditions when they aren't benign. To this end, we procure from a hardware store, a roll of sturdy clear plastic. This is a bit of a pain to carry but while we are still in cold and potentially wet winter conditions of the 'deep south', it is worth the effort. The roads across to Houston were dull, and straight with the ride being non-eventful. The Astrodome was a major attraction that as sports' buffs Lawrie and I couldn't ride by. Our timing was good as there was a Yule-season game playing that night. Grid-iron was a complete mystery to me but Lawrie had followed it in his time in the US and knew the rules and most of the nuances. We hadn't been watching for all that long when all the players stopped and just stood around. Nobody seemed to be injured, but nothing was happening.

"What's going on now?" I ask.

"Oh, it is a live telecast, so this is an ad break! It's one of the reasons soccer hasn't taken off in the US ... they won't stop for ads, so get no live games on TV!"

We had one more night's camping beyond Houston before Mexico. This was New Year's Eve and it was spent in a farmer's field, sober with not even a bottle of Mad Dog to engender some revelry. We could see it was about to rain so settled early, tent-less but completely under our roll of clear plastic. It was so big that we were able to lay it out, then lie down and pull it right over the top of us, tucking it in over the lower layer. It certainly wasn't glamping, but our spirits were high just laughing at the ridiculousness of our situation ... all recalling previous New Years' glories. It had been on New Year's Eve 1971, that with much fanfare, I had sailed from Auckland. Many hundreds of streamers connected us passengers on the SS Australis, to our loved ones on the wharf below. A band played and fireworks soared, tears flowed and the excitement in the air was palpable. Six years later was providing such a contrast that we couldn't help but giggle. Life's a funny old thing. Set your sight's low enough and you'll always be successful and contented.

We'd also come to the realisation that the earlier period of just hanging around and living, had depleted our kitty alarmingly, so had now decided on a regime of extreme parsimoniousness. To this end, our main meal was changed from 'Super Stodge' to 'Basic Regular Stodge'. It would be good to record that one of us was an imaginative cook and that we were dining healthily and well … but that would be a lie. We were pretty much limited to one-pot stuff as we only had one burner, the legendary Optimus 8R petrol cooker. I know we could have several pots and pans etc., and sequentially juggle their time on the heat source, but that seemed way too hard. So it was either a fry-up in the pan, or a stodge in the pot. I have no culinary skills and Lawrie was semi-famous in London when he was part of a clique within Transit House, a big doss-house for returning travellers with Transit Travel. Lawrie's group were semi-permanent and had a roster of each person cooking for everyone once a week. I seem to recall Lawrie's night was Tuesday and religiously every Tuesday evening, he doled out money to each of the group to get fish and chips. This was seen by all as a win-win. Roly was more or less pardoned from cooking because he attended to bike maintenance each evening. No matter the weather or conditions Roly checked the girls out, lubricated and adjusted chain tensions, topped up their oil levels, tightened nuts and bolts etc.

Our ride across Louisiana and Texas had shown up an unexpected issue with both Panthers. They were drinking oil. This surprised Roly as apart from being slightly unusual with a semi-wet sump system of oil containment and distribution, they were an extremely simple four-stroke engine. They were known to have a fool-proof, reliable oil pump. Of course, we were newbies to the marque and there were no publications available to us back in the UK. So apart from a small section in Modern Motorcycle Mechanics which gave basic settings, we were on our own. We'd met a small group of the owners' club before we left but like us, they were just a group of young long-hairs with an affection for these obsolete old treasures.

With the collective knowledge of the Panther Owners' Club's members now able to be shared through the internet … and the fact us young long-hairs are now wizened old white-hairs, who have learned a bit over the years, we now know that the Model 120s were massively over-oiled. Even from new they had what many would deem an unacceptable thirst for the black-gold. Period motorcycle road tests would often list oil consumption and the normal benchmark was 1,000 mpp … miles per pint. Panthers were rarely if ever road-tested, so their performance was not generally known. Subsequent to our adventure I have obtained a Canadian road test of a 1962 model and the oil consumption was not overtly high-lighted but recorded as 1,000 mpg which most of us would gloss over without noticing the change to gallon from pint. So from brand new, they were only getting 125 miles per pint. Another wisdom which even today not all owners realise, is that the screw-in dipstick with its two lines does not mean that you maintain an oil level between the two lines. That would be way too obvious! No, the top line is the level the engine should be filled to when freshly built. The correct running level is between the bottom of the dip-stick and the lower level, so as long as there is evidence of oil there, you are ok. By filling to the top line, as we constantly did, you are over-filling the engine and it will use that additional oil extra-ordinarily fast. To compound our mistake, we economised by buying franchised agricultural oil of a low grade, and low price.

Although disappointed in the oil consumption of Penelope and Samantha, otherwise we were trucking along well. The roads were First-World-perfect but to us the countryside was pretty dull with featureless prairies only occasionally featuring bobbing oil horses to stimulate our interest. The miles seemed pretty interminable and we were excited to finally reach Laredo. We resisted the urge to send postcards to the rugby club because we didn't quite feel we were a success yet. The earlier failure meant I had set the bar a bit higher. I was determined to win back some respect and admiration and hoped Latin America would provide it … as long as we had enough tyres to get across Mexico!

Journeys are made in the imagination. The rest is drudgery.
TED SIMON (1931 –)

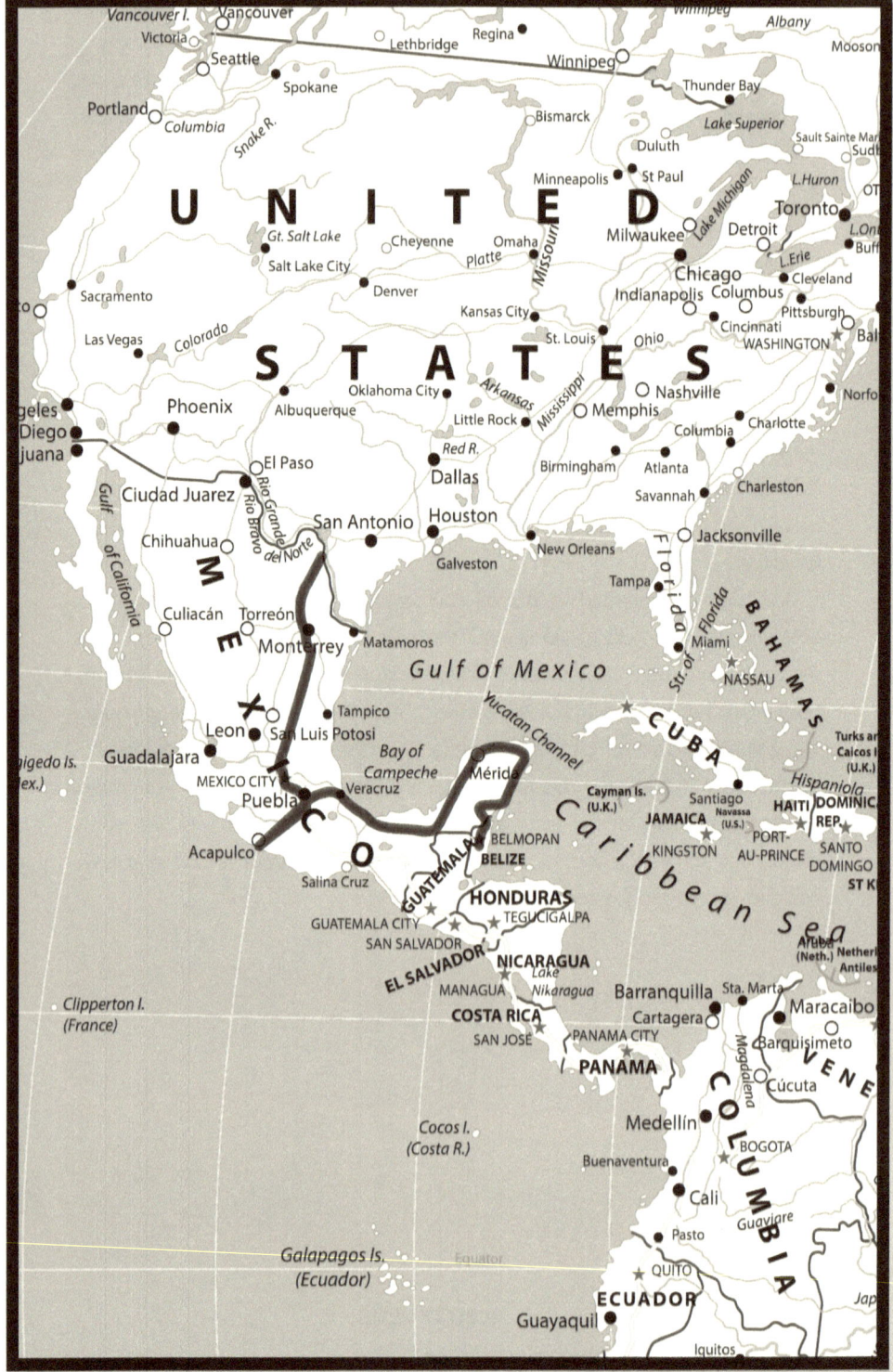

CHAPTER 3

MEXICO

Departing from the US into Mexico really signalled the beginning of a new stage of the adventure. It was like being back in school and leaving the 'primers' and going to the 'standards'. We knew we were leaving what we thought of as the 'civilised' world where everyone spoke our language and we had a modicum of control over our ways. The border crossing introduced us into a world of chaos and excitement. Suddenly we didn't understand what was being said … or shouted in most cases. Navigating the process was bewildering. There were unexplained queues, lines of vehicles and throngs of confused-looking travellers. It was hot and dusty, just like the movies and there were insistent touts who for a fee would take you through the bureaucratic nightmare. Of course this we shunned — to our cost, as it took several hours to get visas checked, passports stamped and most vitally, our carnets filled in. The carnet was a particular problem as most travellers using their own vehicles were just going in and out of Mexico alone and had American bank documentation showing they had lodged a $10,000 bond. Our carnets were substantial documents requiring the right places being filled in and in the case of the Entry Point, part of the relevant page removed. Ours further confused them as they were all in my name, simply because all the bikes were mine. For some reason, this seemed to create suspicion. We knew that this was a key document to be fastidiously completed because if it wasn't, it might compromise the refunding of the monies that had been lodged on our behalf back in London.

Finally, we got through and into the colour and vitality of Mexico, across the Rio Grande, through Nuevo Laredo and on the road to Monterrey. We resisted the fleshpots of Nuevo Laredo as it all looked a bit tourist-tacky and we were eager to get on … we're travellers not tourists … far superior! This was now the 'real deal' or at least the beginning of it. We were naturally quite excited. Our little crew was gelling beautifully with Lawrie's amusing, laid-back ways keeping the spirits high, and Roly's fastidious maintenance regime keeping the wheels spinning. As titular head, and keeper of The South American Handbook, my role was to keep us heading the right way, to look up what we might encounter along the way and impart this knowledge to all.

Monterrey introduced us to city camping. Camping to us had always meant nice green spaces, either ones we found ourselves or the lovely American State and National Parks. This was our first encounter with the philosophy that camping meant caravans or motorhomes, not tents. To this end, the areas available were all either sealed or hard-packed gravel, ideal for vehicular movement, not for tents or tent pegs. Very much here we were second-class citizens unrealistically wanting a grassed area to put up our humble shelter. Monterrey was an important pause for us as it was a 'mail' stop. It was with great excitement that we rode the bus into the centre of the city in search of the Poste Restante. The Poste Restante mail service was traditionally the only way that travellers could receive mail and was simplicity itself. The service was provided by the main Post Office of a city or town. They had a repository to hold mail. No address was needed because the Post Office was in effect delivering to itself. So Steph and others had been told to send mail to the Poste Restante, Monterrey, Mexico. We all got mail and for me, it was wonderful getting a letter from Steph even though it didn't have much to tell me, but sure filled the cockles with much warmth. A letter from home told us that Roly and I now had a second niece, born on Christmas Eve. Mum also passed on the wisdom *'keep well, and always think things through, as often that saves a few mistakes'.* She also urged me to *'try and spare a line or two for us pensioners won't you, and tell us either where you've been or where you're likely to go … and then we'll feel part of our family still.'* Grammatically not up to her usual high standard but I felt for them. They had just had their 38th Wedding Anniversary and their first ever Christmas with no off-spring present.

There had been no news from Anne so we were unsure of her movements or likely rendezvous point and time. Steph was still in London, trying to get a visa arranged to be able to go to Saudi Arabia for a short stint with the nice Arab family she had worked with earlier. It seems that the action of the NZ Government in sanctioning the All Blacks' tour of apartheid South Africa earlier in the year had continuing ramifications. In addition to 25 African nations boycotting the Olympic Games in Montreal, it seems others are not issuing travel or work documentation to Kiwis. We'd known this was a problem when Mark Te Tau from my team had scored a highly-paid job in Saudi because of his specialist farming background in NZ. Thrilled with what was unfolding for him, he'd chosen the colour of the new Triumph Stag he was going to buy. Sadly, the visa never came through and when we had left London he was still waiting … and still dreaming of the sleek sports car.

Life was good, the weather hot, the road-side food cheap and nourishing. The sudden exposure to a hot sun was playing havoc with my exposed nose. With the use of open-face helmets, we were getting hit with both wind and sun. My snout soon blistered and peeled. Of course, this left it tender, raw and ready for the process to start again. Our kit didn't include any unguents or salves to preclude or alleviate this. It was presumed that I would harden up sooner or later. The harmful effects of the sun weren't known to us at the time … we were young and ignorant of many things. The language barrier was a minor one as we always managed to find our way and locate fuel and food. It would have been nice to have a Spanish dictionary or phrase-book but locating one and spending money on it didn't seem a priority. Things were good the way they were, and what you don't know sometimes can be a benefit. One night we had occasion to have to put the tent up very close to the road-side, in full view of anyone passing along the way. At some stage in the night, we hear voices outside the tent, not threatening voices, just curious ones. We respond to their salutations best we can, but it is obvious there is a disconnect. A voice calls *"Muy peligrosa, muy peligrosa!"* That sounds pretty good to us, so we respond *"Muy peligrosa"* a couple of times and ultimately they pass on and we resettle, happy with our meaningful interface.

A few days later we are riding in the mountains and on several occasions encounter signage before sharp downhill bends which also use the word *peligrosa*. It comes to us slowly that our night-time visitors had been telling us that where we were camped was 'Very Dangerous!'

For motorcyclists the perfect ride is infrequent — when the temperature is just right, the road surface is good, the traffic minimal, the radii of the bends matched to the bike you are riding etc. When this happens it is nirvana. For Penelope and I, we hit this heightened state on our last day before Mexico City. Mexico City sits on a high plateau at 8,000 ft and to get there from the north you leave the lowlands and sidle along the slopes for several hours, only slowly climbing. It was a perfect day which morphed into the perfect ride with no traffic slowing us and Penelope performing at her finest. We danced our way along, flopping to the left, and flopping to the right in a rhythmic sequence of moves. It was wonderful and seemingly endless. Soon we had romped away from the others, not caring ... bound up in the ecstasy of the moment. If something happened to one of them and I had to go back ... well, how wonderful would that be! In fact, back behind me, Roly suffered the scary sight of Lawrie sweeping past him onto the wrong side of the road, narrowly missing an oncoming small truck. Lozza had got quite proficient at riding ... but there hadn't been many corners up to this point, and he had just frozen mid-bend. Not for the last time was the omnipotent one above kind to us.

Mexico City was a bit of a nightmare, the camp expensive and barren, the air pollution as memorable as noted by others ... and there was no mail. We did a side trip out to Teotihuacan, the City of the Gods, which we were very impressed with. Here were pre-Aztec pyramids to rival those of the ancient Egyptians. This had been the largest city in the pre-Columbian Americas with possibly 125,000 residents, which would have made it the sixth-largest city in its epoch. Often attributed to the Toltecs, the construction still contains many mysteries and for me rivalled the old-world magnificence of Ephesus and Persepolis visited on the 'Ernie' ride. Even still being fit from rugby and the continued exercise, walking around the vast plazas and concourses was debilitating in the thin air.

Roly had decided that the oil consumption of the Panthers needed to be addressed and to that end, we managed, with much sign-language and hand waving to obtain correct size piston rings for both Penelope and Samantha. These were for a Dodge truck but deemed fit-for-purpose and fitted. Only time would tell if they made a difference.

We still had a few days up our sleeves before the 15th Jan, so decided to relocate to the Pacific Coast at Acapulco, to rest and recreate. This was another magnificent day's ride as it was all downhill to the coast. The road down twisted and turned, with spectacular drops ensuring that we kept the focus on the riding rather than the views. Later we would read in an English-language publication that recently there had been an appalling bus accident on this very road. Something like 45 people had perished, with only one survivor. When asked what was the driver doing at the time

Our Mexican family

of the accident he responded: *"He was peeling an orange!"*. The girls had been pretty enfeebled in the rarefied air up on the plateau so appreciated the move.

I'd had a day in Acapulco on my way to Europe so knew it as a resort town famous for the rock diving. I'd thought it all a bit lame, especially as Elvis wasn't there doing the high dive. We avoided the township all together and rode a little north to a beach area where it seemed like a small grouping of houses had been started, then abandoned ... and that was exactly what it was. A small family (Mum, Dad and three wee ones) indicated it was fine for us to set up in a roof-less structure. We loved the way that as we moved in, they sent over the six-year-old boy with a machete almost his size to trim away a few large weeds. Quickly they became our surrogate family, and the mum was engaged to provide cooked evening meals for us. Of course, that is a winner all round, as they got hard-cash and we got tortillas with frijoles and occasionally eggs. They'd put a thatched roof on their dwelling making it a bit more four-seasonal than ours. This was a great place to while away the days. Roly claimed his best ever sun-tan after only four days and Lawrie and I ran the beach as well as spending endless hours diving in and out of the pounding surf. It was pretty idyllic. Oranges and coconuts completed our diet.

We finally left our little patch of paradise and our nueva familia with a little sadness, but I was pretty excited as the looming rendezvous at the Central Post Office on 15th January was something I had been hanging out for ... with all the expectations of the besotted. So we moved back to the barren camp in Mexico City, dropping the carburettor needles a notch to lean the engines off a little so as to run a bit better at altitude.

It was a shattering disappointment to find no welcoming arms on the 15th, nor any mail. A few days later I write home recording *'We haven't found Anne and don't know where Steph is or when she is coming. Learnt yesterday that she's in Saudi Arabia ... so she's on the way, but we have no address for her. Mo has gone to Canada for three weeks so we can't ring her to find out. Isn't life complicated?'* Meanwhile, we had been struck down by our first bout of *'Montezuma's revenge'*. Lawrie had both ends going ... the full-Monty, so to speak, whilst I was spared the vomiting. Roly seems unscathed and a little bemused by it all. In the camp, we've been doing a lot of communal cooking with other campers and we'll take liberties and blame some Aussies for our temporary demise. We've been pretty productive and got the requisite jabs for the areas we are heading, and also procured malaria pills. We've decided to head off to the Gulf of Mexico to find a beach to lie about on, while we wait for news of Steph.

Meanwhile, an ocean or two away Steph has got her visa and made it to Saudi Arabia. In a letter to my parents on the 14th Jan, she pours her heart out –

'Tomorrow is Jan 15, the day I was originally due to meet Des in Mexico City but I am just hoping he has received at least some of my mail saying it would now be the 30th. In his letter which I got just before Xmas, he said not to worry about getting there by then as he did not think that he would manage it. I had letters yesterday from my Annabel and from Mo. The latter had received one from Lawrie (dated Dec 22nd) and they were in New Orleans awaiting the arrival of the two Panthers. Bessie had already got there and they were well. Naturally I am panicking a trifle in case Des has not received any of my mail and gives me up as a bad job or else breaks his neck and everybody else's trying to reach Mexico City by 15th and I cannot imagine the Bionic Woman (alias Ann Betts) wanting to wait two weeks for a short fat girl she does not know – and probably does not want to know. So I worry myself to sleep each night wondering if they are all right as it is so horrible not knowing. However, I have great faith in Desmond Joseph and although it gets shaken from time to time, I know he will

Camp in the trees, Veracruz

be ok and will ensure Roly and the others are also.'

Shunning the obvious holiday parks, we found a suitable beach a bit out of the sizable town of Veracruz and established a camp in the trees. With the idleness that only the young seem to be able to tolerate, a pattern was established of lazing around for most of the day, working on our tans, reading a bit, walking a little, doing a bit of exercise, having an evening cook-up and fire. Pretty damn good, if you ignored the fact that we weren't going anywhere, or doing anything. We'd created a relationship with the local fishermen who brought their catch ashore nearby for sorting. We'd been surprised that one fish, a green one was always thrown aside. It was of a nice size and we enquired why they didn't keep them. We were shown that the flesh inside was also a greenish hue and apparently were not saleable because of consumer resistance. However, they were perfectly fine to eat if you ignored the colour. Once this was established as a fact, it was a high-point of our day to meet with the fishermen each day and collect 'our' fish. This made such a nice change from the rice-based stodges we were still enduring each day. Especially when eaten in the dark, the colour was not an issue, and we loved our free fish meals.

One evening we were disturbed by a small group who looked like a rebel militia, suddenly appearing by our fire. Some of these grim-looking characters had Pancho Villa moustaches and were visually quite threatening. It is moments like this when Lawrie shines. In no time, his easy laughter and engaging ways had diffused any potential for conflict. I think they could quickly sense our impoverishment and that we weren't worth rolling. Unlike the other gringos they'd encountered, we were Australianos. This made us pretty interesting, and soon liquor was being passed around to the enjoyment of all. They became regular nocturnal visitors and almost affected my life's destiny … but more of that later.

We learned that Steph would be arriving at the end of the month, and I left the boys to continue beachcombing. Taking the 12-hour train from Veracruz back to Mexico City, I expectantly made my way out to the Airport. A saga wouldn't be a saga without drama and disappointment. Like the Cher song, *'You wait and wait … girl don't come'*. There was no clear knowledge regarding the exact when and how, but I hung around for a few days, toughing it out during the nights in the terminal and striking up a friendship with a homosexual American guy also waiting for his beau. This took me a little out of my comfort zone, but he was really interesting and for a period had operated a Wells Fargo mail delivery run in California using a horse, like the real thing. Now he had a goat farm down in Costa Rica, and we were invited to drop in and stay. Taking a break from the terminal, I had a daytime exhaustion-induced nap outside in the sun on a grassy patch near some trees. It wasn't really my intention to fall asleep, but I did and when I awoke, I found two young street-kids snuggled into me. We had no common language but I suppose I'd served a purpose, maybe providing a bit of perceived security. They constantly passed a drink can between themselves. Clearly, it contained glue and one of the two had a very scabby upper lip and the part of his nose between his nostrils had been eroded away, presumably by the corrosive effects of the adhesive fumes. These kids were about 12 years old and didn't ask for anything from me.

On the 30th Jan, I left a card at the Poste Restante: *'9.00am Going to Airport. I'll wait to 7 tonight. If we have missed I will check Poste Restante 8.00pm. Then must return to VERACRUZ. If you are coming next week, catch train to Veracruz. Evening about 9.00pm. I'll meet it at the other end – 35 Pesos 2nd Class but be early or no seats available and it's cold inth the mountains. Sorry but only one letter today – dated 4 Jan so don't know much. Annabel doesn't either. Love Dez.*

With a sinking feeling of disappointment and confusion, back I went to the boys via another pretty gruelling train ride, having to stand for many hours. Life on the beach was resumed with the small adjustment that I would rise early and go into Veracruz to meet the train.

Each day I was hopeful and eager … and day after day my optimism was not rewarded. We were running out of reasons to stay. Our suntans were complete, my nose had hardened up and whilst neither Roly or Lawrie suggested moving on, I was a bit sensitive to our position, stationary as it was. I knew Steph had to be coming, but how were we to connect? How was I to find her? Was I to wait forever?

On the 30th Jan Steph had overnighted in Paris, so we had not quite been in town at the same time. Upon her arrival at the Mexico City Poste Restante, she was shattered to find NO letters or messages from me. She then checked into a cheap hotel and went to the British Embassy, campsites and other likely places we could be, but all to no avail. With no other guidance to suggest a different course of action, she repeated this for several days and also made numerous trips back to the airport … and checked the hospitals as well. Nothing, nix, no ay nada! Deciding on needing to move on, she bought a train ticket coincidentally to Vera Cruz, and made one last visit to the Poste Restante … joining the queue behind an American who could speak fluent Spanish. When she again was greeted with no mail she called across to him "Can you get them to check the male 'M's for me?" Eureka … pay-dirt!

It was an oddity that the Mexico City Poste Restante sorted the incoming travellers' mail into male and female. We'd spotted errors when checking our own mail, knowing that Daphne Harris was never going to see her letters when they were with the Hombre 'M's. I thought I had been pretty clear when I left my postcard there that it was for a señorita. And so it was that almost a week after I had left it there, Steph finally had her sweaty paws on my postcard. With great excitement, she carried out the directive given and was on the train early that night. In Veracruz, Steph had her carriage door open while the train was still doing 20 mph and leapt off at the earliest possible moment, almost spilling to the ground.

To her intense disappointment, there was no hairy beast there for her. Again, nothing! With her optimism slowly waning, she waited for an hour or so before giving up and seeking out the location of any camping grounds … maybe I had been delayed. Finding a camp, she learned, that yes, there had been some Gringo moto riders, but they had left that very day for Panama. Shattered at being so close, yet so far away, she wiped away the tears and joined a couple of Americans going into the bus station, looking to go down the Pan American Highway.

Whilst Steph had been clickety-clacking her way through the night towards me, I was immaturely over-indulging on cheap tequila with the militia and fishermen. I don't know why that crucial night was chosen for a party, but sometimes fate does that. Early next morning I remained torpid and not going anywhere until the sun fully rose and demanded I get up. I probably cast a pretty forlorn figure as I belatedly made my way on Penelope into the train station, fully two to three hours after the train arrival-time. Half-heartedly I asked the only railway attendant I could find about a 'gringa' but he shrugged his shoulders.

I am known as a pretty buoyant person, not given to sloughs of despond, but this was almost the breaking point. I was hung-over and feeling guilty, as perhaps ... just perhaps, today could have been the day my Princess came to town. Pretty pissed-off with myself, on a whim I decide not to go back to the beach yet. I pull over, and go and sit on a park bench in the sun to ponder our next move.

Maybe 30 minutes later, a commotion from the road attracts my attention. Something is happening in a passing bus. My focus narrows on a slightly-open high window where a hysterical Steph is having an explosion of joy and screaming out the narrow slit. As I gasp in amazement, the bus cuts across a lane to the pavement in true Latin style ... instigating an angry blaring of horns from the affected traffic. Seconds later there is a crazy lady running straight through that same traffic. I hear the applause from the bus as this speeding bullet of a young thing seemingly cleaves through the traffic like Moses parting the Red Sea and unharmed, throws herself into my arms. I know my heart nearly falls out of my chest as we laugh and laugh and laugh ... we've found each other. They say that love doesn't always follow a straight path, but this has been a ridiculous journey. This is serendipity!

Steph's arrival gives rise to a celebration. We are now complete, we can now go forth and conquer. What's more, Steph brought with her a much-needed $720 for the coffers. If Anne is still out there, she can have her own adventures. Of course, all celebrations in Mexico involve Tequila. We don't actually like tequila. It comes in differing qualities with prices of $2, $4 and $8 a bottle. We find it best to 'not like' the $2 hooch and another indulgent night follows. Steph has been alcohol-free in Saudi for a month and her resistance seems low and she is soon in the 'Land of Nod'. I don't mind as she looks lovely asleep. Connubial excesses can wait.

We head south, a happy bunch. The ride from Veracruz to Palenque was leisurely and enjoyable as we headed out to the coast whenever we could. Long-since gone was the cold of Louisiana and Texas, now we were enjoying an exotic tropical adventure. We were often riding through jungle with exotic smells and sounds, brightly-coloured butterflies as big as telephones, mysterious birds and even a beach-encounter with a large iguana, which to me looked like a small crocodile and was treated accordingly. Upon spotting a VW Combi van with a dented roof, we realised that the infrequent large thumping noise we had heard at night was the falling of coconuts. Never again did we camp under a coconut tree. We were loving coconuts and learning that they can be used at all stages was a revelation. We'd all only seen them with ¾ inch thick white 'meat' and thick syrupy white milk. We never knew you could drink the milk before the 'meat' formed. In this state, it was semi-clear, sweet and slightly spritzy … very thirst-quenching.

We were now getting to meet more travellers and often the evenings were filled with tall tales and lots of laughter. An Aussie couple in a Combi seemed to be travelling our way and we saw a bit of them in the following weeks. Our interactions with them also introduced a trip catch-phrase. Tony and Vicky were of a similar age to us and being from our part of the world it was natural that we would gravitate towards them. I think Steph also enjoyed a bit of female company. We all liked Vicky a lot … and Tony? Well, he was OK but … he was bone-idle. It didn't take long to notice he did nothing around camp and if he wanted something he would call to Vicky to fetch it for him in a plaintive, pathetic way. *"Vickee"* became our cry when we wanted something passed over or even at times when we wanted someone's attention.

One of these coastal stays also demonstrated a dark side to some of the holidaying Americans. We'd encountered quite a few from north of the border who regularly wintered in Mexico for the warmth and low cost of living. We'd noticed among many that there was not always a respect for their hosts and often an aggressive disdain. We came across a young guy with a big, threatening dog. "It's OK, he's trained to only attack Mexicans!" we were assured. His mates all grinned their approval. We were loving Mexico … their food, their hospitality, their humility, their fun and colour. We were guests in their country and seeing others disrespecting it, was a sorrow.

And so it was on to Palenque, inland and at the foot of the Yucatan Peninsula, for the first of many Mayan ruins. The ancient Mayan site of Palenque was unknown

Mayan ruins at Palenque

to the Spanish when they founded the nearby town, as the jungle had reclaimed it. But since its discovery in 1740, it has been important to the area both culturally and economically. The ancient city was a major one of the Mayan Empire, which was active for more than 600 years from 250AD. The main attractions of the site include the Temple of the Inscriptions and the Palace. Initially, we stay in Palenque town and visit the well-preserved ruins which are only about 10kms out of town. The palace, in particular, is very impressive and substantial with heavily sculpted walls and feature panels. Here we learn for the first time about the Maya and how this was a substantial Mesoamerican civilisation, noted for having the only known fully-developed writing system of the pre-Columbian Americas. They are also known for their art, architecture, and mathematical and astronomical systems. Their influence spread through the areas now known as Belize and Guatemala. Blood was revered in their society, seen as a source of nourishment for the Gods and they indulged in gruesome sacrifices. The victims were often high-status prisoners of war. The poor were kept as slaves.

We're told of some picturesque waterfalls in the jungle about 20 miles away, so move there and make our camp in the carpark. The Misol Há falls are like a scene out of a Tarzan movie. The water drops about 30 metres or more into a circular pool. There is a cave-like hollowing in the bank behind the falls and this makes a beautiful, shady and cool respite from the hot sun. Soon our days were mainly spent in the pool with spells in the sun reading or mini-adventures behind the veil of the cascading water. Small numbers of people come and go during the day, but mainly this is our place. A chatty young American girl came and sat with Steph and me. Clearly a hippie, she displayed a complete comfortableness in her body-image, happy to display lots of natural body hair. Her skimpy underwear covered but a little of what our conventions normally called for. Our evenings were solitary as no one else chose to camp in a sealed car-park with no facilities.

It was here that we met Tom Beers. Tom was an ex-Vietnam veteran who had a humility that we warmed to, and he became part of our crew. He told us great tales and listened to ours. Of slightly unusual appearance due to the fact that some infection at puberty had robbed him of ever having body hair. This meant he was totally bald and had no eyebrows or eyelashes and always wore dark glasses. We got great amusement from his light-hearted proclamation that the town he came from boasted a sign saying *'The Home of Fred MacMurray'*. That cheesy actor was so much pro-establishment that Tom wanted to one day be responsible for the sign being amended to read *'The Home of Tom Beers, the Man Who Killed Fred MacMurray'*. We'd never talked directly to Vietnam soldiers before and he said he was typical of the ordinary squaddie. They didn't know why they were there, they didn't want to be there and were scared shitless. They tried to venture out of their camp into the jungle as little as possible and to make as much noise when they did so they wouldn't blunder into any Vietcong. It was normal to smoke dope all day and count off the days till they went home. He said he always felt like an invader and none of them ever saw themselves as potential liberators. He'd been to Mexico before to get away from the Illinois winter and he knew where the area's legendary 'magic' mushrooms were. These had to be gleaned immediately after a rain-shower and preferably from under a cow-pat … or so he said. Lawrie took him off one day and they returned with the goods.

None of us were into any sort of drug taking … or narcotics in any form but with the rationalisation that these were gifts of nature, we had a portion each of the mushrooms under Tom's guidance. Steph and Roly reported very little effect. Meanwhile Lawrie and I just slowly moved along into a euphoric state where everything was hilarious and worth laughing at. The beautiful greens of the surrounding jungle became just ever-so intensified and we marvelled at how wonderful our lives were. Our days here were blissful and meaningless. I remember thinking how lovely Steph looked in her shorts. She made me think of how Elizabeth

Taylor would have looked when she was young. I walked up the path behind her one day admiring her legs, thinking what a lucky, lucky man I was.

Finally, it was time to say goodbye to Tom and head further up and around the Yucatan Peninsula. The jungle was so dense that apart from when we could get out to the coast, our nights were spent in quarries which at least enabled us to get off the road. We headed to Mérida, the principal town of the modern Maya. We've enjoyed our small interactions and observations of this gentle race. Almost all the women wear their traditional brightly-coloured long skirts and the men startling white tops. Anywhere there is a settlement or a few dwellings, we'd see the washing all hung across stone walls, letting the sun keep the tunics bleached white. It was interesting that in contrast, our white tee-shirts had slowly become a light grey …
"Someone's mum just doesn't know, What someone's mum really ought to know. What someone's mum better get to know. Is Persil washes whiter."

Good beach time was spent out near Campeche and it was here that we encountered the Airstream caravan phenomenon. We'd never seen these cigar-shaped, polished-aluminium capsules in the flesh before. But here was a whole cavalcade of them. It was interesting to find them so far from the main-stream tourist spots like Acapulco, Oaxaca, Guadalajara etc. Many of the owners we spoke to were quite timid but with complete faith in their autocratic 'Captain'. It was an extremely well-organised troupe with road-leaders and tail-end Charlies. There was radio contact between the front and the back. Parking and camping were organised ahead and nothing was left to chance, and definitely, there was not the opportunity to free-hand an opportunistic adventure away from the team. There were about 35 of these space-craft-like caravans and it was like a small village on the move or even a reminder of the covered wagon expeditions going west across the USA. It wasn't our scene at all and we thought it looked a little incongruous in the old-world Mayan villages and surroundings. Too intrusive when en masse.

Merida didn't thrill us at all as it is just a market town and when you've seen towns all over the world, it takes a lot to excite us. It just became a transit-stop on the way to the well-known ruins at Chichén Itzá … although I did buy a pair of tyre-tread sandals to supplement the wooden clogs I had been wearing since London.

It was amazing to wonder on how the Maya had such a sophisticated and dominant civilization, which had withered away 1,000 years ago leading to the gentle folk subsisting today in small clusters. Typically, apart from in Merida, the Maya live

Temple of The Warriors, Chichén Itzá

Strolling through the concourse at Chichén Itzá

MEXICO

in neat thatched-roof 'stick' houses of one room in which the whole family sleeps in hammocks. Chichén Itzá was as impressive as all the photos show and we enjoyed the exercise of climbing all the structures we were allowed to climb. Youthful exercise in the sun is so invigorating, especially when surrounded by over-weight middle-aged American tourists. After Chichén Itzá we were aiming for the tip of the Yucatan Peninsula to a place called Cancun. Some pretty well-healed travellers had enthused over this supposedly idyllic spot, urging us to go ... *"You'll love it! It is a patch of paradise unlike anywhere else in Mexico."* It seems that the Mexican government had scoured the area looking for a spot to develop. They found a 22.4 km stretch of gleaming white beach backed by a blue lagoon and made the decision to pump money into making a resort which would bring tourists directly from Miami and there would be a regional boom from the inflow of money.

Deep down, we were a bit suspicious, because we know that we are not quite like most of the travellers we meet. Some seem to look upon the area almost as an outdoor Disney World, but they also seem to pine for a bit of sophistication and their own junk-food etc. And so it was that we were shattered to find the most magnificent natural setting despoiled by high-rise hotels and thousands of tourists for whom the effort of getting there was no more than saying yes to their travel agent. There had been no struggle ... no experience of the Yucatan, just an airport terminal and a quick transfer to an air-conditioned hotel and then it was beach-fun and cocktails at sunset. Of course, to support these hordes there were American supermarkets selling exactly what they could get back at home. Vacuum-packed, safe and hygienic. There were no local tiendas offering unfamiliar and exotic items for sale, no roadside stalls selling tortillas, tacos, tostados, empanadas or enchiladas. In other words, Mexico and the Maya had once-more been purged and subjugated. We hated it, we railed against it and found a spot a bit out of town at the beach and had just one night there, significant only for spotting a scorpion. I don't think we even swam in the glittering waters. We might be impoverished and a bit ragged around the edges, but we took the moral high ground. We wouldn't be going out to the Isle Mujeres (Island of Women), we wouldn't be lingering here spending money that would be going back to Uncle Sam, we'd sidle down the Caribbean coast to Belize, which was a new name for British Honduras.

Further justifying our loathing of the spot, was our passing through a shanty-town about 20 kms away in the jungle. Here was the housing for the workers needed for the resort hotels and service industries. We slept that night in a small quarry, listening to the jungle sounds and feeling so pleased with our lot. Yes, we'd had to wriggle around to get our hips into corresponding rocky depressions, there were probably mozzies, but we wouldn't have swapped our locale for a clean-sheeted, soft bed in a high-rise Sheraton in Cancun for all the tea in China or even all the tequila in Mexico.

We'd enjoyed a lot about our time traversing the Yucatan albeit that there was an over-arching sense of unfairness of how things had turned out in the latter half of the 20th Century. Once upon a time the cultivated areas grew sisal and produced a huge proportion of the world's rope. The more jungley parts produced chicle … chewing gum, which had been used by the Maya and Aztecs. Consequently, it was quite productive, but ultimately both gave way to synthetic alternatives and prosperity withered. We had enjoyed seeing part of the Monarch Butterfly migration, which is a true wonder of nature. Monarch Butterflies live between two to six weeks normally, except for every so many breeding cycles, there is one that gets the signal (with hundreds of thousands of others) to leave Canada and the USA and fly to Southern Mexico, hibernate over winter, fly back, mate and die. They fly to the same trees every year even though they are maybe eight generations removed. I also loved the Yucatan because Steph was proving to be a wonderful pillion and from time to time she would squeeze me almost to death, calling over my shoulder that she was having a 'gust'. I am not sure my mother even had 'gusts' of love as demonstrative as these air-restricting ones were, certainly no one else had … and it made me feel pretty special.

We hopped our way down the coast, staying on white, white sand beaches, backed by azure, blue seas. We were absorbing as much knowledge as we could relating to the new nation of Belize. The South American Handbook gave us the bones only. We knew it was the only British Territory in Central America, we knew it still had British Army bases, we knew it was anti-hippie, we learned it was pretty empty, we knew it wasn't very Spanish … and that Americans rarely, if ever, visited. Very few travellers we'd met had been there but the word was we'd never get in with long hair and big beards. To this end we had a big clean up, washed all our clothes, Steph cut our hair, we trimmed the trimmable, and we made ready for another border crossing. We also smugly reflected that the *Septics* had been wrong about the tyres!

> To accomplish great things, we must not only act, but also dream; not only plan, but also believe.
>
> **ANATOLE FRANCE (1844 - 1924)**

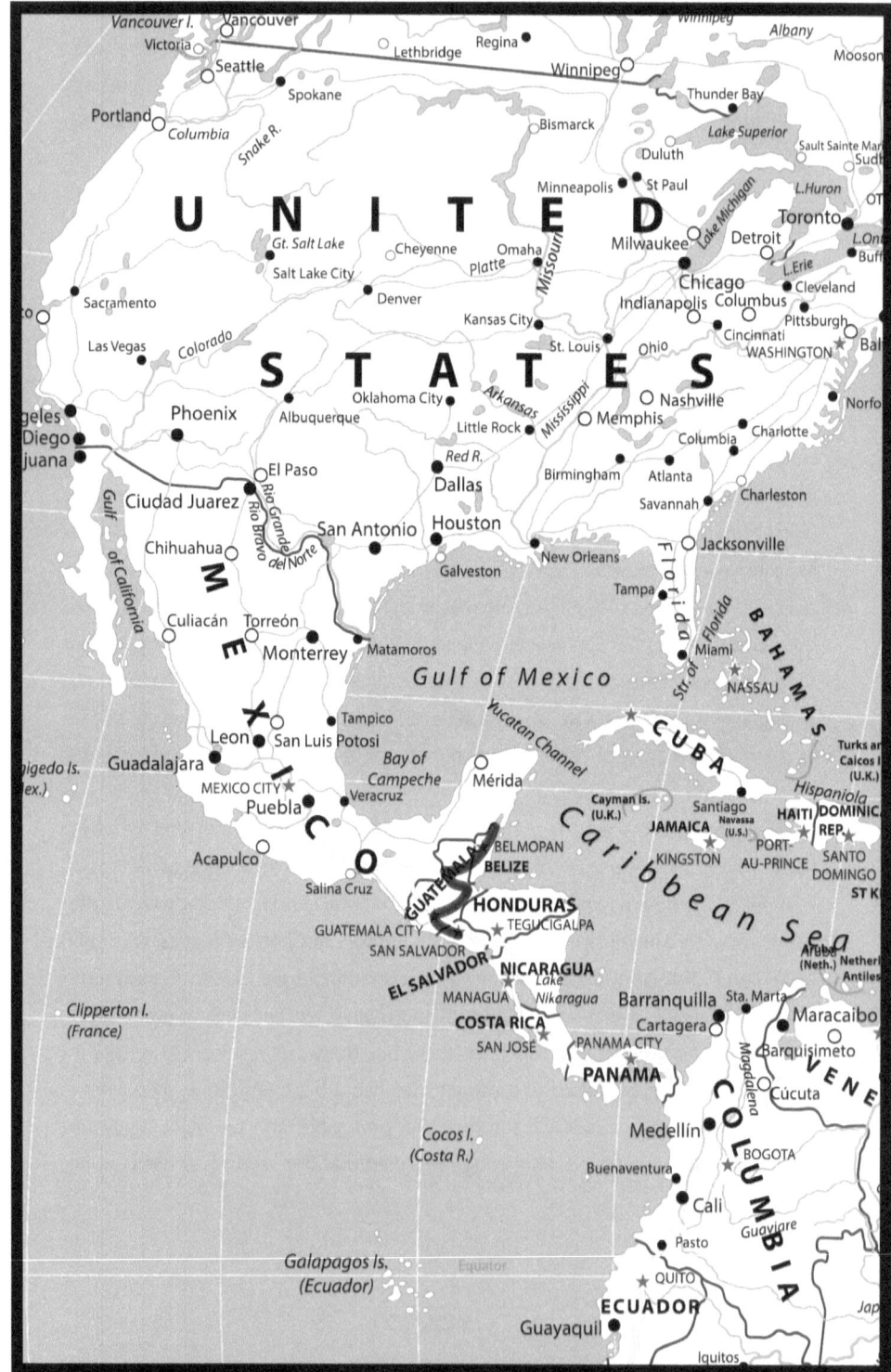

CHAPTER 4

BELIZE AND GUATEMALA

Belize welcomed us with the most amazing tropical downpour, right when we were in the middle of the border crossing process. We'd exited Mexico but hadn't yet been accepted into Belize. It is an interesting reflection, recalling how these countries didn't have to let us in, and consequently, we were always a little on edge. Belize didn't have much in the way of tourist attractions, as the small coastal area is swampy and 90% of the land is forested. It is also at the top of the area known as The Mosquito Coast. As a consequence, not many travellers came through this way. We were on one side of the broad, dusty thoroughfare and just as we completed the initial part of the 'getting through' process, when a deluge started, the likes of which we had never seen before. It was like a river was being poured from the sky. There was no way we could just dash across the road … there was no room between the raindrops. Fortunately, after 30 mins or so 'Her upstairs' threw a switch and it stopped, just as quickly as it had started. This meant we could finally get across the road to our drug interrogation. Belize has a reputation for being really strict on marijuana possession or usage, so the big, Caribbean-Black Border Guards put the frighteners on us before we could even get in.

I'd been through a similar process a few years earlier entering Turkey. There, they had a poster that they took us through, with the lengths of prison-stay for the various quantities of dope possessed, all listed. It included the death penalty for a decent amount. Our crew weren't users and were totally sobered by the lecture …

then in the first town, a guy saunters up and asks "You want Afghani Gold?" "What is it?" we ask ... and he opens a big paper bag of green leaves. We almost shat ourselves on the spot, imagining our instant incarceration. It was a bit like that here in the sultry heat of Central America. Of course one of the problems was, that we did look a bit like extras from Easy Rider. I can see why border officials were suspicious ... we weren't very appealing-looking. We were pretty tatty, young, bearded, our bikes had a dusty oil-ingrained patina and quite clearly we weren't going to enhance the economy of anywhere we travelled through. Were we worth the bother, you could almost see them asking themselves? Roly and I wore army-surplus trousers which we found ideal for riding, as they had lots of pockets and baggy crotches, meaning they didn't ride up and cause strangulation of the male soft bits. I also wore a matching combat jacket, so probably looked like a failed guerrilla ... someone Che had sent packing.

Initially, the authorities seemed pleasant enough, but after processing Steph and Lawrie, they decided they didn't like either of the Molloy boys, even with our fresh hair-cuts and clean clothes. This quandary was only resolved with a bit of old-fashioned baksheesh. Begrudgingly we parted with some money, and finally, we were in ... and pretty relieved. We won't be tarrying in Belize. It is a very small country with only two roads and we're using it to get through to Guatemala where we will spend time in Tikal, the biggest, most famous of the Mayan ruins, before getting onto the route south. We are fascinated to find English being spoken again. Some of the border guards spoke with posh Oxford-type accents, certainly putting our efforts to shame. Others had more of a Caribbean Rasta lilt, but the lack of Spanish being spoken is most novel. Although completely different from Cancun with no resorts or tourists, there was the similarity of no tiendas. The stores carried imported foods from Britain and whilst it was quaint to see the familiar brands in the shops, the prices were off-the-scale and we bought very little. More than 25% of the total imports to Belize are food. Apparently, there is a drive to make the country self-sufficient in food production but it is a long way off. After the loss of the mahogany timber trade ... and the chicle bleeding, the old British Honduras fell into decline, needing to be supported by Mother England. There are only moderate exports of citrus, sugar, bananas, cacao beans and coconuts.

Mennonite communities have established themselves to do agricultural work and whilst these Anabaptist church members farm as was done 150 years ago ...

shunning all motorized equipment or vehicles ... they are major contributors to the economy. The Mennonites are very similar to the more well-known Amish and both come from the same roots in Switzerland. The Anabaptists separated from the state church in 1693, as they believed religion was a grown-up's thing and adult baptism was central to their beliefs. The Anabaptists had a minor scism later, to bifurcate into the Amish and the Mennoniites. The Mennonites still speak Plautdietsch, which is a German dialect of the East Low German group with an admixture of Dutch mixed in.

For our first night in Belize, we take advantage of finding a formal camping ground near the border town of Corozal. Here is a scattering of fellow young travellers and somehow we end up with a cabin of some sort, sharing with others. After all the usual socialising and tall-tale telling, we had semi-settled when an American couple knocked on the door. "Hey, we're going over the border in the morning ... so enjoy!" With this, they handed over a big brown paper bag of marijuana and left. We weren't sure if things were looking up or down. Roly says we smoked up a storm ... but as I am a non-smoker I have my doubts. In the morning we found another Yank and gave him only half a bag of dope, urging him to take care as already we'd found there were regular road-blocks where documentation was checked.

On our way to the capital Belmopan, we had an irritating although minor break-down. We were struggling in the mid-afternoon sun. We were low on water and parched. To our delight, a big American pick-up truck appeared in the distance, the first vehicle we had seen for quite a while. It slowed as it approached and the passenger-side window was wound down and a burly young white guy put his head out and just as they were almost abreast of us he shouted "JESUS LOVES YOU!" ... and they drove off in a shower of stones and a cloud of dust. Our admiration of Christianity plummeted even further.

Belmopan had only been the capital for seven years, replacing Belize City which had taken a huge hit with a destructive tidal wave in 1961. We weren't interested in exploring Belmopan much, as we were aware of needing to keep in front of the approaching wet season, whilst still allowing for a bit of a rest-up in Tikal. Not that there was much to see as the population was only about 3,000. We had more interest in getting out to the coastal Belize City where maybe there would be mail and at least the opportunity to send a missive home. Once there, we set up the tent in another formal camp.

We had zig-zagged a couple of times getting to the camp, and while setting up, we send Roly back to a shop we'd passed, for provisions. Not usually in his brief, we reckoned on it being a piece of cake … no Spanish needed, shop already found … no essence of hunter-gatherer required. So off he goes out of the camp and down the road and in full view of us turns left at the first junction instead of right. With us jumping up and down, shouting and waving, Roly rides off out of sight, going God knows where. We wonder if and when we will ever see him again.

In time Roly found his way back, albeit without the supplies but enshrined in trip folklore. My letter home tells of us all being well and happy with Roly still the only one not suffering from 'Montezuma's Revenge'. I tell of only one snake encounter as being close enough to scare me, recording … *'I suspect it of being a Coral Snake – 20 mins and no more white man'*. I mention the huge mosquitoes and also express a little envy towards Americans with big budgets enabling them to eat and drink well … while we scrape along on a diet of beans, rice and fruit. Our budget is US$40 per week for the four of us, including petrol, so on the face of it, it's not Rolls Royce travel … except in our hearts it is. We're loving it. It is exotic, it is hard and adventurous, it is bigger than Ben Hur, and already we know the memories and our friendships will last forever. The roads are tough though, being unsealed and when wet they turn to mud and quickly become rutted and remain that way when they dry. Lawrie takes a pretty good tumble but both he and Bessie were not too damaged to continue.

It is now over three months since we left London. We're tanned, lean (and mean?). Our thoughts and conversations are now almost always about food, being as we are constantly in a low-level state of deprivation. When we are not listing our favourite meals and salivating accordingly, we are sharing 'Fantasy Land'. We're pretty snug, the four of us in the little tent and most nights when we settle, someone will ask "What was in Fantasy Land today?" During the many hours of riding it is natural that your mind wanders and creates day-dreams to while away the hours. Lawrie's often seem to involve him rescuing a rich and beautiful widow who becomes a generous benefactor … in more than one way. Mine regularly see me unexpectedly called into the All Blacks or getting to race at the Isle of Man … which usually involves escapades of magnificent skill and bravery. The thing about Fantasy Land is that it can be outrageous when said aloud, yet during the day it has seemed real enough to help with the tedium of sitting still for so long. Roly and Steph are a little less imaginative in their out-pourings … or more reserved when it comes to making fools of themselves. We routinely compare notes each night about what has been seen and/or enjoyed during the day.

We camp between Belize City and the border with Guatemala, and whilst tinkering about in the morning before setting off, we see a horse and vintage buggy clip-clopping along with what looks like Abraham Lincoln and his wife aboard. We give a cheery wave, which the two stony visages ignore … possibly not seeing us, or choosing not to. Once we get going 45 minutes later, it is not unexpected that we come across them on the road, and wave again. Their parchment-like faces do not alter. We're disappointed as we like the thought of this slightly oddball sect working away, tilling the fields just as was done hundreds of years ago, having barn-raising parties and the like. Further up the road, we have to stop to adjust the load on one of the bikes. This is a bit of a constant, as we foolishly don't have aerolastics. We rely upon trussing everything up with rope and hitching it on to the bike with dubious knotting skill. Being as none of us had been scouts or yachties, things often come loose. And so it was, that our now favourite, old-time, early-American, film-set extras came past us for the third time. By now we were pretty determined to get a smile or some sort of recognition … maybe a twitch of a hand in a mini-wave. Sadly, their dour, miserable countenances remained frozen as they passed on and out of our lives. No waving infidels were going to get recognition from the Lincolns. Later we look at a $5 bill and reckon we were right … it probably was Abe and the missus.

The border crossing had been no more than a minor irritation and delay. We're pretty excited about getting into Guatemala and through to Tikal. Tikal is deep in the jungle and not normally accessed by land from Belize. In fact, the South American Handbook notes that Tikal can only be accessed in dry weather by road and normally by plane. Road is a pretty loose descriptive term when applied to what we struggle along. We encounter a couple of local buses waddling along through the ruts and hollows at little more than walking pace but other than seeing a tiny two-stroke Suzuki Jeep, we see no vehicles on our way to Tikal. That little Suzuki impressed us immensely as it passed us at a particularly difficult bit of deeply rutted, muddy road leading to a sharp, tricky climb. With its distinctive high-pitched, buzzing, smokey engine working over-time, it wiggled and swayed its way up and over the top of the crest, never to be seen again. The narrow wheel-base had enabled it to make a way between the ruts. We wondered if a bigger, more macho Land Rover could have achieved the same result.

Arriving in Tikal was pretty special because it truly had been a struggle. We felt a bit like explorers finally stumbling into The Promised Land. A jungle-lined clearing opened up before us. The infrastructure of Tikal was pretty laid-back and non-intrusive. The jungle is very dense in this region so everything shares the cleared area. The grass runway for the small planes that fly in every day is bordered by a couple of rustic eateries and a comedor selling a range of foods. We set up our tent off the top-end of the runway, just to one side, about 15m from the jungle's edge. Our guidebook recommends bringing your own food, water, hammock and mosquito net, however, we were happy to use the local provider to top-up our basic ingredients. It was part of the fun of being there … and being different. There were no caravans … you'd never get an Airstreamer along the roads we had endured. Very few people over-nighted, other than the pretty wealthy who had a hotel down the other end of the air-strip. We never went there and they never ventured up to see us either. Good result!

There was a steady stream of newbies arriving each day on the plane from Guatemala City. They'd do six or seven hours in the Tikal park area and depart before dusk. Our previous jungle experiences paled, as we absorbed what we were a part of. Spider monkeys were swinging through the trees like circus trapeze artists … only 10 times better. There were brightly-coloured toucans, parrots and delicate hummingbirds. These, in particular, were high on our list of special birds. Our all-time park favourites, however, were the friendly coatimundis. We didn't know about these odd-looking ground mammals before. They are from the racoon family and are active both during the day and at night. They are furry with a ringed tail which they often hold erect and while their snouts are quite pointed, they are also pig-like. They have a reputation for being intelligent and are happy to walk through your camp at any time … or climb a tree right next to you. We loved them. Also known to be in the surrounding jungle were jaguars and at night we would hear calls that sounded like they were from a big cat. However, we were informed that they were more likely to be the noises the howler monkeys make at night … to frighten the jaguars. Pretty successful as they frightened us as well. We knew this was a habitat of the poisonous fer-de-lance snake and also the tarantula spider, but didn't go out of our way to encounter them. At night there was a deafening cacophony of exotic sounds, all alien to our ears, but nice to go to sleep to. Each morning at 6.00 am while still dark, we would awake to a strident call of "Flores … Flores!" This was the call to the bus which would depart shortly after for the regional town, 64 kms away on Lago Petén Itzá. A few hardy souls would emerge from shadows and climb aboard for this epic ride. Mainly the bus brought in supplies.

It was hot and sticky, but that was ok too, as we were young and durable. It is good to have a base for a week or so, as it enables us to explore and have a bit of routine to our lives. When on the road, you are constantly in 'hunter-gatherer' mode, always making decisions. You've never seen what you are seeing, you've not been around each corner, you don't know where or when you will eat, you don't know where you will sleep … will it be another quarry? … you don't even know where you will go to the toilet. What about fuel? So there are a lot of low-level stressors, which while stimulating, are also a little tiring, especially when you are in the vanguard, making most of these decisions.

The crew is great, we are so disparate, yet so compatible with no semblance of sulkiness. No one is moody or depressive. It is almost like they have been hand-selected! We each have our roles and no one covets the others'. Lawrie is proving to be the most amazing fire maker. His patience is numbing, and watching him layering up tiny twigs with following graded layers to make a wonderful pyramid that has never failed to ignite and please, is a joy. Steph has now assumed the role as the main cook which has elevated things a bit and our stodges are now quite palatable. All the while, Roly tinkers and tweaks, keeping our girls running as sweetly as possible. We let him do the mechanical worrying, so enabling stress-free riding. The fuel available is not always of high octane and the girls complain a bit, but it is what it is. Me … well, Lawrie has now christened me 'Blashers'. Somewhere we had read an account of Colonel John Blashford-Snell's latest venture where he (and half the British Army) navigated the length of the Congo River. Lawrie felt he was an autocratic blunderer and their expedition seemed as poorly planned and expedited as ours. The fact that he wore a pith helmet and probably called to his men in a "Tally-ho" fashion made him a figure we could deride from afar. We had 'toffs' in the rugby club, so felt we were experts in the field. Anyway, I just continued to steer the ship, hopefully providing guidance and blind-optimism.

Tikal is the biggest of the ancient Mayan cities and has five magnificent temples, imaginatively named Temple 1, Temple 2, Temple 3 etc. These rise up out of the jungle to impressive heights (between 50m and 65m) and again Lawrie and I would endeavour to run up these for 'training'. Each day we would independently wander

Looking across to Temple 11 at Tikal

and explore, often with different iterations of the team. Once day, Steph-less, we had occasion to strike up a 'relationship' with a casually-dressed, but elegant Englishwoman. Somehow we decided that this was the famous actress Julie Christie. She was very interested in our venture and told us of some friends of hers doing something similar, riding out to Greece on old bikes. Of course, we thought, that she thought, that we were pretty cool. Steph dismissed our enthusiasm, in an uncharacteristically bitchy way. She disputed it was the actress and we have to admit that we didn't actually ask her for her name … that didn't just fit with the chat. We exchanged pleasantries a few times over the next couple of days, but by then it was too late to ask.

The nights sometimes rained heavily and to this end, we dug a channel similar to the Suez Canal around three sides of the tent after experiencing a major inundation. This seemed to work. Steph and I managed a fair bit of time on our own, sometimes sneaking a skin-on-skin siesta during the day. We were still euphorically enamoured of each other, and any opportunity was an opportunity. I never felt guilty for feeling so happy … just sometimes a little over-awed by it all. We were still getting to know the edge-bits and limits to our relationship, likes, dislikes, phobias etc, when I decided it was a good idea to climb a steel ladder that had been attached to what looked like a mausoleum. This would get us to another elevated surface where we could sunbathe or look out over the available vista. This is when I learned of brave Little Steph's fear of heights. She really didn't want to go up the ladder and resisted very vocally. She'd got halfway up and although she didn't want to seem like a quivering softie, she didn't want to go up any more. An impasse resulted ... with me insensitively cajoling. She wasn't interested in the 'Face the fear ... and do it anyway!' mantra. However, ultimately she steeled herself and trembling and cursing, she went up the last few rungs which got her in a position to pop her head over the top ... and there were a small group of young American tourists lying out in the sun listening to the whole episode. Steph was mortified. Needless to say, there was little interaction between us and we had to out-wait them so we could get down safely and with dignity.

After a week or so we decided we'd sampled most of what Tikal had to offer and it was time to move on. This meant facing the tough section of road out to Flores again. This was duly done with no spills and a sense of satisfaction. We were finding Guatemala quite different to anywhere we'd been to date. Firstly, the population was primarily of local Indian stock, with the Spanish influence being quite minor. This meant the people we encountered mostly were short and stocky like the Mayans and almost always in traditional garb. The terrain we were crossing was tropical and often hilly. Unlike the Yucatan Peninsula where there are almost no rivers (they flow underground), here rivers abound and almost everywhere the road crosses a river, there'd be a small settlement. The acclaimed Lake Atitlan area with its volcano would have to be missed, as it was a day's ride north of Guatemala City. We were coming in from the East then heading South. We'd read great things about the lake ... but we'd heard the same utterances about Cancun. We'd leave it to the hippies, we didn't really want to back-track.

We were just about into Guatemala when upon nearing a small settlement we encountered two Honda XL350s heading towards us. This gave rise to more than just a stop and chat. Almost instantly there was an easy bonding with the riders Mark and Pete. We decided to stock up with some victuals from the local tienda and have a picnic while we caught up with news and advice about the ways ahead respectively. I had spotted some of the locals down at the river just a short way back and it looked like a good spot for a break from the hot sun. The track leading down to the swimming hole looked dauntingly steep but with the bravado of the young and foolish, we plunged over the edge and once on the downward slope, there was no stopping. Gratifyingly, Roly and Lawrie followed and nonchalantly we

First meeting with The Plastics

began our relationship with the boys who would become 'The Plastic Expedition' in our weeks ahead. Mark and Pete were both Englishmen who lived in Tasmania. Their Hondas were bespoke adventure bikes with neat, tidy luggage. In fact, everything about them was neat and tidy, purposeful and tested. We felt a bit clumsy and ill-equipped alongside them. Outwardly our 'expeditions' were polar opposites. They looked the part ... we looked like the Clampetts from *The Beverly Hillbillies*.

Sometimes, a rapport can be struck with people at a moment's interaction and so it was with the 'Plastics'. We instantly liked them ... there was no big-noting, no bull shit, they were of a similar age and from our part of the world. They had started their ride in Panama, so we were able to fill us in on some of the things that we were likely to encounter. Similarly, we could tell them about the horrors of the roads ahead of them as they continued on to Tikal. I am sure they took this on with an internal wry grin, as clearly their bikes were designed for the terrain, whilst ours had been designed for the gentle English country lanes of our forefathers. Not only had they selected their bikes after much thought and research, but they even put one through most of a season's motocross races. It turned out that Pete was a sponsored off-road rider and before finally giving the thumbs up, he even tested with their luggage aboard. We didn't get this info out of them at our first meeting, nor the fact that Mark was the Tasmanian B Grade Trials Champion … 'trials' being the sport where you ride a motorcycle across outrageously steep, and rutted, rocky terrain without putting your foot down. Each 'dab' is a point added to your score and the person with the smallest score wins. Accordingly, it was no real surprise that when we finally decided it was time to continue our respective journeys, they fired up their waiting steeds, quickly stood up on the foot-pegs and neatly 'braap, braaped' up the steep track in a shower of stones and were soon out of earshot.

Lawrie looked at me and muttered, "So, how the fuck are we going to get out of here, Blashers!" The answer, of course, was one at a time with much pushing and assistance of all the team. We were glad the boys weren't there to see our limited abilities. It had been a good break and for once, we really did "Hope to see you again!" There was a strong possibility because they were looping up into Mexico and then heading south because like us, they were heading for South America.

We were within 30 kms of hitting a good road when a lower shock-absorber bolt on Samantha broke. At least this broke at a beautiful river and whilst we lacked a hand-drill to remove the remnants, we got a local workshop to do this for us. They even had a seemingly suitable bolt to insert, although we were a little doubtful regarding its tensile strength. The last few weeks have been incredibly hard on the bikes as they are relentlessly pounded hour after hour, sometimes significant air being seen beneath the wheels. In the fantasy world of tall-tales and derring-do, I'd even reckoned I'd seen Bessie a metre in the air.

The rivers of Guatemala also gave rise to amusing interactions with the local Indian women. Their 'wash-day' was, of course, spent down at the river, where the village mujer did the laundry en masse. It was always fun joining them for this. Naturally, being an emancipated lot, we all washed our own clothes. The local indigenous women could not believe that Steph did not do all our laundry … what kind of woman was she? They also could not believe how inept we all were at river-laundry. We had none of their skills when it came to the pounding of the soapy clothes on the rocks. This they did skillfully and seemingly endlessly, all the while keeping up the general chat, laughter and hubbub that the day obviously called for. Not for them would there ever be the solitary 'wash-day blues' of the developed world's liberated women. The occasions always appeared raucous with only a loose semblance of order and safety. Kids of all sizes played in the river while their mums pounded and wrung and stretched and finally laid-out the clothes in the sun. Steph

Roly observing wash-day

took her rebukes in good fun and always won their hearts by kidnapping their babies and showering them with tummy-kisses and other demonstrations of overt affection. Her ability to engage using her love of the young filled my heart with joy. She was so skilled with them and clearly, her fondness for the wriggling little brown babies was ingrained, not just part of her training as an obstetrics nurse.

Guatemala City was just another large city to be endured, then forgotten. We got mail which was always a high-point but cities always meant spending beyond our budget. Usually, we would have to pay for our camp instead of just finding somewhere to set up our tent and sometimes we would even have to pay a taxi to lead us to where we were going. Our missives home were now restricted to the efficient single-page Aerogrammes, which are light enough to not be too expensive. In one I complain about the postage costs and relay how Steph had attempted to send a substantial letter to her folks, but the cost was going to be $6, which was our food budget for three days ... so no letter went home. Our funds are pretty low and Roly has given mum instructions to sell his Yamaha Trail bike.

The days are hot and my nose is only just holding its own against the ravages of the sun. The heat in the middle of the day is such that we just hide somewhere in the shade. Our days often start in the dark as we like to get on the road just as the sun is rising. We are usually a little chilled as we cut through the dawn air but always with the knowledge, that day will soon warm us and ultimately send us to shelter.

We've found also that if we are resolute in pushing on, we can prolong our time in the sweltering sun by briefly stopping at a river and plunging ourselves fully-clothed into the water, boots and all. This leaves us completely sodden and the evaporating process of removing the moisture from our clothes, replicates refrigeration, and for some time we are quite comfortable.

We're enjoying observing the Latin American lifestyle. Sometimes their lack of material things is balanced by a relaxed quality of life that we nod our heads to. We love the way they enjoy their siestas, usually with mum and dad, affectionately top-and-tailing it together in a big hammock under the trees. We laugh at how sometimes at a small road-side *'tienda'*, you might be served by a kid who never lets go of a rope which disappears through the back, sometimes right out to the trees. The rope is constantly being gently pulled back in forth in a slow rhythmic fashion ... connected to hammock containing a sleeping baby. Family life is very shared and we never see small children having tantrums. They cry appropriately and never seem to whine and whinge. It is not a poor poverty ... it is what it is, and we don't get a sense of deprivation. The small houses with dirt floors and chickens running through them seem suited to their way of life. There is a lot of happiness and laughter about, and we think that counts for lots more than possessions.

We've also been teaching Roly to swim. Being that he has never had any meat on his bones and that mostly our weather in Wellington is at best temperate, Roly always found swimming to be something to avoid where possible. When warm water and tropical outside-temperatures were married together, it was a completely different scenario. Now swimming was enjoyable and something to look forward to. A few more skills were needed though to ensure he could enjoy rivers and beaches safely. Being a typical Ocker, Lawrie swam as naturally as he perambulated. I found I could keep up with his 'crawl' for a while but would always have to give up and watch as he effortlessly surged away. He reckoned I was trying too hard and just needed to be more efficient, I had to truly make it like I was walking, something I could do all day. It should be boredom that stops you, not tiredness. Years later I would achieve this level. Roly never became a strong swimmer but he was at least proficient enough to not need watching over ... well almost.

We chose the Pacific Coast route to head south and into El Salvador. We were keen to see the sea again. This time it would be the Pacific Ocean, which of course connects us with home.

Travel is only glamorous in retrospect.

PAUL THEROUX (1941 -)

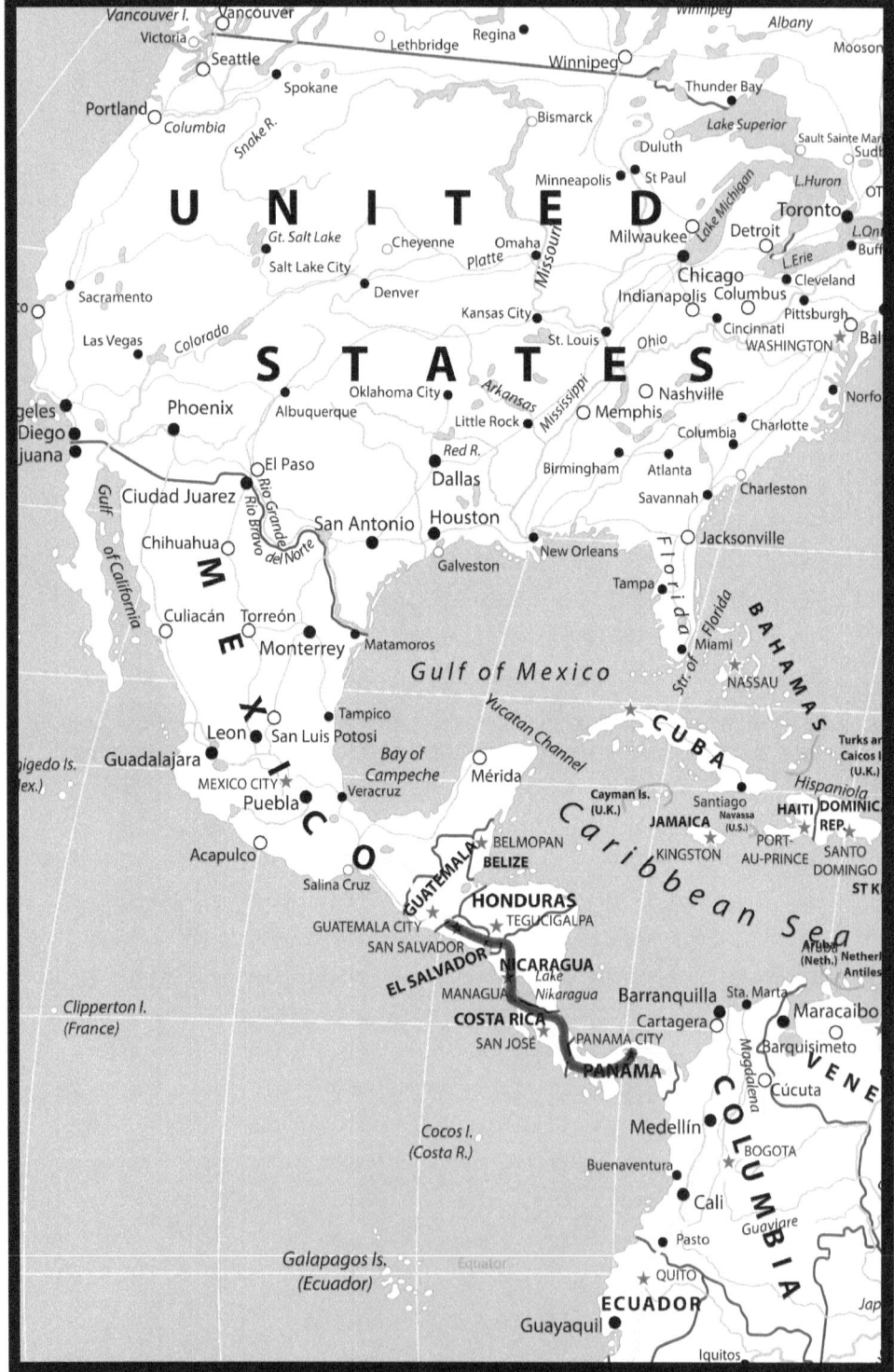

CHAPTER 5

EL SALVADOR, HONDURAS, NICARAGUA, COSTA RICA, PANAMA

El Salvador is the smallest and most populated of the Central America countries and the border crossing is yet again frustratingly slow and bureaucratic. We get sent from official to official, each checking one thing and demanding a small fee. They have a form that requires a lot of stamps and only when these are all collected are you able to pass on to the final and most important guy, the one with the weighted barrier-arm at the end of the border compound. Once he has checked you have all your stamps, he puts the form into a 44-gallon drum which serves as an incinerator ... burning the results of your last three or four hours of toil. With a conspiratorial grin, he then lifts the arm to let you enter. You've been rorted, but you are in. Once through and hopping down the coast, we see similarities to both Mexico and Guatemala but with only a very small percentage of actual indigenous

Indians. Most of the population are mestizos (mixed European and Indian) with a significant number of Central Europeans who arrived in large numbers after the Second World War. A lot of the country we pass through is flat, and we're seeing banana and coffee plantations.

It is on one of the beautiful beaches that we face up to the fact that Penelope cannot go on. For some time, her big-end bearing has been failing and we need to replace it. In a sandy, al-fresco workshop (the beach), Roly goes to work. This is a major job necessitating the engine being removed then totally stripped. We have spare bearings and she will get a good overhaul. It is unbelievably hot, making every spanner and metal surface a touch-hazard if not kept shaded. Although normally a pretty good assistant, I am hardly worth my title, unable to keep with Roly's steady and relentless slog. The heat and humidity drive me into the sea and the shade at regular intervals. Roly doesn't have a reputation as a sun-lover, but on this occasion his stamina is impressive … he pretty much just keeps at it until the job is done. Lawrie does have a reputation of being able to lie in the noon-day sun … but he is useless mechanically.

We've been made aware of a truck and bus workshop about 20 miles away and once we have the flywheels out of the engine, we head there confident they will have the large socket needed to undo the big-end nuts, so releasing the individual flywheels. Big-end replacement is quite a specialised job because of the need for the flywheels to align perfectly when re-assembled or the engine will vibrate and be stressed unduly. To help with this I had used a square to scribe a guiding line across the edges of the two flywheels then centre-punched one and used a compass to score a large-diameter line across both. The purpose being, that if the scriber perfectly follows the line I have marked after the rebuild … then it is true.

The workshop foreman has no English but understands quickly what is needed. He undoes the large nuts and splits the flywheels for us. This reveals a bit of a disaster … the new big-end bearing is the wrong one. It might well be marked as Panther 120 but it has tapered shafts and Penelope's are parallel … bugger, buggery-bugger. But wait … what if the shoulders of our new one are built-up using weld then turned and ground down to the right size? Obviously, this must be done accurately as the parallel shafts need to be a tight, interference-fit in the flywheels. Our man semi-reluctantly agrees to the job and tells us to come back tomorrow. We are appreciative that he is prioritising our work and doing it himself.

The welded-up big-end pin

We arrive back the next day, just as he is tightening the big-end nuts. With a grin, he hands over the assembly. No, no we indicate ... not so fast, you must check with dial gauges that the wheels are true. This almost caused a bit of ill-feeling, as it was like we were doubting his skill and workshop-craft. We know from experience that often the flywheels need to be given a bit of a nudge with a big lump-hammer to align them perfectly. With a little reticence, he fits the flywheel shafts into some vee-blocks, sets up some dial-gauges and turns the crank. Unbelievably it runs almost perfectly true, way, way inside our indicated tolerance of two-thousandths of an inch. The charge is realistic and it is a couple of happy boys who make their way back to the beach for the rebuild.

Putting Penelope back together again was as hot and hard as taking her apart but only three days after reaching the beach, we purred off again, happy that not only did Penelope have a new big-end bearing but she had new main bearings as well. This would make her 'bottom-end' bullet-proof and unlikely we would be going in there again on this trip. Our man at the truck-stop had done a wonderful job

EL SALVADOR, HONDURAS, NICARAGUA, COSTA RICA, PANAMA

as Penelope was now silky smooth ... well as smooth as a thumping 650cc single cylinder can be.

We were finding it interesting discovering how many different sorts of bananas there were. Clearly, there were some that were for cooking, but there were many others of differing shapes and sizes, some not even bent. We sampled some deep-fried banana chips and declared ourselves fans. Coconuts were still a staple for us and we had got to like the frijoles and tortillas. Most days we'd have one meal of these from a roadside stall. These were easy cheap stops and better than our rice stodges. We were still being incredibly frugal and our leisure time was still being filled with tales of our favourite foods. Salivating over foods as diverse as 'Grandma's sugar buns' from Steph's family, to chocolate 'buzz bars on the ice' from most Kiwi dairies, filled in a lot of hours.

About this time, we decided we should try and make our own frijoles, so bought some pinto beans and put them in water to soak one in of our plastic water bottles that rode on the front of the Panthers' front forks. We weren't sure how long we needed to soak the beans ... in fact we didn't know anything about the process but figured this would be a good start. A subsequent perusal of a recipe sees the first line read ... *'Combine water, pinto beans, and garlic into a large pot and cover; Cook over low heat for 5 1/2 hours; stir salt into beans and continue cooking until beans are very soft, about 30 minutes more.'* Well at the time we didn't know about the six hours of cooking ... we'd do it our way. Unfortunately, the process got interrupted when after a couple of days of the beans not softening up, in error, whilst berating us boys about something, Steph grabbed the wrong water bottle and instead getting a slug of clean (albeit a little warm) water ... she got a full and enthusiastic mouthful of fermenting purple pinto juice. We made it worse by guffawing at her spraying it all over the roadside. That ended our experiment with producing our own frijoles.

We hit the Honduras border late in the afternoon and are pleased that there is an on-shore cooling breeze making it not too unpleasant. I do notice though that at 6.00 pm it is showing 98° Fahrenheit. It shows that we are adjusting to the heat when we think that 98° is quite cool. We're going to cut across the Pacific Coast side of Honduras to Nicaragua, by-passing their capital with the beguiling name of Tegucigalpa. We're still staying ahead of the rainy season and are keen to continue to do so. There isn't anything noted in the South American Handbook to entice us further into Honduras. All the countries so far are uniformly poor and all have been very hospitable to us. Both border controls are equally friendly and equally rapacious, but we are pretty used to that now.

There has been a lot of bitterness between El Salvador and Honduras and as recently as seven years earlier there had been a brief and infamous war. This was the so-called *Football War*, also known as the *100 Hour War*. Honduras is five times larger in area with a considerably smaller population. With the squeeze of population in El Salvador, it was pretty natural that a reasonable number would migrate to the much emptier Honduras. The catalyst for their brief skirmish was the two-leg qualification series for the soccer World Cup. The first game in Honduras was won by Honduras and the second leg in El Salvador was won by El Salvador. Particularly after the second game, there was a lot of violence against El Salvadorians living in Honduras, resulting in many having to flee for their lives back to El Salvador. The deciding rubber was played in neutral Mexico City, but when El Salvador won that to go through to the FIFA finals, more violence erupted and again the El Salvadorians in Honduras were the targets and genocide was alleged. Two weeks later on 14th July 1969, after the Honduran government had done nothing to quell the instability, the El Salvadorians attacked both from the air and with ground-forces. The two air forces both had American World War Two aircraft and the air was filled with near-vintage Mustangs and Corsairs. Honduras called for help from Nicaragua as there was a possibility that Tegucigalpa could be over-run. A cease-fire was arranged on the night of 18th July and El Salvador finally withdrew its troops on 2nd August 1969 but it would be another 10 years before a full cease-fire was agreed to.

It is only 140 kms or so across from El Salvador to the Nicaragua border, so we camped near the border once through. The twilights are not long and we settle early. We have a late start to the day (7.00am) due to the ravages of diarrhoea and quite early in the piece, we strike trouble. We were in some foothills, temporarily taking us away from the coastal plains. I slowed for a tight right-hand bend then accelerated hard uphill in third gear and was gently healing over into a left-hand curve when a large 'PING' issued from Penelope like the snapping of a stud or something similarly serious. After a detailed look around and starting and re-starting the engine we can see that, 'oh shit! The barrel is moving about and oil is pissing out!' The two head nuts on the long through-studs on the pushrod tunnel side had both stripped their threads. The nuts were found to be brass, so no wonder really. Unable to find replacements in our spares … probably on the M56 motorway near

Wash day

Liverpool ... we rob Samantha of one, so both girls are running three head nuts instead of four. We tighten down vigorously and cross our fingers. It is not ideal but there is no other option.

Another turgid, stressful border crossing is ultimately achieved and we get into Nicaragua, Central America's largest country. Nicaragua has three distinct geographical regions: the Pacific lowlands ... fertile valleys which the Spanish colonists settled, the Amerrisque Mountains (North-central highlands), and the Mosquito Coast (Atlantic lowlands/Caribbean lowlands). We cut across the Pacific lowlands as it is the shortest way through to Panama. We're now pretty keen to get to South America. We've seen the way so far as being an entrée ... a bloody lovely one, filling and delicious ... but now we are ready for the main course. We're pretty interested in what we will find in Managua as it was largely destroyed by a destructive earthquake in 1972 and we've heard that possibly as many as 11,000 people were killed and way over a quarter of a million made homeless. Our South American Handbook admits to having no knowledge of possible re-build so includes all the out-of-date information in the publication.

Although this part of Nicaragua is a *tierra caliente* (hot land) region, it is undulating enough to not be too unpleasant during the middle of the day. I recall riding into the remains of Managua and some young hot-shots on tiny motorbikes decided to play with us and on a hilly section a 125cc Honda loudly showed us up. Penelope may be 650cc, but her design and performance date from the 1930s … and she is two-up and heavily laden. Bessie is of course from the 1930s but she is light and sporty and we know Lawrie could have bested the young punks … if he'd wanted to.

Four and a half years after the devastation of the earthquake, Managua was still in a state of chaos. Most of the old city had been demolished and a lot of rebuilding had taken place about 15-20 kms away. Tens of thousands of people live in shanty-town settlements surrounding the city. Managua is on the southern shores of Lake Managua and could have been quite picturesque if it wasn't for its present predicament. We're only visiting to get and send mail. We don't have the money to spend up large and contribute to the economy. We've read somewhere that Mick Jagger's wife Bianca is from Nicaragua and feel they can do a better job sprinkling gold dust about.

We learn in Managua that mum has sold Roly's trail bike for a good price and the funds will be forwarded on. That is good news. Lawrie sends mail home and notes that the stamp features a picture of the NZ Coxed Four collapsed over their boat after winning the Gold Medal at the 1968 Mexico Olympic Games. We wonder why, and what on earth would be the connection with Nicaragua in 1977?

Nicaragua's other claim to fame is, that it is where they nearly … and certainly should have built the canal to link the Pacific to the Caribbean Sea. This was first surveyed way back in 1825. The idea was to use the enormous Lake Nicaragua which drains to the Caribbean but is on the western side of the country and is only 30m above sea level and the distance through the land masse to the Pacific is less than 20kms. The US was very keen to carry out this project and did a lot of investigative design and costings. However, at much the same time, the French in an attempt to gain more influence in the Spanish and US dominated region, commenced the Panama Canal. After 15 years of struggle which cost 22,000 lives they admitted financial defeat and sold the 'work done to date' to the US for $40,000,000 which was seen as a bargain as when added to the money needed to complete the project, it would be cheaper than the easier Nicaragua Canal. It is interesting that in 2012 the government of Nicaragua signed an agreement with the Hong Kong Nicaragua

Canal Development Group (HKND) that committed HKND to financing and building the "Nicaraguan Canal and Development Project". It was intended that the new canal would be able to take ships that were too large for the Panama Canal. As of 2018, no physical work has been carried out and the principal investor has gone broke due to 'turbulence' in the China Stock Market in 2015 – 2016.

It is only a short day's ride to the Costa Rica border. We're looking forward to Costa Rica with some interest as it sounds … different. It is the smallest of Central America's countries, more wealthy than its neighbours and has no army … having done away with it in 1948. That sounds good to us as all the others have an omnipresent military. We are however wondering about the demographic make-up which is noted in the South American Handbook as 'very largely white'. The indigenous Indian population in most provinces is less than 0.5% and the black population are limited to small pockets over on the Caribbean coast.

The border does not give us a good welcome. We strike it close to midday, hoping to get through before they all take a siesta and close up shop for several hours as most borders do. The customs officials decide that we cannot enter with all our spare tyres and must surrender them … to them. Yeah, right, that is not going to happen … so negotiations start. Things get pretty testy as we accuse them of wanting *baksheesh* which possibly wasn't the best tactic as they then start to get in a huff because we have insulted their integrity. As time goes by their stance moves just a fraction. They will let us take any new, unused tyres in but any second-hand ones we had to surrender. They are resolute and immovable. This is a little better, but as we've recently swapped some tyres over it means we're still going to have to give them three tyres. This was even after we had swapped over some of the recently changed tyres. That in itself was a massive effort. The day was baking and Roly and I changed both of Bessie's tyres over and one of the Penelope's. There was a steady stream of border-crossers all wondering what we were doing and why. I remember in particular a whole bus-load just gawping at us … no one works outside in the midday sun. Finally, we were done and we insisted that the confiscated tyres were destroyed in front of us. This was a bit petty as they could have been put to good use somewhere, although that is a bit unlikely as they are all 19" which is not a size used by any of the modern bikes. At least we left feeling only half-rorted.

So we got off to a bad start in Costa Rica, and it didn't get much better. We did find it more affluent than its neighbours but matching this was a lessening of their friendliness. There were times when farmers declined us an overnight tent site. This had never happened before and the hospitality was nowhere near the levels of any of the other countries traversed to date.

It often seems that the poorer people are, the more likely they are to share.

Not only have we been teaching Roly how to swim and be at ease in the water, but I have been teaching him how to dive. Not a natural, he has gained a little proficiency in the standing dive and is ready to move on to 'the running dive'. Now it should be pointed out that both us Molloy boys are myopic. We are both quite short-sighted … to the level that requires glasses for all normal activities. The river where our latest lesson is taking place is pretty damn good with some shallows, quickly deepening to good swimming areas. The beach is a little too stony to be picture-perfect but overall it is a lovely spot. Roly warms up with a couple of well-launched standing dives. These are done from knee-deep, into the nipple-high swimming hole. I demonstrate a couple of running dives … quickly across the stony beach, into the shallows and arms-over-the-head … 'woosh' a nice elegant dive into the deeper water.

"Just like that Rols!"

Roly takes up his position 10m back and starts running. It seems to be going quite well … he looks confident and the take-off is impressive. Not quite an elliptical arc follows … but not far off it. The height is good, the distance exemplary … only the launching spot is 3m too soon. He has not even waited until he has reached the water and consequently his landing is in about an inch of water at the river's edge. Oh dear, we can't help ourselves … it is like something from a 1920s black and white comedy movie. Instantly and insensitively Lawrie, Steph and I fall about laughing, not even pausing when we see Roly's gravel-rashed, red-raw nose and chest. Roly's running dive attains instant trip folk-lore status. He never attempts this again … there is no getting back on the horse.

Costa Rica had a couple of other exploits for us … challenges to overcome. The poor fuel has been hard on the girls and Penelope has been giving out signs that she is maybe burning a valve. Finally, she decides she is not really going to go any further and she won't be waiting until the cool of the evening or a nice shady spot. Damn, we are caught again out in the blazing heat of the day. There is one small tree with just a small ever-moving shadow. I rate this roadside repair as one of our most memorable, because of the achievement of success without the required tools.

To remove a valve for replacement or 'valve grinding' you need a tool like a big G-clamp called a valve-spring compressor. This holds the valve's head tight against the valve seat in the cylinder head while the valve spring is compressed at the other end by the tool, so allowing the small retaining collets to be removed from the end of the valve. This then allows the removal of the valve. Even with the right tool, it can be a traumatic operation as the tiny collets can spring away into oblivion either when you are removing the valve or putting it back in. Without the G-clamp to hold the head of the valve, the compressing of the springs from the other end is almost impossible because there is nothing to compress against. Note that I said 'almost'. There in the hot, hot sun Roly and I combined to achieve the almost bloody impossible, and we never lost the collets. I think we sourced a combustion-chamber-sized rock which pressed against the valve. I applied downward pressure on the cylinder head, keeping the rock hard against the valve while Roly somehow compressed the spring and delicately removed the collets. This same operation had to be repeated with the installation of the new valve. I am so proud of this effort. It had so many opportunities to have sunk us. The tiniest of slips and we would have been dead-in-the-water. But no, the rabble live to rumble on. Maybe someone upstairs really is looking after us, but just having a laugh occasionally by giving us a tortuous path.

We're normally pretty structured in how we ride. We ride at our own pace, not often lined up close but usually strung out like a navy flotilla heading to Murmansk keeping apart to confuse the U-boats. We check on each other at regular intervals so if someone goes missing it is not half a day before the others notice. I tend to ride in front because I enjoy front-riding and I usually know where we are going … and have the South American Handbook. I also have Steph who keeps an eye out for whoever is next back. Roly has always liked riding at the back. He hates having someone 'up his arse' and likes to ride at his own pace, undisturbed. He also has most of the tools, knowledge and skills for our road-side maintenance etc, so it makes sense for him to be Tail-end Charlie. Which of course leaves Lawrie to ride in the middle, and being the affable mate that he is … he doesn't care where he is. After San Jose (Costa Rica's capital) we had a high pass to cross. We were quite looking forward to this as we were longing for a bit of 'cool' and being that this was 11,000 ft we expected it would be cool. This would also be the first time that our Derriboots would be of any use. Derriboots were insulated rubber 'gum' boots which I had sourced in the UK and had sent out to us in Mexico. They would be invaluable in the Andes I felt. To date, however, they had been a bit of a nightmare as they certainly were not designed to be worn in the tropics, especially without socks. None of us actually have any socks.

I am not sure what caused us to be at the back, probably we stopped to put on some more clothes and waved the others past … maybe I needed a pee. Just as we began to climb away from the plains we hit rain, and as we climbed higher, the heavier and colder it got. This was not the 'cool' we had been longing for, this was teeth-gritting misery. Visibility was limited and we saw no sign of the others, but this didn't worry us as we were probably gaining on them, and sooner or later we would be where we usually were … out in front. But remember our omnipotent one up there with the sad, sick sense of humour? When we were high on the pass, way up in the clouds, grimly hanging on to the enjoyment of the moment … NOT … the supposedly benevolent one throws a puncture at us. We're cold, we're wet, we're miserable, we have no tools … and we're alone!

"Just kidding!" the prick upstairs says and sends a small flat-deck truck our way. I know I said the folk of Costa Rica had been not as friendly or helpful … but I had also said there weren't many Indians. So this squat little Indian assesses the situation and determines we must get Penelope on the back at all costs, as well as Steph and me somewhere aboard. He is not going to leave us up there. Probably one of the only benefits of being young is that you are strong. And so it was that with some difficulty we got Penelope up on the tray of the truck, Steph and I jammed inside and we made it up and over the top of the pass. Well down the other side out of the rain, sheltering in a roadside coffee shop we find the others. They were moderately concerned and had been considering mounting a rescue effort but needed to warm up first … and besides, there was always the possibility that we might turn up any minute.

The Panama border is no worse than any of the others but no better. It is amazing that it can take up to six hours to cross a border. I'd experienced this before when crossing in and out of communist countries … and here with right-wing republics it is just the same, layer after layer of officialdom and endless queues, offices which shut on a whim for several hours. It seems to be all about power and control and always keeping you on the back-foot, worried and confused. Roly includes in a letter home that *"I hate all this petty and unnecessary bureaucracy. I don't really have all* that much to do with it as I always 'go lost' and things are usually a little more sorted out by then."

It takes us a few days to get to Panama City. We're not really rushing and Samantha needs a bit of clutch work. The Panther/Burman clutch includes rubber shock absorbing washers in metal cups to enable a bit of 'give' in the drive, negating some of the thumping single cylinder's harshness. This helps with primary chain life and niceness of the ride for the rider. Some manufacturers do it with a spring-loaded face cam on the engine sprocket … robust and fool-proof. Panther and Burman have conspired to make something that possibly works but also deteriorates quite quickly it seems. The clutch chain-wheel has eight holes but into six of them go the metal cups and odd-shaped rubber 'buffers'. Samantha has been destroying these and whilst we have replacement rubber buffers, we don't have the cups … why would we … they are made of metal? Well, the bloody metal cups have been disintegrating and Roly's only option is to distribute the remaining three cups evenly and button her up again. It is wing-and-a-prayer stuff. We're not quite sure what we'll do about this for 'the main course'.

You enter Panama across a mile-long bridge over the canal. We have been made aware that the Panama Canal Yacht Club is known as the 'crossroads of the world' … and it has a legendary bar. We've been hanging out for a worthy occasion and it must be said that our last couple of weeks have been extremely hard and at times stressful. We needed a blow-out … as well as a decent scrub-up and some personal-maintenance time.

I wrote in my diary: *'Because our travels were being funded on a budget smaller than a gnat's nostril, we did not have any allowances for frivolous or indulgent behaviour. Fortunately for us all, Lawrie had frailties that surfaced from time to time. At regular intervals, he would crack and demand to treat us all to a deserved good time. This was done by writing in the diary that he owed the expedition the required money needed to have the blowout. This way we could revel in the thought that the treats were costing us nothing and our great mate, who was the mate of all mates, was shouting us all. This was a fine system as it meant we never felt guilty about spending the expedition money and we could wallow in debauchery with impunity. Lawrie's tab grew over the months to rival the national debt of some third world countries. This was great as we all knew just how good it would feel one day to be able to say "Forget it, we've wiped the slate!" This illusion of parsimonious behaviour was clung to for many months.'*

The Panama Canal Yacht Club was one of the occasions when Lawrie's wonderful frailties surfaced and we celebrated like never before. We even managed to ring home ... collect of course. We were so relieved to have made it to this iconic spot ... intact. There were a lot of laughs and self-congratulatory high-fives happening. The room had numerous old salts who had sailed the world and of course had massively bigger adventures than us, but we were still pretty full of ourselves. I felt it was almost impressive enough to start sending postcards to the boys at the rugby club ... surely they'd be impressed now! It might have taken a while, but we had reached PANAMA! With us on a macho-man cycle of beers and cheers, it took us (the boys) a while to notice Steph was over at the notice board and seemingly writing on a card there. This was the notice board where crews were advertised for ... and we found Steph was posting a 'position wanted' card for a sailing home to New Zealand. Maybe the gin (Mothers' ruin) had made her maudlin and homesick, maybe the last couple of weeks had been the 'tipping point', maybe we were blinded to the arduous nature of the ride because she'd been so good at it, no matter what the deprivation ... and what about me???? What about the infatuation and the 'gusts' of love?

Well, it took a few more drinks and the promise of good times ahead ... more food, more money, more bathing. It was a very relieved rabble of boys when she took down her posting, and with a grin ordered another drink.

There are no foreign lands. It is the traveler only who is foreign.

ROBERT LOUIS STEVENSON (1850-1894)

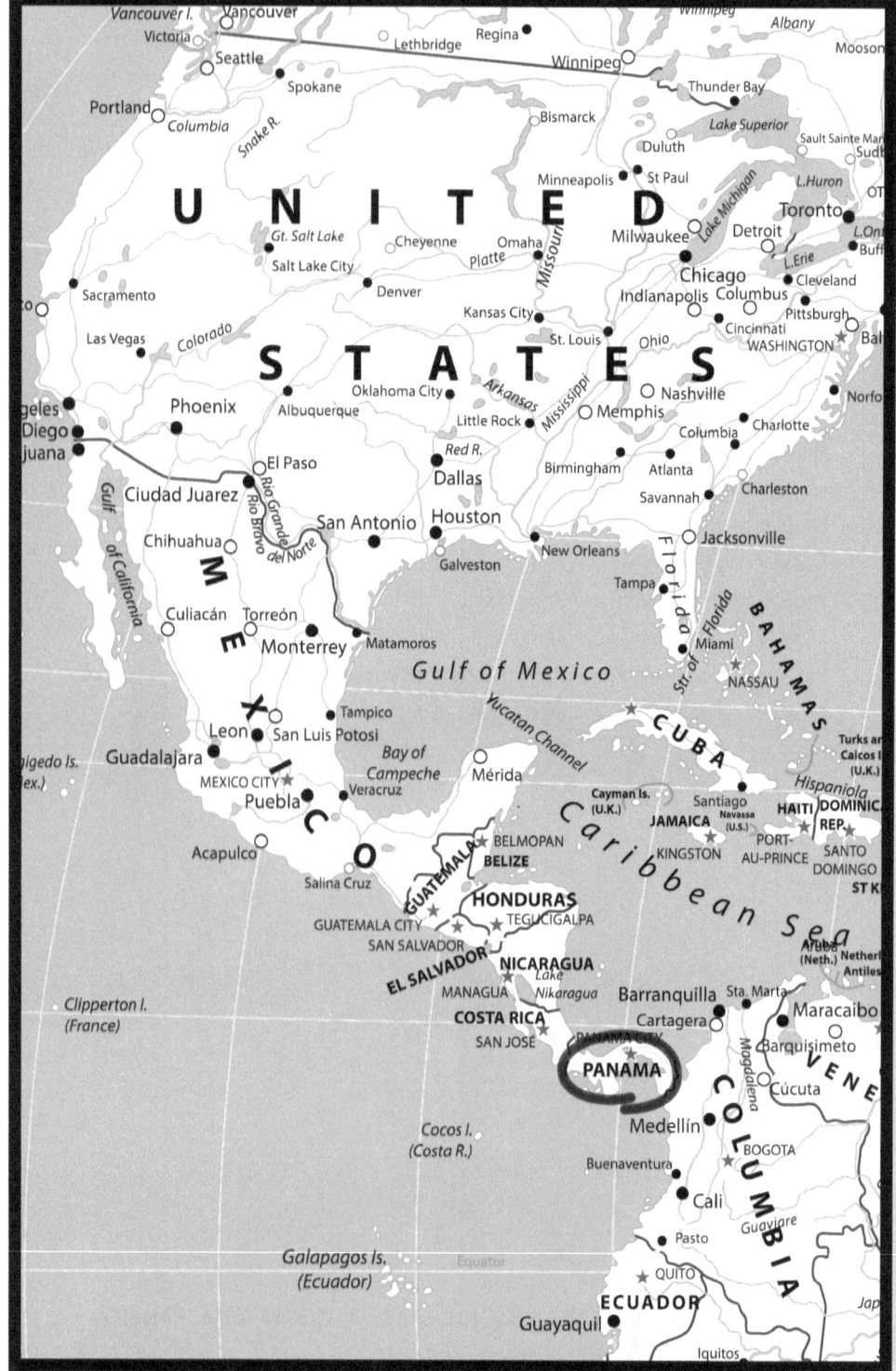

CHAPTER 6

PANAMA

It was a sluggish start after our celebratory blow-out. We'd made it to Panama … but what now? We didn't have much of a plan. By now we knew there was no way across the Darien Gap, so we'd need to find a boat … or ship. A ship is the big one because it has lifeboats. I think we'd prefer a ship. We'd need to establish a base and get our ears to the ground. To this end, we rode into town with no clear intent. We encountered a couple of Panamanian motorcycle cops on older full-dress Harley Davidsons and when we asked about camping, one indicated "Follow me!" With this, they graunched into gear and were off in an impressive flurry of splayed legs and 'attitude'. I can't remember if one put on his siren, but I do remember struggling to keep up with the pace as they weaved in and out of traffic with alarming speed. It was like we were part of a crazy cavalcade, cop bikes leading some foreign dignitaries maybe, except we didn't look the part. More likely, people would have thought we were possibly part of a comedy movie being filmed, as definitely cops don't escort rag-tag motley folk like us. Carving our way through the city in such fashion was pretty invigorating, especially as we didn't know where we were going … or to what.

They take us to a stadium of a sort which had a grassed area surrounding it. Not ideal, but we decide this will do for now. Fortuitously, a day or so later when we are in town, another cop waves us down. He is not like the Latin cops, this one is an American, a Canal Zone cop. He wants to see our old bikes. His name is Tim and he's an enthusiast. Finding we have nowhere really suitable to stay, he says "Follow me!". A short while later we arrive at a large grassed lay-by area on the actual canal-side. Here were several BBQs, sun shelters and quite a few windowless buildings that turned out to be 'boatsheds'. We had hit pay-dirt. These boatsheds were mainly owned by 'Canal Zone' employees and it was where they kept their toys and based their leisure time. At the time, the Panama Canal Zone was an Unincorporated American Territory. They'd bought the rights to complete the canal and run it back in 1904 and whilst there were moves afoot to transition it over to the Panamanians, the reality of that was still more than 20 years away. It was an unusual situation … this whole sliver of Panama landmass was administered by US Government departments. The workers were paid American wages, plus allowances for remote and primitive living conditions. This meant they lived very well with large amounts of disposable income. Very few of the people we came to meet over the following weeks were actually from the US. Mostly they had been born in the 'Zone', gone to high school in the US, but returned to highly paid, low-stress jobs.

Soon we were soon ensconced in Tim's air-conditioned boatshed, and minor attractions in our own right. Our old bikes and the fact we were Kiwis made us exotic and interesting. Lawrie was happy to be a Kiwi at times because he had lived there for a period. The boatshed folk were all petrol-heads in some fashion and it was wonderful, slowly finding out what was where. It was like an archaeological find. Discarded toys of different ages showed the leisure-time activities of different times. An activity would be discovered, all the toys bought and subsequently when boredom set in, they would be laid up. Clearly, they had done speed-boats, yachts, stock cars, enduro bikes and now some were doing classic bikes. Tim had a Velocette that was nearly going, one of his mates had a nice Norton ES2, there were various old Indians, including the oddball parallel twin from the post-war era that was credited with sinking the once dominant Springfield factory. These were copies of British bikes of the early 1950s and seen by the Chairman at the time as the way forward. Sadly, they were flawed and the American buyers didn't take to them … they weren't vee-twins. We'd never seen one before so were interested in the technical aspects.

Soon we had our favourite boatsheds. We slept in Tim's but often worked at another which had an ultra-sonic parts wash, something that we were totally in awe of. Not only could we de-grease and clean engine parts, but we could also wash our hands in it. Seemingly the fluid was only water with the addition of washing-up liquid. It was an odd sensation feeling your hands gently tingling … then coming out clean. Such fun. Roly was in demand because he was a proper mechanic and knew about things. Soon he was not only trying to upgrade our girls but also working

Tim tries out his Velocette in front of the boatshed

on Tim's Velo and ultra-sonic-man's Austin 1100 which was of course totally alien to Americans but grist-to-the-mill for Roly. Roly also got to give his opinion on someone's MGB being as he was now seen as the Brit-expert. Ultra-sonic-man also had several Chev Corvairs which were as alien to us as the Austin was to him.

There was a constant flow of Canal Zone folk coming down to meet and see the Kiwis and their old bikes. There was also competition to take us on outings. So it was that we got out on speed-boats, we saw the workings of the locks and we endured BBQ after BBQ. They bought us beer, and they bought us more beer. They seemed to like us. A lot of them were Canal Zone policemen and it was quite amusing that a coterie of the young wives would uplift Steph mid-morning and they would disappear for most of the day. Subsequently, we learned that there was no sight-seeing, they just went off to a causeway and smoked dope.

Our new friends weren't all that knowledgeable when it came to things out in the wider world of Panama City, so didn't have advice or connections about getting across to Columbia. Lawrie and I would venture out and try to locate shipping companies and travel agents. Our skills were possibly better than theirs but still, we weren't getting the answers we needed. A couple of memorable days stay strong in our memories. We didn't have a preference for where we would leave from or where we would go to. I knew from coming through the canal in 1972 that there was a port at either end, Cristobal and Balboa. We decide to go to dockland bars in Cristobal and see if we can make a connection. Possibly we will find a stevedore who can get us an 'in'. We presume these will be rough places and Lawrie and I go together. We don't want to go mob-handed but also feel that two will be safer than one person alone. The day ends up unsuccessful with regards to finding a passage across to Columbia, but we have an outrageous time. The clientele and bar staff are most surprised that 'white folk' would venture in … and stay. This is the Chameleon at his finest and I am his 'wingman'. There are a few Caribbean blacks there with some English, but mainly our afternoon is sign-language and pigeon Spanish. Of course, this is long before the days of responsible drinking and abstinence, so it is a very merry couple of lads who report back in that night. We'd had such a good time and made firm drinking friends, so the next afternoon we return with Steph and Roly. This really rocks their socks off. They'd never had a white woman set foot in the bar before. It is rough and skody, but again we have a wonderful time.

We're getting rumours that there might be a ship from Balboa at the end of the month. In the meanwhile there is a lot of fun to be had. Tim's Velo is completed enough to be fired up and we all ride it up and down the area past the BBQs. It is a fine beast with plenty of urge. It is not the only Velo in the Zone, but the other is a legendary short-track race bike. The night before we met Tim, the race Velo had cleaned up the local short-track championship against much more modern machines. That was the last race meeting for the season so we don't get to see it in action. Apart from the fact that we are not getting any closer to South America, life is great. People are always dropping in to see us, often bringing us their toys to admire. We also have a notable thru-visitor. Word has got around and not only have The Plastic Expedition found us but one day a magnificent Vincent motorcycle rides in. It is a Barry Howell from NZ who has disembarked in Panama with the intention of riding to Canada for the International Vincent Owners' Club Rally. We know of Vincents as being things of legend … there is a picture of one in the back of our Motorcycle Mechanics book. They had gone out of business in 1955 but because of their size and speed, they were revered for decades after. They were by far the fastest things on the road at the time and one had broken the world land speed record in NZ back in the 1950s. So here we were drooling over Barry's 1,000cc shiny black vee-twin bike. It looked and sounded magnificent. Barry wasn't actually a Kiwi but he'd lived there for many years and was going the long way home to Britain. After a couple of days, we fare-welled him and revelled in the 'crobba, crobba, crobba' sound of the 55-degree engine … an aural delight! Years later, we learn his ride was successful. We also learn how the wicked wits in the club twist his name so he is known to all as Harry Bowell.

It is great to have The Plastics with us as now our ability to find a passage is doubled. They are also good to play with during the day. They call us the 'Cast-iron Expedition' and there is always a lot of banter. The days are hot but never too debilitating and now we have an air-conditioned haven, life is good. One day there is a delivery of CZ Moto-cross bikes. These are uncrated and fettled. Pete from the Plastics is sent off on one to report back how good they are compared to what he raced back in Aus. He and one of the local hot-shots have a seriously good play and reckon they are pretty good straight out of the box. There were also Montessa trials bikes for Roly and me to play on, as well as a new PE250 Suzuki. PE stood for Pure Enduro and was more or less the RM (Racing Motor) with a light on it to be legal for the cross-country races. We found this an astonishing beast which lofted its front wheel at the twitch of the throttle. The local lads have a buying entity, enabling them to trade as dealers. Years earlier they had bought some of the first Norton Commandos and of course abused them in cross-country races in the jungle, which as road bikes they were totally unsuited for. Interestingly they quite quickly broke their frames and this news was imparted to the factory. The steering head area of the frames were subsequently all braced. As a student, Plastic Mark had worked at Norton and had many horror tales to share with us. Knowing what he knew, he would only ever have chosen a Japanese bike for a serious world adventure.

The BBQ area was the site of an interesting and amusing interplay with a local 'Zonie'. Lawrie had gleaned a decent supply of wood, we'd had a big fire and there was a great bed of glowing embers for us to start cooking on. A young-middle-aged man wandered over from a neighbouring BBQ.

"Nice fire, what's your fuel?"

We're a bit confused and ask what he means.

"What's your fuel?" he says, nodding to our embers

"Wood!" says Lawrie

"Come again!"

"Wood!"

"Wood? ... ah don't know that one! Sure works well"

"Wood ... from a tree!" We show him our supply of small twigs and the like. He is gobsmacked.

"Well, I never ... Goddam, that is as good as the real stuff!" He shows us his bag of store-bought BBQ charcoal. God knows where he thought that came from.

We've gone from being on a diet of one meal of gruel a day to living like kings with fawning admirers hanging on every word we utter. We've even had caviar, which I have to say I hated and struggled to be appreciative. This was supplied by a slightly older, silver-haired guy who I don't think worked. He had a wonderful backstory which involved hooch-running between states in the US and many other exploits which didn't always meet the full letter of the law. A man of great and exciting tales. Apart from the caviar, and a day out on his speed-boat on Gatun Lake, he opened my eyes to tuna. Tuna was not something we had in my Kiwi life but I had discovered it in England and it came in a tin with a picture of a fish on it. For whatever reason, because it came in a small tin and had an accordingly small fish pictured on the side of the tin, I presumed it was a small fish ... well, it had to be, didn't it? I had been surprised when I had read in a Time magazine that there was now an international requirement for tuna to be caught on a line, not in a net. I knew that tuna boats were striking over this and many were tied up in Balboa. I was pretty sympathetic to them. Our caviar friend said one day "Do you want some tuna steaks?"

I probably gaped gormlessly at him. He took us into his chiller and hanging there was a fish that stretched from floor to ceiling. I was speechless. He carved off great slabs of pinkish flesh with instructions to "Throw that on your BBQ!"

Probably not the night of throwing the tuna steaks on a barbie, but one night at yet another gathering of what are now firm friends, Lawrie and I are chewing the fat with three of our new mates. For whatever reason, one is trying to give another a $20 bill for something he feels is owing. The other guy is resolutely refusing it and the note is going backwards between them, never looking like getting near a wallet. "For fuck's sake you guys!" says the third guy, reaches out, takes the note ... and eats it, washing it down with a healthy draught of beer. Lawrie and I are spell-bound. $20 is our budget for half a week's food, fuel and accommodation.

Our excursions out of the Canal Zone and into Panama City itself are always an interesting contrast. Those in the zone have so much and those outside of the zone have so little. The zone workers don't really see themselves as Panamanians even though they have been born there and lived their whole life there. Of course, they have their own supermarkets and Americana is everywhere, even down to 'Little League' baseball. Like the rest of Central America, Panama is not a wealthy country and most people subsist. There are numerous rough areas and dodgy parts of town where the Zone People would never go. Of course, we have the complexion of the Zone People but none of the trappings. Apart from trying to get shipping updates, we have been waiting for much-needed funds from home. Mum has told us that the funds have been sent but the banks here have been consistently saying "Nada!" to our daily enquiry.

One day Roly and I venture forth again into town and do the rounds of the banks. We've learnt from previous experiences that money isn't always received by the bank that the sender thinks it will be. It is a pretty disheartening day and we are hot, footsore and forlornly making our way back to our bikes. Deep down I know the wise and cautious person would stick to the main roads and go the much longer, safer way to the bikes. But no, I decide to cut across the square so to speak, making our route the hypotenuse of a triangle so it would be much shorter. I can see it is dodgy but always feel we should not cower away from unsavoury-looking things and places. Because we are tired we are no longer chatting away and for whatever reason Roly has lagged back a few metres, not far and not of any consequence. We are cutting through a real rough barrio but the odd person is responding to my smiles. I am walking confidently, showing no trepidation or concern … I am not a victim! Roly has our passports and money etc in a cloth 'money-belt' bag. The bag is in one of his front thigh-pockets which are buttoned down and has a cord attached to his belt. Before he knows it, someone from behind has cut the cord and yanked the passport bag from his pocket and is away. I only hear the slightest of noises behind me and don't pause. Meanwhile, Roly is in hot pursuit. Roly may not be big, but he is wiry and angry. The thief ducks into a decrepit doorway and as he crosses an empty room, Roly throws his helmet with all his might at his departing head. He misses by a whisker, they thunder up some stairs with Roly now a bit back. Not sure where he has gone, Roly bursts into a room and finds there is just a young woman breastfeeding a baby. There is no sign of our thief. Defeated, Roly retraces his route and finds me still blissfully walking down the road. Bugger, bugger, bugger! Possibly this is a bit of a payback for all the easy-times debauching we have been engaged in lately. It was interesting that about the time the robbery happened I was smiling at an old guy who was facing down the lane we were walking through. He would have been watching it all unfold. Such a shame we can't wear signs saying we are not rich Americans or Canal Zone people. It is hard to be bitter and twisted when you see what little they have in these shanty-town areas. The guy saw an opportunity and took it in the few seconds it was available. We might not have agreed at the time, but his need probably was greater than ours.

Clearly, this is a bit of a setback. The banks are now closed so it wasn't until the next morning that Roly could cancel his travellers' cheques. A refund cannot be arranged on the spot and we are told the money will be available when we get to Quito in Ecuador. The British Embassy acts on behalf of us Kiwis … I know this because this has happened before to me, in the backblocks of Romania. Luckily we are still hanging around waiting for this rumoured ship to return from Columbia. In due time and with the reluctant payment of much-needed funds, Roly and I are issued with British Passports. They are temporary, but still pretty impressive. Unlike the Kiwi ones, they are hard-covered and very formal looking.

Of course, back at camp, we share robbery stories and we're not sure if ours out-trumps the one of *The Plastics*. A while back, but also in Panama, Mark and Pete were confronted with a guy with a knife demanding their valuables. "Bugger that!" they thought simultaneously, and both pulled out knives from their calf-sheaths. Now it was two knives, faced off against one much bigger knife in the hands of a desperado who actually looked like he knew how to use it. An impasse results … a stare-down! Over the shoulder of the bad guy, they then notice a group of street-traders running towards them. Thinking they will be going to help out their countryman, who is inexplicably seeming to be having trouble robbing two soft gringos, our boys prepare for the worst. They'll go down together like Butch Cassidy and the Sundance Kid … but no, the street-traders chase off the bad guy. Mark and Pete are then showered with hospitality to make up for the shame that the other guy has brought on the Republic of Panama.

The rumoured ship is no longer a rumour. We are in the loop with the middle-men and although Easter is holding up its return, we just need to keep checking in and sooner or later we will leave this idyll and get back on the road.

Meanwhile, Steph has been learning to ride Bessie around our area. Together they look a delight, both trim and sporty. Bessie has been amazing to date, relentlessly

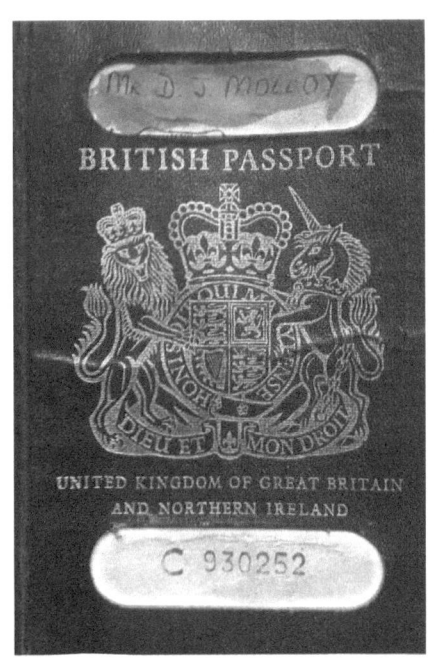

Impressive British Passports

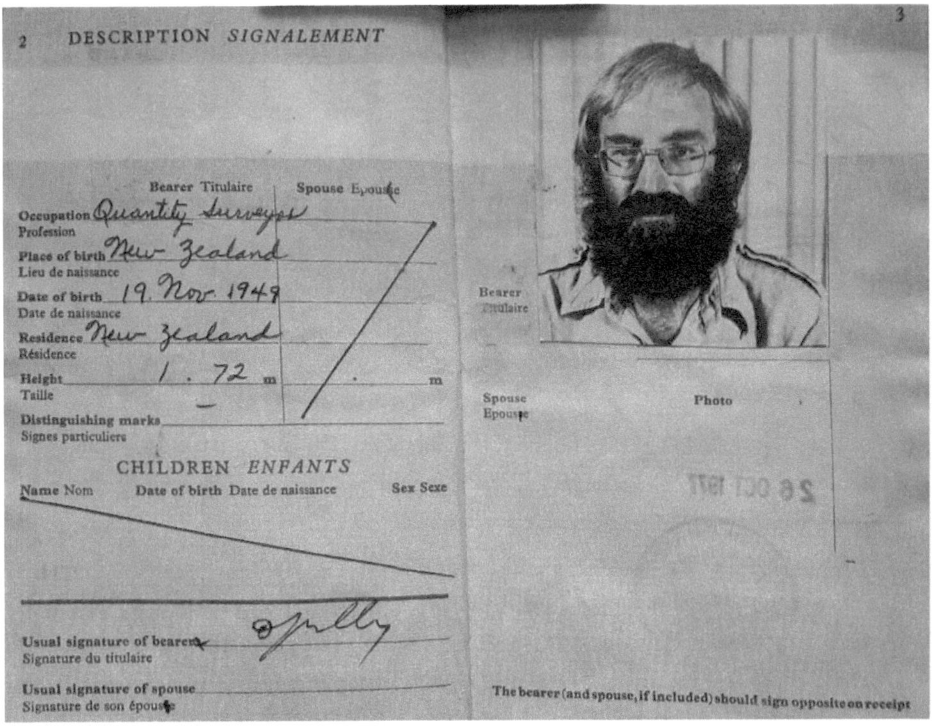

PANAMA

Steph and Bessie - two of my favourites

giving her best. She doesn't drink oil, need constant attention to her clutch or anything and the astonishing thing is that she is 40 years old. She is also wonderful to ride because of her nimbleness and eager performance. She is the only bike I have ridden where I can consistently do figures-of-eight circuits with the handlebars solidly on full-lock. We deem that Lawrie is now proficient in riding, and Roly will get his reward for coming along, by being the pilot of Bessie henceforth and Lawrie transfers to Samantha.

There are a few minor amusements in our days. On one occasion a young lad, seemingly barely old enough to have a licence, yet apparently, the owner of a brand-new Honda 400 Supersport, comes to show off this little jewel of a machine. The Four cylinder Honda was the current sensation in Europe. It was styled in a café-racer fashion with the four exhausts coming together into one muffler in a most attractive way. It was sophisticated and very refined. It was the bike of every adolescent's night-dreams. In the world we've come from young guys never have brand-new anything, so there is a little envy, along with the obvious interest. Anyway, the young guy cruises up and makes a decision to 'impress' with his arrival. As he comes to a stop, instead of putting his feet down then flicking out the side-stand … he does it in the opposite order. At five miles per hour he reaches back with his left foot and engages the side-stand, pulling it out to right-angles … and then with both feet back on the foot-pegs he stops the bike on the front brake and leans to the left. Now if this move had worked and he and the bike subsequently achieved a 'parked' status, we would have been very impressed. Sadly for the young lad, the side-stand had not quite gone over centre past the 90°, so when he leaned to the left, it just folded back and bike and rider fell impressively to the ground. There had been no time to remove his feet from the foot-pegs. The only real damage was to his ego, and we duly oohed and aahed over the bike, which really did impress … wouldn't go where our old girls have been though!

One of the Zone crew let Steph loose in his car one day. It was an enormous coupe as long and wide as a road could accommodate. Roly recalls it was a Buick … or could have been an Oldsmobile. Either or, it was a behemoth. Only the Americans

Harry

could think these things were a good idea. Presumably, it was powered by an enormous V8. Steph looked quite lilliputian behind the wheel, and I worried a little when the car surged away with a roar. At the entry to our clearing with all the BBQs, sun-shelters, boatsheds etc there was quite a narrow bridge on a slight angle to the approach. From a distance, it looked no wider than the width of the enormous sleaze-mobile Steph was now piloting at some considerable speed towards it. We all held our breaths as this really did look like it could end in tears. But no, the car slewed at the appropriate last-second and made it through, popping out the other side like a cork from a champagne bottle. No paint was lost in the making of this excitement!

I hesitate to record my last tale from the boatshed as I am sometimes reminded of my mother's almost constant urging "If you can't say something nice about someone, don't say anything!" I justify myself by knowing that in all fireside yarns there are those that are a bit close to the bone, and perhaps should have been held back … but everyone has a chuckle anyway and tut-tuts later. I know also that all our pasts are never always exemplary paths of flawless behaviour. It should be pointed out that as mentioned earlier, the boatsheds are windowless, also for the air-conditioning to work, the doors must be closed … so at night our time after 'lights out' is in the pitch-black. On this night of infamy, possibly more than the usual libations were partaken of. In the middle of the night, we are awoken to the clear stumbling of one of our number. Even in our blurred semi-comatose states, it is obvious that the person involved has lost his bearings and in the pitch-black cannot find his way out. There are incoherent mutterings, the creak of what we sense to be a cupboard door … and then the ominous sounds of a waterfall. Our camps are never all that tidy and contained, there is often detritus spread in quite a large circle, poorly delineating our living area. The details surrounding the rest of the night and the morning's clean-up have been purged by time and denial … but Lawrie was suitably contrite the next day and he is not the sort of person you can stay grumpy with.

Lawrie also starred with 'Harry'. I can't remember who supplied Harry or why, but he provided us with quite a bit of amusement. Harry was a life-like latex rubber mask which portrayed a bald, incredibly ugly, almost neanderthal visage. When Lawrie pulled this on, he became another persona.

By now we were on a daily watch regarding leaving and many farewell parties were held as each tomorrow was probably it. We'd found the ship two days after it was supposed to be in port, but it was aground on a sand-bar. For some time now we have been getting a daily 'mañana' to our questions about its arrival. Interestingly, we have become nervous about our forward ride. We want it badly, but are also now daunted by it. Here in The Zone, we are cosseted and have all the needs for a good time. We have shelter, we have good friends, and our good friends have great toys that they like sharing with us. Life's great. Steph and I have a secret spot away in the long grass that we retreat to each day, more or less at the same hour … probably siesta time. It seems that every time that we engage in a bit of physical affection towards each other, a military helicopter flies over. Never directly overhead but near enough to be an intrusion. I have to assure Steph that they cannot see us, or what we are doing. Happily, she is satisfied that these are not aerial voyeurs and there is no reason to 'cease and desist'. Strange that it is always there though!

There is one other tale that needs to be told and it involves Roly and some selfless heroism and apparently some needless criticism from me. Motorcyclists of a certain age will remember the chain-lubing system sold by Duckhams. This was a large round biscuit tin of solid black grease which purportedly contained a high degree of lubricity and magic. The methodology of using it was as follows. First, you removed the chain from your bike and hung it up using a suitable piece of wire. You then washed the chain, best you could with kerosene or similar. Next step is to coil the chain up and place it on top of the solid grease in the tin. The tin had a handle which needed to be unfolded and made secure so it did not allow the tin to tip when you moved it. The ensemble was then placed on a heat source, possibly even your mother's stove (this often ended in tears) or in our case on the Optimus 8R. The heat melted the magic grease which then infiltrated every nook and cranny of the chain. The chain duly sank to the bottom of the tin. Once this has happened and you are brave enough for the next task, the whole kit and caboodle is removed carefully from the heat source and whilst the grease is still in a molten liquid state, moved to where you are going to hang the chain from a height so the excess molten grease will accurately drip back into the tin, solidify and be available for use another time. Removing the coiled-up and now very, very hot chain is a delicate manoeuvre to be done gently and without breathing, tongue held just so.

Even writing the above brings back several bad memories. There is not a regular user who does not have a terror tale, and most have more than one. So we marry this tricky paraphernalia to a petrol cooker which has 'foibles'. The Optimus 8R is a wonderful and legendary travel aid. Whilst the manufacturer's instructions point you to various proprietary fuels, in reality, they are just fancy, cleaned-up, unleaded petrol. For us, the beauty is that it is unfussy about the bad petrol we throw in it straight out of the tank of one of the girls. We don't need to carry cooking fuel. They do have a propensity to get hotter and hotter as the shielded tank gets warmer, and they begin to roar like a dragon. If, and this should not happen, the pressure in the tank gets too much, there is a pressure-relief valve which would let the compressed and heated petrol vapour escape and no explosion and loss of life would occur. We had noticed that the pressure-relief valve did sometimes leak just a fraction and sometimes a wee flame would appear there. We would blow this out and turn down the cooker a bit.

Being that this job was done in simpler times, there was no work plan, no hazard analysis, no JSEA (Job Safety and Environment Assessment). We'd done this before … we knew what we were doing. We hadn't really taken cognisance of the fact that the tin was so large and overhung so much that we couldn't reach the cooker's speed control. Reflection tells us that we could have carefully lifted the tin off the cooker and turned it down, but that wasn't what happened. Of course, the 8R began to roar, and roar mightily. Just like the little engine that could, the pressure relief valve finally blew and like a flame-thrower from a war movie, a jet of fiery liquid was projected metres across the workshop. Roly was the first, and the only person to react. With some bravery, he grabbed the whole flaming assembly and attempted to get it outside before it exploded. Trying to keep the tin of molten grease on top of a roaring flame-thrower was impossible and lots of the black liquid spilt before Roly could throw the whole thing out onto the grass outside the boat-shed. Roly's burns were fortunately minor but all the Duckhams was now lost. Roly tells me I seemed to have more concern for the lost chain-lube and even dished out a rebuke for being so clumsy. The clean-up was not insignificant because the grease does indeed have good lubricity and slipperiness. The workshop floor still had greasy areas when we left. At least the concrete will never rust.

The *Santa Lucia* finally got off the sand-bar and into the small river jetty that it operated from. This was not a main port ship … it may even only be deemed a boat. Even once docked, there were further delays because of the absence of an available truck to unload into. Another 'mañana!' We're ready and luckily we had also just found the money from the sale of Roly's trail bike. For some reason, it had come in two instalments. We might not have Roly's travellers' cheques, but we have enough funds to get us to Quito. An additional financial bonus comes to us by way of the numerous small gifts Steph had been given in Saudi Arabia. We've belatedly twigged to the fact that mostly she has been given tasteless trinkets ... all made of gold! Apart from a watch which she keeps (pawned years later in NZ to stem another financial crisis), Steph is able to exchange everything for cash. Every little bit helps and her selfless contribution is appreciated. We've been told the voyage shouldn't take more than two days but we should bring food and water for a few more just in case.

We've been in Panama a month, but finally with some expectation and not a little excitement, *The Plastics*, us, a BMW motorcycle couple and a few others, all finally board for an early-morning sailing. We've had our final farewells. Of course just because we were on-board didn't mean we were going anywhere. Apparently, they hadn't yet loaded their fuel or water. There seems to be quite a degree of secrecy surrounding our departure. It is not a passenger ship and we are just a financial bonus. We'll all sleep on deck somewhere. We notice an *Explosivos* sign at the front of the cargo área and a soldier who never moves far from it. A day later, somewhere around 4.00am, with no fanfare and in total darkness ... no lights showing, we slip away. Next stop Columbia, 560 kms away.

Travel brings power and love back into your life.

RUMI JALALUD-DIN (1207-1273)

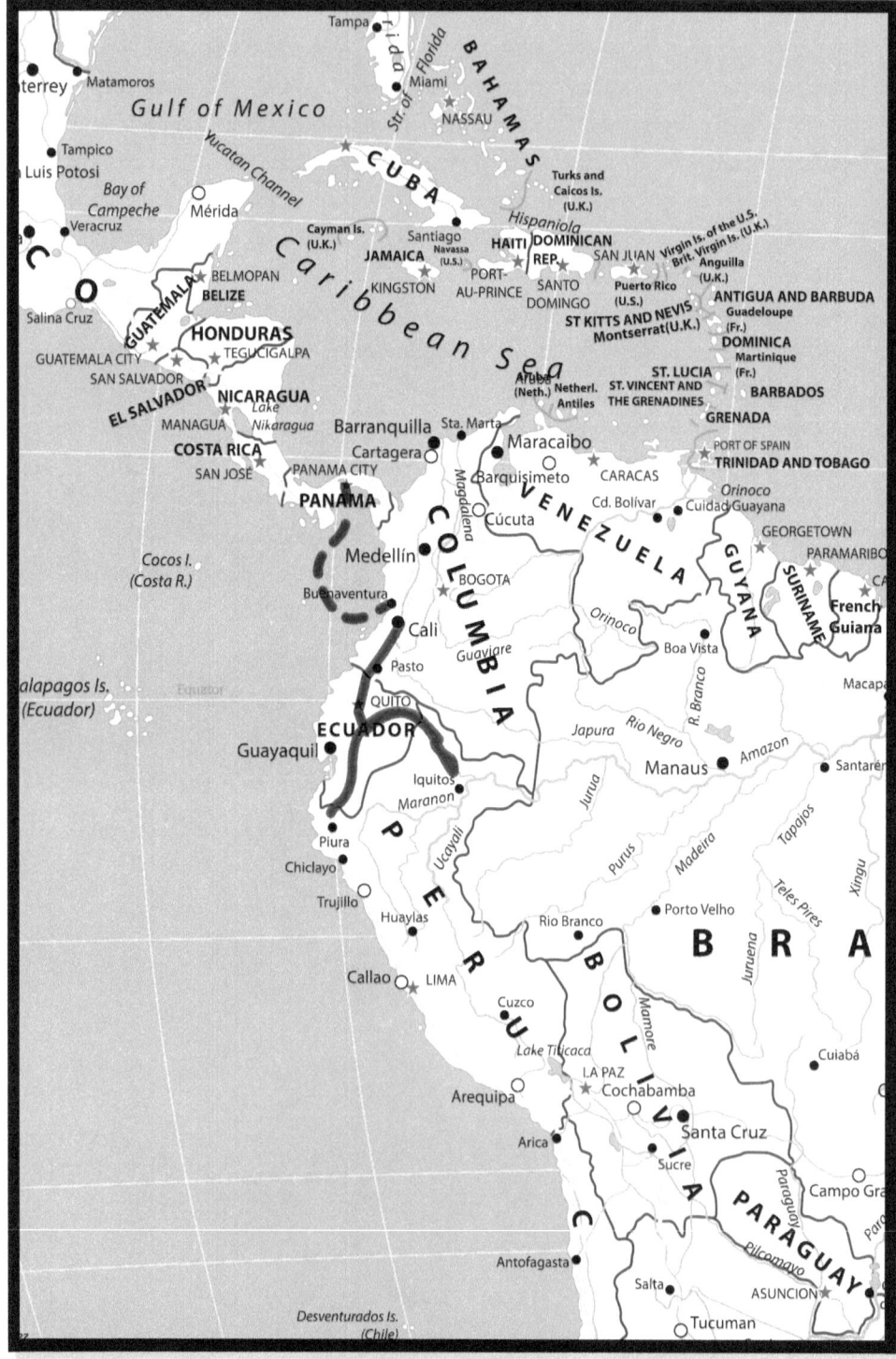

CHAPTER 7

PANAMA TO PERU

The *SS Santa Lucia* was to be our home for significantly longer than the two days anticipated, but what is an adventure without a few hiccups. She was what would be described as a 'tramp steamer'. She's not very big, but she's not tiny either … we hope she is just right (Goldilocks?) for our ocean voyage. There are about 20 of us 'hitching a ride' across to Buenaventura on the Pacific Coast of Columbia. There is no accommodation for passengers and we bring our own food etc. It is an unusual bunch with one Columbian family taking home a brand-new Mercedes Benz, some guys with a big American pick-up truck and a missionary couple returning to Ecuador. He is American and she is Ecuadorian. We hope to stop with them on our way through. Of course Pete and Mark, The Plastics, are with us and so is an English couple on a new BMW motorbike. This gives rise to a strange relationship, quite an unusual and slightly distant one. The problem is that they are not motorcyclists and possibly are a bit 'monied'. BMWs are seen as the ultimate touring motorcycle. They are shaft-drive, smooth and powerful but with renowned reliability and comfort. I'd never even seen one in New Zealand as they weren't sold there, and in the UK they were only offered in posh shops at extremely high prices. I'd seen a few on the roads of Europe and in the car-park at the Imola race-track in Italy but had never spoken to an owner. These were bikes of legend and here is one up close. We couldn't even imagine how they had got a Carnet for such an exotic machine … 'twice the new value of the vehicle' was a figure that would buy a house in most of the developed world and indeed for their new Hondas *The Plastics* had arranged a mortgage over a family house.

"What's the Beemer like?" I opened with, like an excited fan.

"I don't know. OK, I suppose ... I've never ridden anything else." It transpired that the rider knew nothing about bikes and cared for them even less. It was just a means of transport. I was a bit deflated and not a little nonplussed. I had expected some enthusiasm and passion, a confirmation of the selection of the world's most suited bike for what we were doing. Of course, the bike gave no trouble because it was new ... 'and why would it?' They weren't heading south quite yet as they were heading to Bogota to have the bike serviced at the BMW car franchise. They had an itinerary of service pauses to their ride, all done by local BMW-approved technicians, probably in white overalls wearing gloves. BMWs were also known for the quality and completeness of their supplied-as-standard tool roll. They couldn't comment on that as they had never seen it. "It is probably under the seat" I offer as sage-advice. I can sense that any discussions about the bike are awkward for him. He has no mechanical knowledge and needs none. He is the owner, not the servant who keeps it going. The apparent ease of their journey contrasted so much with ours. There was no struggle, no real emotional investment, the bike had no name ... it was just a way of getting from one place to another. Thank God our girls were in the hold and never heard that one. I wonder if it is envy that keeps us from connecting. I know they won't be envious of us and our obvious inadequacies ... and I try not to wonder what it would be like to be effortlessly cruising along on a magic carpet ride, money in pocket, food in the belly. I recollect that the green-eyed monster is pernicious and let it go.

In contrast, there is almost constant playful banter with *The Plastics*. We'd gelled back in Belize and had a good time in the boatsheds learning about each other, our backgrounds, our experiences etc. We even share 'Fantasy Land' sometimes. We knew we would intermittently meet on our way south. We'd already arranged to be with them for their next oil change. Their Hondas were of a design which has the overhead-camshaft running directly in the alloy of the cylinder head. This is fine as long as there is always a supply of good and clean oil lubricating the interface between moving and stationary components, otherwise, the actual cylinder head wears and replacement is costly. To this end, they religiously replace their oil every 1,000 miles. We figure that as Penelope and Samantha are still drinking the precious stuff at a rate that is still higher than we would really like ... we should collect the old Honda oil and recycle through the girls.

But back to the voyage. We'd struck up a reasonable rapport with the captain

Lawrie working on his tan on the Santa Lucia

who was a ginger-haired Caribbean native, so we managed a few updates on how things were going. Early in the piece the radio failed, but they could manage without that, then at 3.00 am one morning we nearly hit some rocks … but didn't … so that was ok too. But then one engine conked out, which meant we were now slower than before, and as the departure had been delayed for a day, we're running a bit short of food. We'd seen a note from a previous voyage pinned on the notice-board in a small kitchen/common-room we get to use, and it alarmed us a bit as they had taken seven days. This concerned us a bit as we clearly didn't have that much food.

When you learn something for the first time, or see something that you struggle to believe, it can be a jaw-dropping moment. For us, there was one such experience on the *Santa Lucia* when we saw what we now know as flying fish. Initially we couldn't make it out. Our logic told us that what we were seeing was not a fish, as it could fly quite long distances at high speed. Yet when they would dive back into the water, they wouldn't re-emerge like a bird would. These wonderful creatures entertained us no end. Obviously there was no Google hidden within a cell phone to elucidate, and no one was carting an Encyclopedia Britannica along, so we remained in reality-suspended awe. We'd already seen phosphorescence in Panama along the edge of the canal. This unearthly glowing of the water had similarly excited and confused us. We all thought we were grown-ups, yet our knowledge of the world around us was clearly child-like.

Early on the third day of sailing, we reach South America ... quite a thrill. Already it looks huge, with soaring mountains. We ease up and turn to starboard (There's a little port *left* in the bottle) and gently head south. The captain has his binoculars out and is determinedly scanning the shore. He then calls below and a young lad we've never seen before appears and takes over the binoculars. It seems that earlier in the trip they'd done a few zig-zags at night as they left Panamanian waters, to avoid the unlikely happening that guerrillas or pirates would try and get our 'explosivos'. We weren't lost, as clearly we had found South America ... we just didn't know where we were.

"He lives here!" the Captain assures us, pointing to the young lad who looks border-line under-age to be a crew member. We head south for a while before there is a bit of excitement and the lad has recognised a land feature. We turn 180° and head north.

We reach Buenaventura on Thursday afternoon. We anchor out in the wide stream that leads to the port. Friday is taken up with paperwork and visits from officialdom. We can see that there is no urge to get us into the port proper and away south which is a bit of a bugger. Disappointingly, the landing process is not completed and the port is not open over the weekend. Once it is realised that we won't be getting off the boat until Monday at the earliest, we enter into negotiations with the crew's cook for food. We will be matching the previous sailing of seven days if we get off Monday. Now that we are not steaming, we move into the wheel-house as our 'spot'. This is like having your own little cave for gatherings, tales, sleeping etc. It also provides us with shade during the hot part of the day. Also, it is the location of the infamous 'wheel-house fart' which was never, ever owned up to. The wheel-house was evacuated for quite some time and the fug discussed and argued over for weeks.

The cook does well out of us all, as we don't actually get to dry land until Tuesday. The unloading is pretty interesting and a little scary. As soon as we see the stevedores, we know we are in for a daunting time. These are seriously-hard men. Interestingly they are almost all obviously from the Caribbean. To a man they are impressively muscled but lean and mean ... their eyes don't smile, but their

Samantha swinging in the breeze

biceps bulge. Our girls are ripe for the plucking being as our whole lives are strapped to them. We split our resources and Pete and Roly go into the hold to cover the hitching up, etc. Later Pete tells us that during the period he was in the hold trying to ensure nothing was filched, every one of his pockets was 'touched-up' at some stage. He was constantly swivelling to ensure he was not ever blind-sided. Roly was down there to make sure that the lifting points on our girls were suitable and these guys didn't hook onto something not strong enough. He also recalls being physically afraid and was very glad when the bikes are hoisted out. They were out-numbered by the stevedores and from his experience in Panama City, Roly knew that it only took a second's inattention and any opportunity offered would be taken.

It wasn't much better once on the docks. There were still more hoops to be jumped through and it would not be until Thursday 13th May that we finally got away from the port … 10 days for a two-day voyage. Whilst on the docks I could sense we were never safe, so split our crew (including *The Plastics*) into shifts so through the nights we always had two visibly up and on watch. I don't know what happened to the BMW couple, maybe their money saw them away quickly, as they didn't end up being camped there with us. The family with the Mercedes Benz paid

We're always of some interest

Indoors at last

NO ONE SAID IT WOULD BE EASY

to have a soldier remain overnight with it, and it still got broken into. Our sorties out to get food etc were always done mob-handed and never did we allow ourselves to be pushed into close-contact with anyone. We usually walked down the middle of the lanes and little streets. We don't think we are over-reacting and can constantly sense the threatening atmosphere. We are not newbies, but even Lawrie's skills are pushed to the max here. We are not enamoured with Buenaventura, especially as it takes $100 to finally get our freedom. We have been severely rorted.

There is already a little trepidation in facing our approaching time in Columbia, as all the reports and warnings make grim reading. The South American Handbook warns *'... don't wear personal jewellery, take your glasses off if you can see without them, and never walk into a crowd.'* We hear what we are sure are exaggerated tales of hands being cut off for ostentatious watches, and jacket-fronts sliced away to get your inside pocket. We figure that we don't have watches and don't look like obvious targets, but we are still a bit spooked and intend heading to Ecuador with as much haste as our girls can muster. Our time on the docks has done nothing to assuage these concerns. We've always gone with the philosophy that everyone has two arms and two legs just like us, so we can do what they are doing and similarly we've got nothing more than them, no more skills etc. We're all matched, so may as well get along, drawing knowledge and experiences from each other. It usually works.

It is interesting that at the end of the day's riding away from Buenaventura, we stay in a hotel (first of the trip) with *The Plastics* and compare notes. I feel I have lost an edge, an accuracy to my riding is missing and I wonder if anyone else feels the same. They all do. We are so used to riding every day over all sorts of terrains and road surfaces that we are highly-tuned. The day has been great, we are riding on pretty good surfaces and we're amongst green, verdant hills. It is wonderful.

Motorcycling is a tactile, almost sensual experience that is both active and passive. Your input and skill immeasurably contribute to the enjoyment. You participate in so many small ways. You put the bike exactly where you want it in a corner by a series of tiny manoeuvres of your body. The moving of a buttock, a knee put out, a dropped shoulder, a weight transfer from one foot-peg to another, a twitch of the throttle hand, all affect where and how the bike tracks. It is your individual skill that does it. You counter-steer by pushing your right bar away to turn right quickly. The bike starts to fall to the right and without realizing it, you catch it with a reactive adjustment, and together you glide and swish around bends. It is like ballet with a machine. With competence gained, it is uplifting. It is an extension of your body, not a vehicle to be guided by remote controls of steering through a transfer box of worm gear and racks, pinions and the like. You think through bends, and the motorcycle listens to those thoughts and movements reactively.

The passive component of motorcycling is the environment you ride through. You are in it, for better or for worse, be it wet, cold, miserable, hot, smelly or windy. There is an immediate consciousness that you are in contact with. You are not viewing through a TV-like window. This is part of what makes the whole experience uplifting and sometimes joyous. Every ride is an adventure to be savoured, leaving behind the constraints of the repetitiousness of our everyday life. Some people think that adventures are only done by adventurers, which is so sad and inaccurate. Adventurers tend to be elite athletes who drag husky dogs across frozen wastelands (snacking on them when hungry) or row tiny boats across large, open oceans. But reflect … life is an adventure. Watch children as they discover in life, they rush to the next stage, corner, hill, whatever, with excitement and eagerness … because they have never been there. They run ahead because they want to find out what is around that next corner. Sadly, we seem to lose that eagerness and thrill as we mature into the plateau that is so often our 'grown-up' state … and then it is time to ease up, and prepare for our own demise and transfer to the next world.

Popayan is a very Spanish town. Collectively we do our laundry in big concrete tubs. The hotel is old, cheap and most suited to our needs. They let us cram into a couple of rooms for the six of us and as there is an internal courtyard, our bikes are off the road and safe. The boys do an oil-change and we keep the old oil. It is a good result. Popayan is in a garden valley at 1760m and was quickly seen by the conquering Spaniards as being a lovely place to retreat to, away from their sugar estates down in the hot and wet areas below. It has always been an aristocratic reserve, lived in by mainly peoples of pure European descent. It has a lot of old heritage architecture and whilst our hotel might be old and a little crumbling, it has a yesteryear style we admire and like.

We are now truly in the hills and our riding takes us to giddy heights and dazzling lows. There is a constant smile on the lips. The eyes are devouring a sensory banquet. I feel Steph squirming from side to side, altering her view almost constantly. She wants to miss nothing … and there is so much to see. This is the beginning of the

Andes. The Andes will be our friend and foe for the next couple of months. At times the peaks tower over us and at times the valleys stretch out below us almost to infinity. We put in a decent day, independent of The Plastics. We'll see them again, we know that. We like to run our own race. Informally we have agreed to rendezvous at the missionaries' place in Otavalo, Ecuador. We see a suitable camping spot in the late afternoon and seek out the small-holding farmer who seems to be linked to it. The farmer is more than happy for us to put up our tent and insists we join him and his family for an evening meal. They are potato farmers and clearly not wealthy. Our meal is convivial and consists of boiled potatoes with a small bit of hot sauce you can dip into. We have no real shared language skills but it is a special night. I think we both felt privileged. They didn't have much, but so wanted to share it. In the morning, quite early the teenage daughter comes over with coffee. These are special people who we know we will never see again, but their hospitality has been moving. We wish we could give more than memories.

I've been looking forward to Ecuador for a long time. Mum used to often quote parts of W J Turner's poem *Romance* when we were growing up. It always sounded so exotic and I knew she'd be so excited for us, knowing we'd be riding through this dream-like world.

When I was but thirteen or so
I went into a golden land,
Chimborazo, Cotopaxi
Took me by the hand.
My father died, my brother too,
They passed like fleeting dreams,
I stood where Popocatapetl
In the sunlight gleams.
I dimly heard the master's voice
And boys far-off at play,
Chimborazo, Cotopaxi
Had stolen me away.
I walked in a great golden dream
To and fro from school--
Shining Popocatapetl
The dusty streets did rule.

Steph and Des in earnest discussion... probably over shopping

> I walked home with a gold dark boy,
> And never a word I'd say,
> Chimborazo, Cotopaxi
> Had taken my speech away:
> I gazed entranced upon his face
> Fairer than any flower--
> O shining Popocatapetl
> It was thy magic hour:
> The houses, people, traffic seemed
> Thin fading dreams by day,
> Chimborazo, Cotopaxi
> They had stolen my soul away!

Chimborazo is the tallest peak in the world, in that it is the furthest from the core of the earth ... or the furthest poking up towards space. The Equatorial Bulge means that it is not the highest above sea level, however. Cotopaxi is the second-highest peak in Ecuador and confusingly Popocatapetl is in Mexico ... but I never knew that when growing up. Ecuador has more than 30 volcanoes arranged like a ladder, the ones in the Cordillera Occidental (Western) and ones in the Cordillera Real (Central) make the rails of the ladder and are separated by a 400 km wide trough, the Central Valley, which has hilly rungs caused by the rims of the volcanoes overlapping. This makes for spectacular riding with very little in the way of flat plains. East of the Cordillera Real there is The Oriente, the eastern lowlands from which flow the tributaries of the Amazon. A lot of this area was lost to Peru in a disastrous war in 1941.

Ecuador also has some of the cheapest petrol in the world. It is only 20c a gallon compared to over $1.00 in most of the other countries we have travelled across. Unfortunately, Ecuador is also pretty small, the second smallest republic in South America. It does make us want to ride around and around purely because of the savings, which are dear to our hearts. We are running pretty short of funds again.

The ride through to Otavalo was stunning as I wrote in *Sloper* magazine.

Riding through Columbia and into Ecuador exhausted our vocabulary of superlatives. Riding in clear weather in the Andes for the first time was a very moving experience as the immenseness of the mountains is incredible, with patchwork-quilt-like pastures on almost-vertical sides of all the hills in Columbia and Northern Ecuador. The grass was so lush and green that the temptation to leap off the bikes and eat some was very great indeed. Although we were travelling across the equator at this time it was never hot because at times we were riding at between 10 and 12,000 ft. Occasionally there was a descent lasting perhaps three hours or more and dropping us 4 or 5,000 ft. These were very enjoyable as at these heights the bikes were very weak and going downhill is the only time any speed is reached.

We'd got on quite well with the missionaries on the Santa Lucia and they had helped greatly in the bizarre processes of the navigating the bureaucratic minefield to get us into and away from Buenaventura. Without them we'd probably still be there and even poorer than we now are. Otavalo is on our way through the central valley … which as noted above, we are loving. The population is overwhelmingly indigenous and they almost all still wear their traditional dress. They are short and stocky. Steph towers over the women who rarely touch five feet, and many are closer to four feet. It seems like the country is primarily made up of hundreds of small villages and not many bigger towns. Spanish is not the first language of most Otavalo Indians.

Although with only 8,000 population (and 8,000 ft altitude), Otavalo is a successful commercial hub for the region. The Indian Market on Saturdays is a big attraction for both the locals and tourists alike. Beautiful shawls and multi-coloured woolen fabrics are displayed and sold, as are the distinctive regional ponchos and hats. The colours are bright and include lots of blues, yellows and reds. It is interesting that the hats the locals wear are what we would describe as 'Panama' hats, which we saw no evidence of in Panama. The men often wear white trousers under their blue ponchos and most will still have the long, braided hair which is a regional tradition. We learn that the area is quite matriarchal and that alcoholism is rife and of great concern to civic leaders … and missionaries. It is interesting that tourist-demand for lighter garments to send home has introduced lurid synthetic materials to the market-place. To our eyes, they detract from the wonderful traditional woolens and felts.

We soon find our missionaries and they appear to be pretty pleased to see us. Their residence is humble but quite large. It is large enough for them to have a 'church' area where they hold prayer meetings and there are enough rooms to ensure that Steph does not sleep with me. They have ascertained that we are not married and it would not be appropriate for us to be together in their house. We respect this, knowing that our parents would probably have similar wishes.

Due to our diminishing finances, it is decided that Roly and I will go to Quito and uplift the travellers' cheque refund which he had been assured would be there. It is only 90 kms and we decide it is an easy option to catch a local bus … cheap and fuss-free. This gave us more of the same magnificent Andean travel, yet when framed by a bus window it is a pale alternative to what we are used to. We are not 'in' the picture … we are viewing it as spectators. The difference between four-wheels and two-wheels is immense.

Motorcycling is an addiction that, for those of us so afflicted, we are hopeful they'll never find a cure for. To try and describe the freedom and enjoyment of motorcycling has challenged even the most erudite. My own attempts usually involve a lot of arm waving and exaggerated superlatives. The unconverted have no idea of the quantum leap that is taken when the tin-top box is exchanged for a freedom machine. Riding the Andes with towering peaks leaning over us fills us with awe. We can also look down thousands of feet into valleys far below, the details blurring with distance. We can feel the scale of the mountains and smell the countryside. We can sense the enormity of the slopes seeming to rush away to infinity below. In the bus, it was pale and puny, barely worth remembering. The writer Robert Pirsig puts the difference quite well.

You see things vacationing on a motorcycle in a way that is completely different from any other. In a car, you're always in a compartment, and because you're used to it you don't realize that through that car window everything is more TV. You're a passive observer and it is all moving by you boringly in a frame.

On a cycle, the frame is gone. You're completely in contact with it all. You're in the scene, not just watching it anymore, and the sense of presence is overwhelming. That concrete whizzing by 5 inches below your foot is the real thing, the same stuff you walk on, it's right there, so blurred you can't focus on it, yet you can put your foot down and touch it anytime, and the whole experience is never removed from immediate consciousness.

I wonder if the 'only-a-means-of-transport' BMW couple have had an epiphany yet.

Quito is a disaster. The Panama thief had managed to cash-in most of Roly's travellers' cheques before we had got a stop put on them. Only $80 remained and was made available for him. We feel further 'down' as there is no mail at the Poste Restante. Spirits are a bit low. Roly writes home advising the folks that he wishes to cash in his superannuation fund from the Wellington Hospital Board where he has been working. It won't be a massive cash-injection but it will see us along a bit further. Hopefully, this can be got to us in Lima, Peru.

We're never maudlin for long and our time in Otavalo is interesting. Our hosts are generous with their time and show us lots of the region. Roly took the husband for a ride around the area on Bessie. They visited several farmlets and artisan workshops but had an occasion when up in the hills, to be bowled over by a sheep that randomly charged into their front wheel. Roly fell heavily then was further smashed into the ground by the quite large missionary. They managed to get themselves upright and the immediate concern was for the still-stunned sheep. The missionary was aware of how precious the sheep would be to the farmer who owned it and if it was dead, there would need to be compensation. Fortunately, it soon got to its feet and staggered away. Bessie was righted, kicked into shape and a hasty retreat was made in case the sheep's recovery was only temporary.

The missionaries are from a born-again sect and seem particularly to hate the Catholics ... who of course have been here for 400 years. The Catholics run hospitals and schools, which doesn't seem to count either. Our people are more interested in souls, not the physical and scholastic well-being of the potential parishioners. We are in an interesting and slightly difficult position. We like these people on a personal level and can even live with them trying to subtly convert each of us, but we don't see any Christianity in their lives. They have little compassion for the locals. We'd been a little surprised when we offered them some books for their flock. We'd decided that we need to lighten our load. But no, they didn't think they could find homes for our books among the English-speakers. The wife is a mestizo not an Indian and her attitude towards the locals is slightly dismissive. We're there for a Sunday and have been made aware that they would prefer it if we would be out of sight when their congregation of well-heeled mestizos assemble. Shortly beforehand Steph finds an Indian girl of about 10, asking for food. She is carrying a younger sibling of about two in a wrap-around shawl. The missionaries are initially reluctant to let us share food with the two but ultimately do so, ensuring we are around the back with instructions not to let the girl go until their service starts, telling us that the parents will be in a drunken stupor somewhere. The older girl refuses to eat until

Steph doing what she does best - helping others

Just a chat with the local Policia

the wee one is replete and only then does she voraciously devour our offerings. We admire her a lot more than we do the missionaries.

We've been in Otavalo a few days when to our surprise *The Plastics* arrived with one bike on the back of a small truck. We stifled our joyous glee, and feign concern. It seems that a couple of days back in Columbia they had paused for photos high on a mountain-top. Pete had then free-wheeled down the road without starting the engine. He silently rolled along, descending for something like 23 kms before the lack of gradient slowed him and whilst still moving, he gave the bike a lusty kick to start it. The mighty Honda responded by immediately locking up solid. Pete hadn't taken cognisance of the fact that the engine and gearbox are lubricated by the same oil and when free-wheeling sans-moteur there was no oiling of the output shaft spinning in the stationary idler pinion. This got extremely hot and the action of trying to kick-start the bike was enough to move it minutely and the hot and cold fused together ... irrevocably. No amount of pounding with hand-tools was going to separate the two. Roly's prognosis was that it needed a seriously big hydraulic press.

We learn of a suitable press in the next town. I lead the way with Steph on the back of Bessie. It is not often we get the opportunity to abandon Penelope and have a romp on the lighter, more nimble BSA. Mark is following with Pete on the back. They have the gear assembly with them. We reach a long uphill and Bessie applies herself with her usual resolute endeavour. After a while I notice the Honda getting slightly smaller in our mirror. Yes … Yes! Birmingham's finest from the pre-war glory years is vanquishing Sochiro Honda's latest pretender. I chuckle knowing that we have won some respect. Later, the boys say they could have possibly dropped down a gear or two and revved the nuts off the Honda to keep up … but gracefully admit admiration.

The 60-tonne press grunts a bit before finally parting the two fused-together gears. The ride home is uneventful. It has been a good day out. After a bit of dressing with a file and sandpaper, the Honda gearbox is re-assembled and pronounced fit for purpose again.

It has been decided that both the *Cast Iron Expedition* and the *Plastic Expedition* will go to the Oriente, so we can say we've been to the source of the Amazon and we are aware there are places you can see the famous Vampire bats and also Tarantula spiders. We know from the South American Handbook that it will be an adventure but is achievable. It is spectacular and it is difficult, and to their surprise, the Plastics find that we don't travel a lot slower than they do. In fact, Penelope can match them. The Panther M120s are long and skinny but known as sidecar tugs. Solo use is rare and often derided by the riding cognoscenti … but on gravel roads, they track confidently straight and true. I give the old girl a good fistful of throttle and she keeps the Hondas at bay. Lawrie and Roly are never far back either. It is interesting that the girder forks of the BSA make for very accurate steering, and Roly can scoot along the side of the road where the Indians have worn it smooth with their shuffling feet … and where there are no pot-holes.

The Amazonian Basin is wet and we shelter under a big sunshade, finding the concrete floor slab to be too flat and hard for comfort. Give us a quarry with undulations, peaks and hollows every time. The bats and spiders impress but we have no desire to take them home … give us a cuddly coatimundi any day. The ride back to civilisation is quite similar to the ride in but I must admit to a bit of youthful competitiveness creeping in. I'm now pushing Penelope hard, stretching The Plastics, giving them something to talk about. Deep down I know they are the hot-shot riders on the real dirt bikes, but hell we'll show them that even with a pillion on-board we're a force to be reckoned with too. It all becomes a bit helter-skelter and frenetic. Steph has already morphed into the Best Pillion in the World (BPW) so her presence is of no concern … until she twists to look at something just as I am pitching into a left-hand corner. Suddenly we are going down in a shower of gravel. Because of Penelope's relatively long wheelbase and steering angle, things happen slowly … we're over to the point where the muffler is scraping along the road and we are spectacularly slewing sideways during our descent. There is enough time for me to twist the throttle on and to my relief and joy … and to Pete and Mark's amazement … Penelope climbs back from the brink of disaster, onto her wheels again and nonchalantly we continue without a pause. The requisite changing of undies can wait. Chalk up another to the *Cast Iron Expedition*.

All too soon we have run out of roads in Ecuador and Peru looms ahead. We've enjoyed our time here immensely. Seemingly we gravitate towards the Indian culture, with their quiet deference appealing more than the mestizo's forwardness. One thing we have noted with some disappointment is the prevalence of goitre among the residents, particularly in the Oriente. This extreme swelling of the throat is very noticeable and sometimes there appears to be no neck at all. It is as a result of the tyroid not functioning properly and the cause may be as simple as not enough iodine in their diet. Alpine countries traditionally had similar high levels of goitre and Switzerland largely removed the problem with the introduction of iodised salt in the 1920s. It is sad to see something which seemingly could be cured so easily.

The cheap petrol is a great incentive to stay, but our dwindling funds mean we must get to Lima directly. On our last day in the country the road conditions were very challenging. At the end of the afternoon, we encountered Mark and Pete again and they asked how long we had taken to get from where-ever to where-ever, and upon assessing our response, they replied … "Oh, about the same time as us! How many times did you fall?" When told none, they looked at each other and laughed. They'd both taken a couple of tumbles that day. Tick!

We reach the Peruvian border at noon on Friday. We're all let out of Ecuador, but getting into Peru is a different story. Roly and I … and Pete and Mark, of course, all have British passports, so are given the immediate go-ahead to enter. Lawrie and Steph are told they must go back 90 kms to a consulate to get visas. We split our remaining funds into two. Knowing it will be touch and go to expedite the entry requirements in the time left in the day, we part with the agreement that I would be at the Peruvian side of the border at noon, every day until we are together again.

Traveling is a brutality. It forces you to trust strangers and to lose sight of all that familiar comforts of home and friends. You are constantly off balance. Nothing is yours except the essential things. – air, sleep, dreams, the sea, the sky. – all things tending towards the eternal or what we imagine of it.

CESARE PAVESE (1908 - 1950)

CHAPTER 8

PUERTO PIZZARO TO LIMA

It was like bloody déjà vu. "I'll be there at noon!" Of course, when parting from Steph and Lawrie, we weren't through into Peru and had no idea where we would be making camp. Even if they had everything go right for them ... and they not only got back before closing but managed the exit and entry processes ... they probably wouldn't find Roly and me.

Unlike Veracruz, there was no militia, there was no tequila, there was no party and hence no excuse ... none needed, as I was back at the border well before noon. The night before, Roly and I'd found our way out to a nearby beach and settled in. The Plastics had moved on. With the blind optimism of youth, we presumed our paths would cross again. We weren't sure how or where, as they were faster than us ... and being well-organised and well-mounted it was not likely they would suffer the inevitable hiccups that regularly hinder and delay our progress.

Before they'd moved on Pete shared one of his *Fantasy Land* moments. He felt that he and I should somehow go racing motocross in the UK on the powerful, four-stroke CCM machines. There was a connection I would enjoy ... the engine was originally sourced from BSA. Fantasies like these are fun to unroll in our heads. We all know they can't and won't go anywhere. Pete probably didn't realise just how much Penelope does to make me look good on the gravel either.

I was a bit surprised that there were no compadres coming through at noon on Saturday. I waited all afternoon in case it was 'just one of those days'. We knew from experience that border crossings can drag on for many hours. Niggling away was the thought that they could have struck trouble. We'd played the odds. *Bessie* has been relentlessly reliable to date. We knew Lawrie had few mechanical skills and accordingly no tools … not even the wherewithal to fix a puncture. He was however very enterprising and resolute. Any failure would only be temporary. Sooner or later they would meet the noon rendezvous … and there'd be a tale to tell.

Sunday, also found me spending yet more fruitless hours staring across no man's land. Nix, no hay, nada … just shimmering mirages. The heat is pretty relentless, the boredom tedious. The day creeps away, and I return to an equally bored and frustrated Roly. His day is even more solitary then mine. At least I have border interactions to look at. It is too early to plan for us to embark upon a rescue sortie. Plan A, which is, of course, our only plan, will be adhered to for a while yet. We can't help wondering what is keeping them though. Our beach site is pretty good. We're close to a small village called Puerto Pizzaro with a comedor and a cantina. There is an island just off-shore that begs to be explored. A few fishing boats are based here but don't seem to be keen on selling fish. It all goes in a refrigerated truck.

By Monday I am starting to make friends at the border but my concerns have not lessened. There is absolutely no news of our other half. I have a glimmer of hope when I see a big 4 x 4 ex-army truck which is decked out for adventure travelling. It has mainly Aussies and Kiwis aboard. I ask if anyone has seen Lawrie or Steph, hoping they would notice an old bike and my scruff-bag crew. The response is almost like I have leprosy. No one wants to talk with me … or even meet eye contact. People scuttle away in all directions. I cannot believe no one wants to engage with a fellow Anzac, or be interested in our plight … or our story. Quickly I ascertain that they have a self-contained truck-life, and somehow I have the possibility of upsetting that. I sense a lack of confidence once their insular world is intruded upon. Of course, that is probably why they are on a group-tour anyway. It is frustrating because I am not asking for acceptance of our lifestyle, nor judgement of it … I am just trying to find out if anyone has seen Bessie et al. Were they at the other border post?

I've become quite pally with a young Peruvian guy of about my age with an old World War Two WLA Harley Davidson. He is trying to ride north, back to a job on an oil rig in Venezuela. I am impressed by his ambition, but he has also struck issues. We're border regulars. His paperwork is not satisfying the Peruvian authorities to even let him out of the country. I doubt he would get into Ecuador even if he got

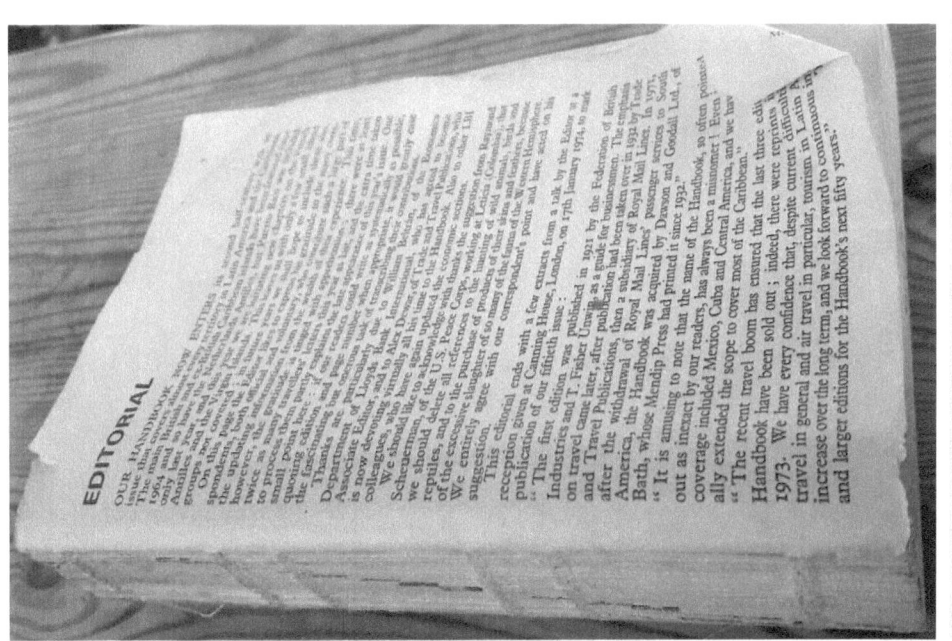

The two bibles - The South American Handbook and Modern Motorcycle Mechanics

through. He has a pretty girlfriend with him, although I am not sure if the plan is for her to tag along for all of the ride. They are pretty naïve and youthfully optimistic … but haven't we all been there? I offer encouragement.

I'd felt Monday would have to be the day if for some reason the consulate closed early on Friday and was not open over the weekend. A lot of possible scenarios play out during the slow-motion torture that is my day. I am also pretty conscious that once again we are spending money doing nothing, making no progress. I worry about the others too … what about their funds? I know they won't be wasting them, but maybe the visa cost more than they had … what then? I bury that thought and search for other possible reasons for their lack of appearance. There is nothing I can do from my side, but I need to tough it out for at least another day. Tuesdays are always lucky days … actually, I think Tuesdays were the days we were meant to take our anti-malaria pills. These had proven to be so hideous that everyone would ignore the fact it was Tuesday hoping Steph wouldn't remember and get out the awful white pills. I think there were weeks when Steph couldn't face them either.

My young Peruvian is now talking about giving me his WLA Harley as he is running out of time to get back to his job. His delays to date and lack of information regarding entry requirements have him at the point of baling. I agree that I can look after his old war-horse and will get it to Lima, somehow send it to NZ and in time he can come and reclaim it. We'll have huge fun exploring NZ with me as a guide. Nothing is impossible when you are young. To this end, we go and get a *Notario Público* to draw up papers transferring ownership to me. This is pretty exciting. I am not looking to take advantage of my new friend, and I am already dreaming of the big Kiwi adventure on our old-timers. Steph will have to ride *Bessie* to Lima.

Tuesday does prove lucky and with big smiles, the missing duo come under the border barrier in the late afternoon. I was right, they'd tales to tell. The consul had decided to break early for what was a holiday weekend in Peru. He'd already gone before they arrived and no one else could issue visas. The consul had stayed home in Lima for Monday as well and it wasn't until Tuesday morning that he was back on deck. In the interim, our likely-lads had holed-up in a very squalid hotel. It was just a matter of toughing it out and trying to eke out the funds for as long as it took. The bloody long-awaited visas had been quite expensive and Lawrie and Steph are fully cleaned out. We need to seriously think about our position as we don't have enough funds to collectively get to Lima.

Getting the WLA back to camp is interesting. We'd looked at a dark and threatening sky and said: "Looks like rain!". No, we're told it never rains in June. It often looks like it but apparently, it will not rain until July. Well, this turns out to be one occasion when we were right and the locals were wrong. The sudden and short deluge turns the dusty track to our campsite into a muddy and treacherous challenge. The WLA is quite alien in that it has a hand gear-change and a foot clutch which has an action that is more or less the reverse of what you have on a car. To let the clutch out to start moving, you push it in. This feels counter-intuitive … but as I mentioned earlier, I have two arms and legs like all the previous owners and riders. And so it was that I slithered successfully back to camp and Roly and I sat down to closely investigate the old beast. In New Zealand, these were unheard of. We'd got the rival 'Army' Indian 741B. Interestingly the Aussies got the WLA, and seemingly a large number ended up in Holland … and at least one in Peru. Dusk was upon us and when fired up, the WLA could be seen to squirt fire out of the head to barrel interface. We laughed at being able to 'see' the combustion as well as being able to hear it. Being a side-valve it will run hot anyway. Roly admires the fact that it has been able to be kept going for all these years using local parts as replacements when needed. How we will fund freighting it home has not yet been resolved.

We're still formulating plans when the owner and his girl-friend come into our camp. Seemingly she is distraught and feels they should leave the bike with her grandma who lives up at the border town … could they have their bike back? Of course, there is only one answer to that one. We have a laugh, tear up the notary's papers, shake hands and finally, the old Harley rides out of our lives … with its syncopated beat slowly diminishing away into the distance. Chalk up another 'nearly-was'.

It is interesting to ask why did we not have even a provisional or tentative 'exit strategy' … why did the crew blindly follow along in this constant state of purgatory and penury? Why was there not a rebellion? Possibly my blind optimism was pervasive? It has to be admitted that we were having an amazing adventure, and I suppose that a state of constant hunger was a small price to pay. Not everyone gets to have fun like this. My mother would say "Cut your coat according to your cloth." I suppose I would have to respond that it was just a bit of a bad estimate regarding how much cloth was needed. Sorry, mum!

Back in Ecuador Steph had sent a postcard to her Arab family asking about little Faisal. The family had great faith in Steph because, in addition to having good skills with him, she'd also been the one to diagnose that the lack of eye alignment and focus was more than just a baby's development. Steph also knew that shortly the family would be returning to the UK where Faisal would have an operation to correct his squint. The included message was just a chatty overview of what we had achieved ... but was also done with the intention of sewing a seed ... bringing her back into their consciousness. The family had always wanted Steph with them, and when told she was going to join her boyfriend in Mexico, their response had been. "Don't go, we'll bring him here!" Maybe ... just maybe we can get at least one 'out'.

Lawrie had tapped-up his brother and there should be some funds waiting for us in Lima. It is decided that Lawrie will leave us in the beachside camp and take an express bus to fetch the money. After the ticket is bought, we divvy up the remaining kitty. Seeing as he is going to money we only allocate Lawrie £2. The balance leaves us with about £5 which is less per person but we have some food and there is an 'economy of scale' to feeding three together. It is a 1,300 kms bus ride but it doesn't stop. We are hopeful of 'day there, day for the money and a day back'. Maybe we will see Lawrie in three to four days. We decide we won't do an "I'll be at the road intersection at noon every day after Saturday." We know Lawrie can bludge a ride down to the village or if he has to walk it is only about five kms.

In some ways, our life at the beach camp could be seen as an idyll. The sun had come back and was a constant, we didn't have to go to work, the sea was blue and warm, always inviting. When the tide was right Steph and I would wade over to the island (Isla de el Amor) for our still-eager private times.

Needless to say, Lawrie didn't return in our anticipated time-frame or anything like it. We'd thought this might happen so had gone onto even more frugal rations. We were a bit over rice and were no longer in the lands of frijoles. We had re-discovered porridge ... that breakfast of childhood winter mornings. We would each have two bowls of porridge a day and one banana. Steph and I would cut one banana in half in the morning and have it with our milk-less porridge and repeat the dose in the evening. Roly would match us in the morning ... then sometime during the day would crack and eat his other half ... then in the evening be banana-less, pissed-off and covetous of ours. Along with our bag of oats, we had a block of raw sugar. This was a local thing and we would parsimoniously shave a bit from the almost-black block. Very, very occasionally we might shave a bit off during the day for a bit of energy.

One afternoon Steph was carrying out a bit of sewing maintenance up in the dunes. She was sitting on our little wire stool and the garment being repaired, was stretched fully over her legs and down to the ground. I was nearly to her after coming out of the briny from a dip, hopefully, all muscles and sex-appeal … when

Des noting something at the bird net

Tranquil scene immediately prior to the snake arrival

she lifted the garment. There was a shriek and she leapt to her feet, spilling from her thighs a sizeable snake. A SNAKE!!! At full pelt, I fled back into the sea ... no point in having the fearless leader go down with a snake-bite or constriction. Needless to say, I took a bit of ribbing over this lack of selfless bravery. Steph always reckons it was me showing my true colours. I was 'a-tremble' for some time after.

About 20m from the shore, a bit down from our camp, was a shipwreck which I had already investigated. With Roly not being fully at ease in the water, he had not found the tide-timing right to get out to have a look himself. Finally, one day I saw him make a move and get out to the wreck. Steph and I were just coming back from the island and were aware that the tide was already rising. I hoped Roly's visit would be short ... but no, there was quite a bit to see when you are mechanically interested. He went below deck and out of sight. From afar I monitored the sea's rise. Soon it was what I knew would be chest-height or more ... and still no Roly. Finally, he appears and ultimately has to do a bit of frantic dog-paddling and neck-high wading and bobbing to get to safety. He never goes out again and in fact, this was probably his last swim. It is interesting that a herd of cows wade and swim out to the island every morning, returning in the late afternoon. I wonder about whether a percentage get taken by sharks. It makes me think about our daily venturing too.

We've found a middle-aged American who is connected to the Chicago Museum. He is an ornithologist and is collecting specimens for his students to study. To this end, he has a net stretched across an opening in the scrubby trees behind the beach. Every morning he collects the birds from the net and soon we become his helpers. Initially, we couldn't see how he took live birds from the net yet laid them out motionless on his tarpaulin. He explained that birds have very weak hearts and that a gentle squeeze stops them and they are effectively euthanased. We find this technique is not difficult to manage and it means no blood and gore. Our birdman has a supply of formaldehyde back at his motel unit where he stores the birds before dispatching them. We learn that he is actually a 'world-expert' in ornithology and has written a book which he says shows that birds have long been wrongly categorised. His assertion is that it is the thorax that defines the family. He has a rival with an opposite opinion and it all sounds pretty intriguing to us … who are experts in nothing. We suspect he is a little lonely as he seems to like our help and visits. One night when we go over to his unit, either we are a bit early or he is a bit late finishing his meal. I am mortified to see that my off-siders are openly salivating over his food. They are hypnotised by it. There are times when he pauses with a morsel on his fork midway to his mouth and explains another bit of bird-lore. Steph and Roly's eyes engage solely with the food. I can see there is no concentration on the dialogue … they are just watching the fork's path to his mouth. This is about five or six days after Lawrie left. Our money is gone and our food supplies pretty low. Later that night we decide we will have to ask our birdman for a loan. We are pretty sure Lawrie will be back soon.

We do indeed borrow $20. This keeps us going until finally Lawrie shows up after more than a week has gone by. He'd got to Lima and found no money at first so had to pawn his treasured Swiss Army knife to the hotel for a room. He then got sick and took to his bed. Finally, he recovered … and located his money. The bad news was that there was not $600 … there was $200. This would not get us to La Paz where we think we have organised some funds to be. With Lawrie back, we repay Birdman and have a proper meal in the beach-side restaurant with him. It is a convivial night and the repast sure beats porridge and banana. While we rest up and cogitate on our forward moves, Lawrie and I decide to try and swim to the island. I reckon I can do it and the tide timing means that at worst we can stand and wade. Soon I sense Lawrie slowly easing ahead. Just minutely he is quicker and inching away. Every few breaths I raise my head slightly and look to see where he is. For a while he is a few metres ahead, then I realise I cannot see him. I swim on, re-adjusting the area I scan in the brief time my head turns and I breathe. I keep swimming and I keep scanning, but I can't see him. Surely he can't have romped away that quickly and that completely. I know my vision without my glasses is not great, but surely I would see his strong crawl wind-milling along ahead of me. I can't help but think of sharks. What if the sharks, who apparently do take the odd cow, had decided on an Aussie? "Don't be silly … keep swimming, and go a bit faster!" I plough on, trying to dismiss my thoughts of the sea turning into a red soup courtesy of a Great White. Of course, just this once … the only time ever … Lawrie had run out of puff and decided to stand up and wade. He was behind me, and my concerns were of no matter.

For us, it is four days ride to Lima and they are pretty dull and of little note. The Pan American Highway runs near, not at the coast. It is sealed and straight, both of which are pretty alien to us. There is almost no shrubbery or foliage of any sort. There are also not the closely spaced villages like we have been used to. This is real desert country. When we stop to have a break, Steph is needed to find us rocks to rest the bikes against. Both Panthers only have a main-stand which is legendary as being very difficult to hoist the bike onto … when unladen. In the state our girls are in, it would take Andre the Giant to get them on their stands. Normally we just lean them against something like a tree, a wall, a kerb, or a bank. It has never been a problem. Here on the plains of Northern Peru, there are none of these, so we need big rocks. Often this results with Steph scouring the nearby desert and being most annoyed when we call "Bigger, bigger!" which we invariably do. Luckily she is a strong girl and usually is able to stagger back with the requisite boulder. She also resents having to walk so far away into the desert to get privacy when she wants to pee. "I'm coming back as a man next time!" is an often-heard refrain. Due to falls on the earlier bad roads, Samantha has lost both foot-rests but Lawrie has used the 'wood-saw' attachment on his Swiss Army knife to cut suitable forked branches to use in their place. They work well enough.

At the end of another great riding day we end up closer to the sea than we had been for a while, and across the sand, we saw a rough shelter. We struggled across

Leaving the fisherman's hut

to it in the soft sand, deciding it was ideal for our purpose. It didn't have a roof but the walls were woven out of thin branches and layered up to be quite thick and substantial. We could see that we'd be out of sight and the annoying on-shore wind could be evaded. There was a little evidence of previous occupation but not enough to make us think anyone lived there. We settled in, cooked-up and got ready for the long night. Our nights without lights always seemed long, but we would be up at dawn. The occupant of the shelter then arrived back, giving us a hell of a fright. It seemed he was a fisherman and he was OK about us usurping him. He would have no part of us moving out, and he grabbed a couple of things and disappeared out into the darkness to hunker down somewhere else. Next morning there was no sign of him.

The only upside to the ride is knowing we have not enough money to get us to La Paz ... but plenty for going on with, in the short term. This enables us to eat three times a day with at least one being a bought meal in a café or comedor. A couple of times we are lucky enough to find a dish called *lomo saltado* which has strips of beef with rice and fried potatoes. It is a Peruvian specialty and we love it. Sometimes

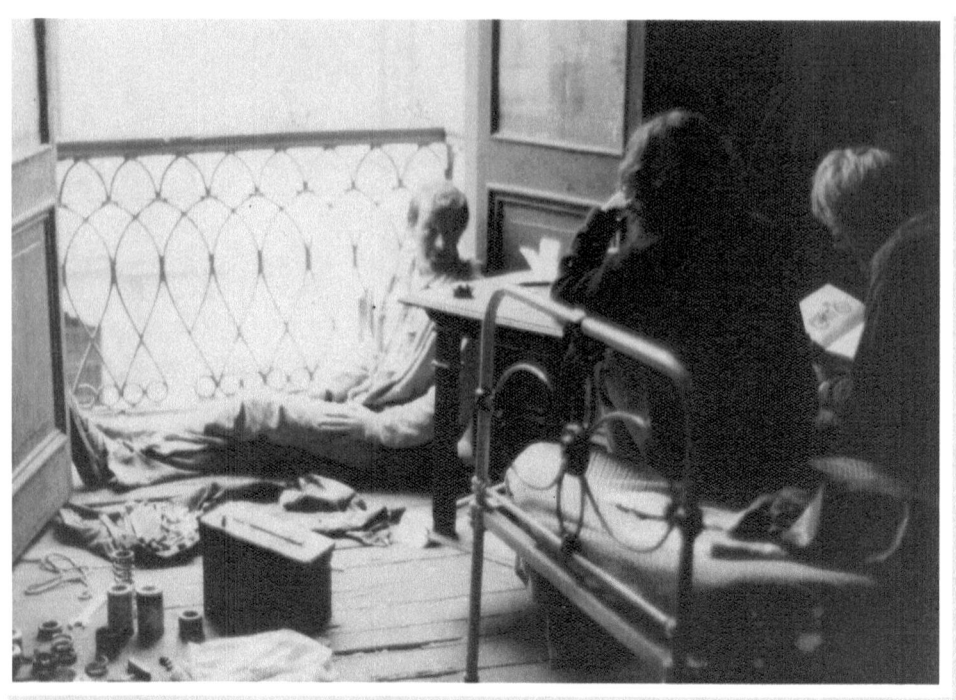

Des browsing Modern Motorcycle Mechanics. Lawrie and Steph probably talking about food

we even wash our meal down with a beer. Petrol has been a shock though as it has recently gone up 50% to $1.00 a gallon. Makes us miss Ecuador even more.

Lima is just another big, bustling city to us. We don't really give it much attention as we're not tourists with fat wallets or time to explore and visit the city's offerings. It is interesting to us only because of the number of old cars still being used as taxis. One we enjoy seeing from time to time is the early 1930s Ford that is the Model A ... but with a little flat-head V8. We think it is all original and quite a testament to their longevity and also to the mechanics who have kept it on the road for more than 45 years. I've always said the less-developed the country, the better the mechanics ... as needs must. Roly had been a little appalled in London to find that very little was being fixed, it was just replaced ... not the background he had come from. Of course, we are benefitting from Roly's training and skill which fortunately is a blend of the developing and the developed worlds. He is by far the most important member of our troupe. We've met a BMW rider who has done a lot of the roads we hope to travel. He has broken his frame in two places, which tarnishes the gilded pedestal we have been holding the Teutonic machine up on.

We've also met two riders with the super-expensive, clip-on Krauser hard panniers. Both have had them break their mountings and bounce down the road. Probably our problems are about par for the course. We don't expect to see sealed roads again until we hit Argentina. All the Andes riding will be on what we call gravel roads, although that makes them sound pretty benign which is far from the truth.

Our time in Lima is spent based at an old, once-elegant hotel opposite the main Railway Station, which is guarded by a military armoured car. There has been recent unrest in Peru which is worrying our outside family followers more than it is us, as we've seen no sign of it. This is only the second time we have 'hoteled-it' in seven months. It is only costing $1 per day for our room which is big enough that Roly uses it as his workshop for some of the fettling needed. The two Panthers are suffering on the bad roads and from being over-loaded. They have been 'bottoming' so badly that the tyres have been getting abraded on the big hits. As well as the deterioration of their suspension units, the seats on both Panthers have collapsed. Bessie has broken the anchor plate to her girder fork friction damper. A bit of welding is needed … and some more of Roly's magic. Lawrie finds the musty, dusty old hotel is playing merry-hell with his hay fever and we all hate the toilets. For our ablutions we've become outdoors-orientated, mainly due to the fact that since leaving the US, all the towns passed through do not have sewage systems with the capacity to handle the demand … so NO toilet paper is ever to be put down the pan, or hole (most toilets are 'hole in the slab' bomb-aimer jobs). In theory, there should be (but never is) a receptacle for the wipings. As you can imagine this is pretty gross. Of course, there is no supplied toilet paper and it is a 'use what you brung' scenario, so usually torn pieces of newspaper. On occasion, you are nearly knee-deep in soiled paper. We far prefer to do our thing in the wilds and tidy up after ourselves. Due to the scarcity and expense of proper toilet paper, we also use everything we can lay our hands on including all our letters. They get one last read before helping with our hygiene. We've even learned that if you carry the envelopes in your back pocket, they will time-soften and when opened out give you one extra swipe.

Steph rings home and her mum hits her with the news that the Sheik has rung. "Where is Stephanie? Where is Stephanie?" This is pretty good news as it means they probably want her back in London when the time comes for Faisal's eye operation. We now have the telephone number of the Sheik's brother in London and we decide that in a week or two we will ring him directly. This could be one 'Get-out-of-jail-free' card. Steph has arranged for some money to be forwarded to a bank here in Lima. Roly writes home, noting the beauty of the young city girls, he tells mum we are thriving and hopefully impresses with his linguistic skill assuring her "no es problema". Roly once more asks if the olds can arrange for his superannuation to be cashed in and also alerts them to the fact he has instructed his bank in the UK to send out his NZ return-leg air ticket, which they are also to cash in. This was mine and Roly's 24th day in Peru but we have ridden on only four of those!

We were still buoyant and facing the final 10,000 kms with enthusiasm. I have always espoused that five months is the ideal length of adventure, being that three months leaves you wanting more, whilst six months often finds you pining for a bit of luxury and familiarity. This leaves five months, as being 'just right'. Here we are seven months in and I am writing home, telling the folks that we intend to cross the Andes through Peru and Bolivia, traverse Paraguay, into Argentina … have a look around Uruguay before crossing the Andes again into Chile and ending the ride at the port of Valparaiso. Our letters home also include tentative mutterings about a return to New Zealand. But anyway … time will tell. I know there is no such thing as a free lunch and there will be a time of reckoning … and pay-back. The 'work and play' has just got a little out of balance. We're in deficit now, but this won't be for always.

Finally, our time in Lima is up. It is time for a real bash at the Andes. We've quite enjoyed the city's cheap food and got a real liking for dulce de leche which is our treat for when we've been good. Roly's done as much as he can with the girls, we're more or less monied-up, although there is to be one more 'collection'. Our first day will be a legendary one … we just know it. We have not been able to get confirmation of what roads are back in use after an earlier earthquake, but we do know it is open over to La Oroya. The day will take us to just on 16,000 ft over the Anticona Pass, reputably one of the highest publically-navigable roads in the world. It will be cold. Both us and the bikes will be short of breath. This is the real-deal.

The bank pick-up is mundane but time-consuming. For some days we have been collecting newspapers and now in the age-old way of our enterprising motorcycling fore-fathers, we have stuffed layer after layer down our jackets and jerseys. It is known as good insulation. Apart from Steph, we have got on every bit of clothing we possess. In the sun outside the bank, we wait and we wait while she gets our latest cash-injection. Of course as usual a crowd forms around us. This is not new;

it is something we just have to put up with. My long ginger hair and contrasting darker beard seem to fascinate the people in countries where hair is naturally black. Soon there are probably 50-60 people of all ages up close and staring at us. A guy attracts our attention from midway back … there are probably three rows in front of him and three rows behind him. He is American and chatty. That is OK, but naturally, he is attracting attention to himself. He wants to know the who, why, where etc. This is all going fine when suddenly he shouts out "My passport, my passport … they've got my passport!" Of course, he is agitated and has swung around to find and confront the thief. The mass of humanity moves not an inch. The faces all remain impassive and curious, no one runs off, they all feign normality. There is no one to confront. He is devastated. There is no one to grab, no one to hit. Our thoughts go out to him but we need to move on as a big day beckons. We can't buy into his nightmare. A little guiltily we have to ignore his situation. He'll have an embassy to sort out his plight.

Finally, Steph re-appears from the bank and it is time to split. While she dons her cold-weather gear I wave the others off. We've been sweltering with all our gear on for long enough, and need to move off the coastal plain and into the hills. Roly and Lawrie have been briefed on the route out of town. It should be a simple matter of following their noses. I perceive no difficulty in this and am happy to send them off. Steph and I are probably seven or eight minutes behind them. It is good to get some air movement playing upon me and I gradually cool a little as we make our way through the suburbs of Lima. We've been riding for about 15 minutes when I see a couple of motorbikes heading our way. To our mutual astonishment, it is Roly and Lawrie. "Where are you going?" we all ask. They are amazed, thinking that somehow Steph and I have got ahead and seemingly are now coming back looking for them. They do not believe that we are riding out of town … and they are riding into town. There is a lot of confusion and vehemence. Ultimately, but with some suspicion they accept my determination that the highway is my way.

> Travel is fatal to prejudice, bigotry, and narrow-mindedness, and many of our people need it sorely on these accounts. Broad, wholesome, charitable views of men and things cannot be acquired by vegetating in one little corner of the earth all one's lifetime.
>
> MARK TWAIN (1835-1910)

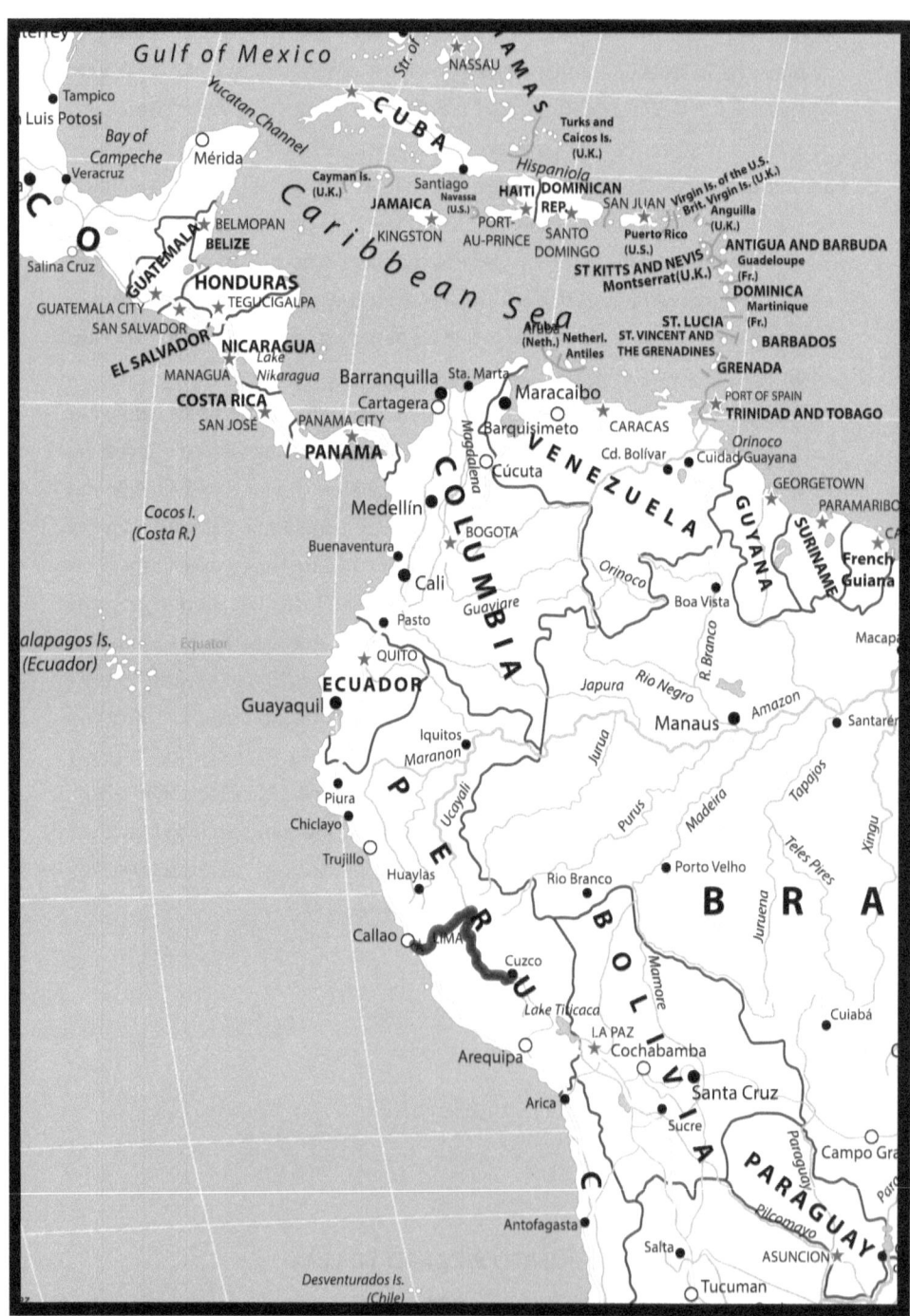

CHAPTER 9

LIMA TO CUSCO

From sea-level to 16,000 ft in one day makes for an amazing ride. We know this is a special day. Not every man and his dog gets to do this ride. After convincing Lawrie and Roly that they were heading the wrong way, our normal riding pattern was resumed and soon we were gently climbing away from the coast. For a couple of hours, the ride was undulating and relatively mundane. Then we started to climb, and climb, and climb. It was steady and relentless, all the while we accordingly cooled. It had been a later start than we would have liked but by mid-afternoon, we still had smiles on our faces. The road was ok, we were chilled, not cold and already we were over 10,000 ft. By the time we got to the height of NZ's Mount Cook (12,349 ft before a bit fell off the top) we were pretty cold and hanging on for the summit. Just to throw a bit of difficulty into the day, Samantha went down with a puncture. Of course, to attend to this meant removing a few layers of clothes and locating our last good tube. This was not a quick repair and by this time we were not confident of reaching La Oroya. Every bit of clothing including our waterproofs was put on and our balaclavas were donned. Such a shame that there was no bank up here, or we could have waddled in and asked for some cash. I am now wearing my old racing leathers that I have lugged along through all the tropical times. Now they will come into their own. We surged on, as best we could. We were now a bit clumsy and the bikes were anaemic. The air was so lacking in oxygen that the required mix for good combustion was well askew. Now the carburettors were dispensing way too much petrol for the amount of air available. The girls ran slower and slower as they puffed their way to the top of the Anticona Pass. Disappointingly it is only 15,807 ft, but we're happy to 'round-up'.

At the time we crested it we were not all that happy, just simply hanging on. We were frozen, dark was upon us and we could barely breathe. We'd chuckled, reading about the trains having oxygen masks, but here we were in a right feeble state. By this stage of our adventure, only Penelope had any lights and they were only a 6v glimmer courtesy of a 45w Lucas generator. Joe Lucas, the founder of the giant company that would supply almost all the electrical componentry for the British Auto industry was jokingly known as 'The Prince of Darkness'. We struggled down from the summit and were so relieved to find a small mining settlement only a kilometre or so from the top. We seek succour and get a spot indoors for the night and a meal. The altitude is affecting us significantly. We have headaches and the shortness of breath is beyond anything we have experienced to date, but then again we have never been this high before. The shortness of breath is exaggerated when we eat. Breathing and eating don't seem to be things that can be done simultaneously. The simple meal is a long drawn-out effort. Our night is a nauseous shocker … an ordeal of almost biblical proportions. We're indoors but we are still cold. Clearly, there has been no time for acclimatisation, as only this morning we were sweating away outside the bank in Lima.

The morning brings an unusual sound into our consciousness. I hear what sounds like racing cars going by in the distance. I struggle outside and can see rally cars going by every minute or so. I try to quickly make my way across the soccer field for a closer look. There are kids running excitedly ahead of me. I can barely walk … my chest hurts and my breath just isn't there for me. I am amazed as Lawrie and I have been keeping up our fitness levels and I'd been a fairly handy middle-distance runner in my youth. Bowling off a 10km run is a doddle … yet here I am unable to keep pace with the elderly. It seems that this is some sort of Trans-Andes rally and we are glad that they will now be ahead of us. We don't have much confidence that the organisers would have made it safe for 'randoms' like us. There is very little transport on the road other than a few trucks and the occasional local bus. Our aim is to get across to Cuzco and we're going what we describe as the northern, inland route. We've got over the Cordillera Occidental and now will run south down the middle valleys of the Andes. We know we'll be up and down, on and off the Altiplano. We haven't been able to source a map and we know the advice in the South American Handbook is out of date due to seismic action a couple of years ago knocking out some of the roads. We're still hopeful we can get through to Huancayo and onto

Lawrie on Samantha, all togged-up

Ayachuco. From there we should be able to get to Cuzco as we've heard that is open for buses.

Our riding now is definitely 'the real deal'. It is tough but magnificent. I truly can write back to the boys at the rugby club now. Even we are impressed with ourselves. I write another article for the Sloper magazine:

'Fortunately, after a week of altitude varying between 9,000 and 15,000 feet we became more or less accustomed to the environment and only at extreme heights have we experienced much discomfort. Day after day, we made our way slowly towards Cusco, City of the Incas. We would climb high up onto the altiplano, ride for several hours then plunge down into monstrous canyons, sometimes zig-zagging down almost vertical sides for three or four hours. The roads in central Peru are incredibly rough and winding and on one occasion we could clearly see the town which was our day's objective while we were sixty-four kilometres of zig-zags away. Progress was slow and the dust the major problem as it continually clogged the air filters.

For 24 hours we rode on roads that did not exist on our maps and the feeling of not knowing where we were going, almost led us to believe the Peruvians in Lima who said that there wasn't a road to Cusco the way that we were going. However, we popped up on our map again and spirits rose. One of our greatest fears was being trapped on the Altiplano at night and after two successive dangerous night descents, it finally happened. After a frustrating day of not finding any villages that had any petrol, we foolishly set off at 4 o'clock for a town 80 kms away known to have some. Our calculations gave us almost enough petrol to get there and rather than wait for a couple of days we climbed up onto the bleak cold Altiplano once again. Hurrying along, Penelope gave Stephanie and I a little lead over the other two. Just before dusk we finally started to descend and ran out of gas 27 km short but at least we were off the high plain and halfway down the mountainside. As we had seen the boys shortly before we started to descend we weren't too worried and started to wait, running up and down the road to keep warm.

Meanwhile, the boys were in trouble, Bessie ran out of petrol and whilst you may think that transferring some from Samantha would be easy, we suggest you try it at 14,000 feet in Peru. This finally accomplished they rode on, only had to have to repeat the entire operation a few kilometres later ... and then Lawrie was unable to start Samantha. So weak and cold were they that they were now two hours behind and consequently it was dark. Somehow they reached us and more petrol was taken from Samantha. We then crept down the valley still cold as all hell but least off the plateau. Twice more we had to rob Samantha of gas until we finally rounded a corner and there below us in the valley were the lights of the town. Even Penelope running out of gas again couldn't stop our joy. We freewheeled down the long zig-zags towards town and then our long-awaited disaster struck ... a front wheel puncture, no less.

"Get out the pump, we'll make it down there!"

After much fumbling the pump appeared and pumping started.

"The hose is cut through! It's not pumping. Where's the tape? We'll tape it up."

"Wouldn't have a clue."

"Come on, somebody must know where the tape is!"

After a frantic search in the dark, some tape was found and applied, the tyre pumped up and we set off for ... 200 yards. Now had to face up to fixing a puncture in the dark, not to mention the cold. Our torch, needless to say, had no batteries and we had no more good tubes left. Luckily the moon had started to shine through and we reluctantly started the chore while Lawrie went on to get some gas.

Luckily money talks, because that town had no gasoline either, so Lawrie gave some kids our container and said 100 Solas if you fill this up. (Gas price 80 Solas). Instantly *a hose appeared and a nearby truck lost a gallon of petrol. This was repeated then Lawrie returned with gas for us. Meanwhile we had been struggling along in the dark frozen stiff, and of course hungry as none of us had eaten since breakfast. Finally, at midnight we were finished and we hit town. No food places were open and the sleepy hotel owner only reluctantly let us stay, warning us that he would charge us if the sheets were dirtied. We'd just had four days on dusty roads without being near water let alone washing in it, and we were coated in dust. So we removed all the sheets and went to bed exhausted.'*

During our travels to date, we have picked up just enough Spanish to ask for things … and now know not to do things that are *muy peligroso*. We are aware that some Andean Indians do speak their own language (Quechua) but it came home graphically and amusingly one day when asking our way of a young man walking along the road.

"A donde Huancayo, mi amigo?" which was my version of "Where's Huancayo?"

"No hablo español"

We crack up laughing and tell him in English that, that is our line. It is almost an hourly mantra. One day we are caught on the Altiplano and it gets dark before we are fully down into a valley. Creeping along with just the one light glimmering away we encounter an Indian inebriatedly staggering his way along. We're both a bit surprised by the encounter but he is first to recover and he gives me something to drink. Unable to refuse I take a slug of hideous fire-water that will repeat on me for days. Under my breath, I tell the others to avoid if at all possible. Lawrie quickly makes praying actions when saying no and it is taken on-board that his religious obligations preclude drinking. It works but our Indian makes me take another gulp to cement our life-long friendship.

A couple of days later we have an experience I record in a story titled *Acid Rain*.

'It had been a long hard day's ride but all the riding in the Andes had been long and hard. It was late afternoon when Steph and I on Penelope rumbled into a small town in the mountains near Cuzco. A stint of hard riding had seen us pull out a significant lead on the other two bikes. Although we had been ahead on the road by 10 minutes or more, at times we were still in close contact and able to wave because of the winding nature and relentless zig-zagging of the road as it climbed down from the Altiplano. Sometimes we would cross only a score of metres apart grinning with determination and possibly bemusement as we rarely saw ourselves riding towards

High on the Altiplano

each other. I thought we looked great.

Roly on Bessie made a neat, trim, nimble-looking picture. Bessie, an elderly BSA with no rear suspension, was never laden to the levels that Penelope and Samantha were. Being newer and bigger and only fifteen years old, Penelope and Samantha, both big single-cylinder Panther motorcycles, always looked overweight and overburdened but that never stopped their willingness to take us wherever we wanted to go. Panthers rule, OK!

The day was over for us and now we needed food and somewhere to sleep for the night. Hardly had we stopped when as usual an interested throng gathered about us. A sturdy, teenaged Indian girl pushed to the front and tried out her few words of English. She was inviting us to dine at her parents' cantina and it seemed we could spend the night there afterwards. What a relief! Travel always presents the daily challenges of "Where are we going to eat, sleep and toilet today?" Again we had hit the jackpot.

We had often experienced these almost impromptu invitations that at one stroke solved all three concerns. Both sides seemed to benefit, as, in addition to buying an evening meal and perhaps some after dinner refreshments, we would be an easy touch for a morning repast before hitting the road. Often we slept on the floor, sometimes

The 'Acid Rain' family

straight outside the back door or even on occasion, the front door, sometimes remembering to erect our feeble tent, sometimes not. Always the nights were cold and hot coffee was always a morning treat to be savoured.

When they rolled into town, Roly and Lawrie were thrilled to find that we had already sourced sustenance and shelter, doubly pleased that we would be inside for the night. A few days earlier our combined nocturnal huffing and puffing had condensed and frozen to the roof of our cramped single-skin tent. The oft-quoted one litre of emissions per person per night seemed a bit conservative as the sun rose to shine on the glacial nylon creating a chilling drip ... drip ... drip ... drip ... drip ... dripdripdripdripdridpidydripdydripidydripdrip! The threatening precipitation got us all out of our sleeping bags and outside just when we were beginning to warm up after an excruciatingly cold night. Bugger! Tonight, being inside would be an excellent treat even if we would have to stay up half the night drinking until all the local clientele went off home.

I can't remember the evening meal so it must have been forgettable and almost certainly contained tripe. All meals in Peru for the budget traveller involve tripe. It could be that the locals have a secret creed that ensures that no matter what is asked for by "gringos", tripe will be served.

"Give them the tripe! Why should we have to eat it?"
"Get rid of the tripe to these gullible fools, they can't speak Quechua or even Spanish!"
"Ah thank God, here are some travellers, Conchita Maria get out the tripe!"

Research is still ongoing, but there is a school of thought that believes that the eating of tripe was introduced by the Conquistadors as a punishment for the local Indian peoples. Now all these centuries later they are getting their own back by inexplicably serving tripe to every foreigner even when they ask for what should be chicken and chips.

"Si Senor, chicken and chips coming up ... Conchita Maria, more tripe for table cinco!"

I know that we drank coca mate to ward off altitude sickness, revelling in the wickedness of it. I remember the beers and the revelry. I remember Steph disappearing for an age and coming back very flushed and confused. She could locate no women's toilet in the Cantina and had to use an "Hombre's" urinal. This had taken quite some planning and gymnastic ability. Her description of keeping the door closed and carrying out a quite unnatural act whilst also trying to keep feet and clothing dry had us in fits. But then again it could have been the coca mate or the beers!

Finally, all the short, squat Andean peasants were shooed off home. Then our hosts insisted on manhandling our motorcycles up the half dozen steps into the cantina. This tiresome although appreciated custom we had experienced before. Our hosts were always worried that our bikes would be stolen so at all costs would get them all inside. Getting three old road-soiled, oil-leaking, heavily-laden, British motorcycles indoors was always a drama that we never wished to inflict on anyone. We are not talking about putting the bikes in a garage, shed or lockup. We mean in your lounge so to speak! Even at home, we wouldn't do it and we love these motorbikes! Once inside, two large beer barrels were rolled across behind the front door and the bikes adjudged secure.

Then we were shown upstairs to a large room overlooking the main road. It had no beds, only hanging carcasses, but we were used to sleeping in quarries, ditches, cafe floors etc. There was no electricity but that was quite usual, what we did find a little strange was that the family bade us goodnight, then locked us in. Although this was a little disturbing, we presumed they would let us out if anything serious like a fire or earthquake happened. We were fascinated by the thought that they must have assumed the women folk needed to be kept safe from us and locking us up would stop any nocturnal wanderings. We settled down to another cold Andean night thankful to be off the Altiplano and inside at probably only 9,500 feet. It's on the Altiplano between

12,000 to 14,000 feet that it is REALLY cold.

Despite being three lads and one lady of reasonably sober habits, on this night it could be said that we overindulged. Indulgent behaviour often has a payback and for me, this came in the middle hours of the night. It does not take a rocket scientist to work out that if you pour copious quantities of beer in one end of your average antipodean male and apply extreme cold, the time that will elapse before it needs to be released out the other end will be shortened. Unfortunately, there is nothing the mind or body can do to stop the process. There does not seem to be a fluid equivalent to constipation. Every desert on the planet was thought of that night, but inevitably, excruciatingly, unavoidably, the time was coming. All the dry thoughts in the world were not going to save me. We were locked in an upstairs room with no vessels or containers that my now spinning head could locate. Briefly, I thought of using a crash helmet but the thought only threatened to bring on paroxysms of laughter and an obvious conclusion.

It was now near dawn and the only solution, short of banging on the locked door and waking the household, was the balcony. I was now at the point of a major meltdown, this was life and death stuff if I didn't pee I would lapse into unconsciousness and die a watery death. Frantically I flung open the doors onto the balcony. Daylight was upon us, but there could be no stopping now. Unbelievably the handrail to the balustrading incorporated a 10-inch solid skirt at the crucial height. Although the male copulatory member (Dictionary definition!) has some stretch to it on a good day, I

Most days were ones of soaring hearts

LIMA TO CUSCO

can assure you that the temperature-shrivelled member in question was never, ever going to achieve the elasticity needed to pee over the barrier, not even on the tippiest of tiptoes. Adopting a bent-thighed stance and aiming through the bars brought on cramps ... there was only one solution ... I had to kneel and relieve myself through the balusters of an upstairs balcony onto a main road.

Having been brought up as a Catholic, I felt there was a reverence to kneeling and this seemed the ultimate humiliation. It was now almost broad daylight and I was projectile urinating halfway across the road causing a thunderous roar in the still, altitude-thinned air as the arcing brackish stream was arrested by the dusty road below. Even sprinkling didn't seem to lessen the deafening sounds. The road was deserted, the town still asleep, but surely not for long!

As you can imagine, when you fill a half-gallon container with fluid then try to pour it out a small aperture, it takes some considerable time, even if squeezing the container. That morning in the mountains of Peru, whimpering with embarrassment, I set a new record for the longest and the longest pee in unrecorded history. All through the purgatory of my relief, I searched for the explanation, I would give when I was sprung, as most surely I would be. Unbelievably and thankfully no one came along during the act and I never did have to pretend I was Russian or insane or drunk or trying to make a pothole in the road or writing my name for posterity.'

The road, or more accurately, bulldust, provides us with a couple more worthy anecdotes for our trip recollections. Bulldust is created when there are long dry periods and the dirt road composition is such that the vehicles help turn the dust created by their passing into a medium which has the consistency of flour. This flour-like surface is thrown into the air by the wheels, making big clouds of following dust, so it looks like the vehicle is travelling at great speed ... even when not so. The huge clouds ultimately re-settle and cover all the pot-holes and ruts that the road may have. This makes it look smooth and quite tame. Of course, the opposite is the case as in places it is like a rocky stream-bed has had a covering of sandy-coloured flour poured over it. It is so fine that when you walk the dust puffs up at your every foot-step. When riding, you hear a puffering(?) sound emanating from your front wheel as it patters along. We ride well apart.

One day Lawrie took a spill in a bulldust section and 'face-planted'. He did this with some ironic self-amusement and went to ground laughing. A photo we took shows him holding the remains of one of Samantha's plywood panniers and quite

Injury-free face-plant amused all

clearly the covering of bulldust on his face. What is not shown was what we saw immediately after the impact. He even had bulldust covering his front teeth. Quite an effort. Another photo taken that day shows us repairing the panniers. Touring motorcyclists will endlessly debate the use of hard panniers versus soft panniers. Soft panniers allow things to be forced in more and things don't shake about as much.

Samantha's footrest replacement – necessity being the mother of invention

They are also usually able to be lifted off the bike and taken with you at night etc. They have ardent fans but there are also proponents for hard panniers as they often provide more security if they are lockable. However, when you 'go down' it is likely they will get damaged and repairs may be difficult. There are expensive proprietary brands available for the current bikes like BMW. Sometimes I suspect their fan-base defend them because they made the choice to buy. Other times I think it is because they don't go anywhere hard. Ours are low-tech, ply boxes which we have knocked backed into shape many times after tumbles. Sometimes I wish we had a carpenter along with a nail-bag and specialist tools. We make do, straightening the nails and re-fixing with a pair of multi-grips and an engineer's hammer. We'd noted earlier that the Plastics had 'mortice and tenoned' all their pannier joints and mounted them with protective bracketry. The bold and brash side of me would say *'because they needed to!'*

The other bulldust episode involved *Penelope* and sort of shows what a wonderful girl she is and what an impatient plonker I am. On this particular afternoon, I paused for something which resulted in us coming up behind the boys as we made our way along the side of a hill which was leading to the Altiplano. We were sidling along,

Pannier reconstruction while Steph swats up on South American Handbook content

with a big drop into the valley on our right and the land-masse soared away above us on the left. There was a wind blowing from the right so all the following dust was blowing across the road in thick plumes. The boys were following a truck which had slowed their natural progression. They were hesitating to pass because that would take them blindly into the fine dust cloud being as all of the Americas drive on the right ... and overtake on the left. I followed for a bit, then decided that the driver was giving out hints that we could 'under pass' by squeezing along on the right. Maybe I was crediting the driver with more sense than I should have, but I make my move on our lads, follow for a bit and then make the decision that "Yes, passing the truck on the wrong side will take me along the road's edge which delineates the ledge it is on and the fall away into the valley floor thousands of feet below ... but the other side is into the dust cloud and would be playing Russian Roulette ... and I am sure this is what my amigo behind the wheel expects." So with strong thoughts of carpe diem I make my move, feeling Steph's thighs tighten on the seat as I do. Well, bugger me ... halfway along, the truck moves back, giving me the squeeze. There is nowhere to go. On one side are churning wheels the size of horses and on the other a momentous drop of ages. There is no option but to go over the edge.

I am grateful that the fall away is not vertical as many have been … but it is steep enough and goes forever … we'll have to lay her down and slide as far as gravity takes us. As we go over the edge I manage to snick Penelope down a gear and try to point her uphill a bit. I am not sure what gave the throttle a twitch … and maybe it is our watcher from above … but just as all hope was lost and I was anticipating a long and scary slide down the mountainside, bloody 'Nellops' … the magnificently loyal friend, gives a shudder and unbelievably climbs back onto the road … behind the truck. We are safe … and deeply chastened. I won't ever do a rash thing like that again … or not until next time.

My mate Dick (of The Last Hurrah fame) was a wonderful raconteur and his stories were legion. It was fitting that his initials were T T and we reckoned that was for 'Tall Tales' Huurdeman. We never really doubted them but at times they were so far-fetched that they challenged our belief. Into this realm, I toss our contender for the most amazing story. After the night of 'Acid Rain', we went for a couple of days 'Tiki Touring' the region. On a minor linking road, we pause and I took a photo of Roly on Bessie with a backdrop of the snow-clad Andes and in the middle distance there is what looks like the ruins of a substantial abbey. The narrow road leads past Roly and curves around in the distance, disappearing past the lonely church. It is a good evocative shot as it shows rocks on the road and a few scraggy flax-like shrubs which show we are in the valley as up on the actual Altiplano there is no growth except tough grass-cover. Forty years later I am given a bound, very limited-edition copy of a diary done by Ron Rutherford, a fellow Kiwi who co-incidentally had lived in Wellington South as we did. He'd done his South American motorcycle trip a few years earlier than ours on a Triumph, starting at the bottom and ending in Canada. I'd met him later and made saddle bags for him in the late 1970s. By coincidence, we had met again and because of our connection, he had given me one of the diaries. They are a magnificent record, being beautifully hand-written in the day and detail everything that happened to Ron along the way, including petrol purchases, mileage done, food eaten etc. I am gob-smacked when I espy a photo that is almost exactly the photo of Roly and the abbey. I locate ours and compare the two. It is a photographic doppelgänger. My photo looks to have been taken about 15m back along the road so just a few more shrubs can be seen. The coincidence of this is huge but what for me is even bigger, is the realisation … that 40 years after the event, the two photos have found each other. I sense that the omnipotent one is having fun. If only I was a believer.

Ron Rutherford's photo from 1974 and our 1977 doppelganger

Steph providing amusement to Des at Sacsayhuamán

We make a detour off the bypass road into Ayachuco. Here we find the Post Office and after some time, get to make the International call that might see us go 'one down.' Steph gets through to Sheik Monsoor's brother in London and learns that the family is arriving shortly from Saudi Arabia … and yes, they want her as soon as she can get there. It is agreed that she will fly from La Paz and the tickets will be arranged and she is to make contact again soon. This is a good and bad moment. It is wonderful that she will be magically transported away from our caravanserai of deprivation. She'll see her sister Anne, she'll see Mo, she'll have food every day at meal-time. It will be wonderful but it also means that aside from us being separated … she'll no longer be a real part of the adventure. She'll be on the outside, worrying, fretting … well, we hope a little that she will be. While in the Post Office we hear unrest approaching and suddenly the big two-inch-thick doors are pulled shut and locked. All goes silent and we can only quietly hear disturbing sounds from outside. There is lots of chanting and shouting and from time to time, noises like machine-gun fire. We know already that this isn't always the case, as often fireworks are used to foment unrest and fear. It does sound a bit scary though, and we are pleased to have such a barricade between us and whatever is happening outside. A considerable time passes before we are let go. The girls are safe but there are signs everywhere of rioting. We quickly get going and ride back out of town past burnt-out and overturned cars. Probably worth a nod upwards, but we just ride on.

Cusco is as stunning as anticipated, the presence of the Inca handiwork everywhere. There are marvels to behold at almost every corner. Here too are *The Plastics* with tales to tell. They've been roaming far and wide, often off the beaten track. We walk downtown one afternoon and a young man steps out in front of us and in a very strong American accent, implores "Do you speak English?" Without hesitation, Mark responds in his cultured voice "I AM English!" and does not pause his lengthy stride. Later we feel a bit remiss about this, but at the time it gave us a chuckle. It is not often we get one-up on a tourist. We take in the ruined fortress of Sacsayhuamán in wonder. Here are stones of more than 100 tonnes in weight which have been shown to have come from quarries 100 kms away … and the Incas did not have the wheel. The joints between the stones often would not allow a razor-blade to be inserted. There are no mortar joints and often the stones fit on multiple sides. Some have been found with three internal planes rendering the theory that the stones were cut with diamond encrusted string impossible. The ancient stone masonry is bewildering and amazing. The other great thing is that the ancient interlocked walls have survived massive earthquakes in 1650 and 1950. The modern one in 1950 destroyed all the churches in Cusco and 90% of the dwellings. The churches were subsequently re-built as they were prior to 1650.

Cusco is very interesting but the presence of so many tourists is a bit overwhelming. We have struggled for seven and a half months to get here … and look it. Our clothes are ragged, our beards a bit unkempt. The tourists have flown in with money in the pocket and see us as little better than carrion on the roads. The air is filled with big-noting chat around 'trekking the Inca Trail' and 'flying over Lake Titicaca.' It is good to be with Mark and Pete again as we each have a realistic level of respect for each other and our achievements. One night Pete tells us of a dream he had. He related how in the dream, we kept turning up. No matter where they went, sooner or later our ramshackle expedition would roll in and four faces would greet them with cheery grins. He said how then in his dream-world they decided "Fuck it!" and they headed south relentlessly churning through the days at full-speed across the pampas of Argentina until they reached Tierra del Fuego, right at the bottom of the continent. "That's got the bastards! It's a win to us!" he'd crowed … then in the distance, he heard … dooff, dooff, dooff … the unmistakable sound of a Panther just

Plastic Mark keeps his Honda well fettled

over the horizon ... and he woke up in a sweat. We took it as praise.

We've been told of an idyllic camp down the valley towards Machu Picchu. It is at a little town called Ollantaytambo and is run by some fading hippies from the US. For once we agree with the word on the street and it is a wonderful respite. The camping area is rustic and as the town is only at 7,500 ft, the nights are not as bitterly cold as we have been experiencing. The toilets are also pretty rustic being that they are outdoors at the end of the camping paddock. They are unisex and the idea is that you will see if there is anyone there through the foliage long before the winding track delivers you to the branch which suspends you over a fast-running stream. The foliage on the way has leaves that are pretty good for the business too. Steph recalls loving the simplicity of running down the track, plucking leaves as she went. We are still suffering a little of what is locally known as the 'Inca Two-step'. For us, it is just the same old, same old ... no matter what you call it. We do have some Lomotil somewhere but are wary of using it because of the known addictive side-effects.

Ollantaytambo is also the scene of our first encounters with the legendary Rhino Beetles. These gargantuan beetles are not harmful to man as they neither bite nor sting, however being as they are the size of your open hand, we faced them with some trepidation. They have a tusk like a Rhino and an armoured shell. Having them thud into nearby walls at night is somewhat scary and not a little off-putting. Learning that they are often kept as pets in parts of Asia does nothing to make us like them.

We're well and truly in the Andes. We'll do Machu Picchu, then scuttle off to La Paz to get Steph off to 'civilisation'. We're sort-of excited.

LIMA TO CUSCO

Because in the end, you won't remember the time you spent working in the office or mowing your lawn. Climb that goddamn mountain.

JACK KEROUAC (1922-1969)

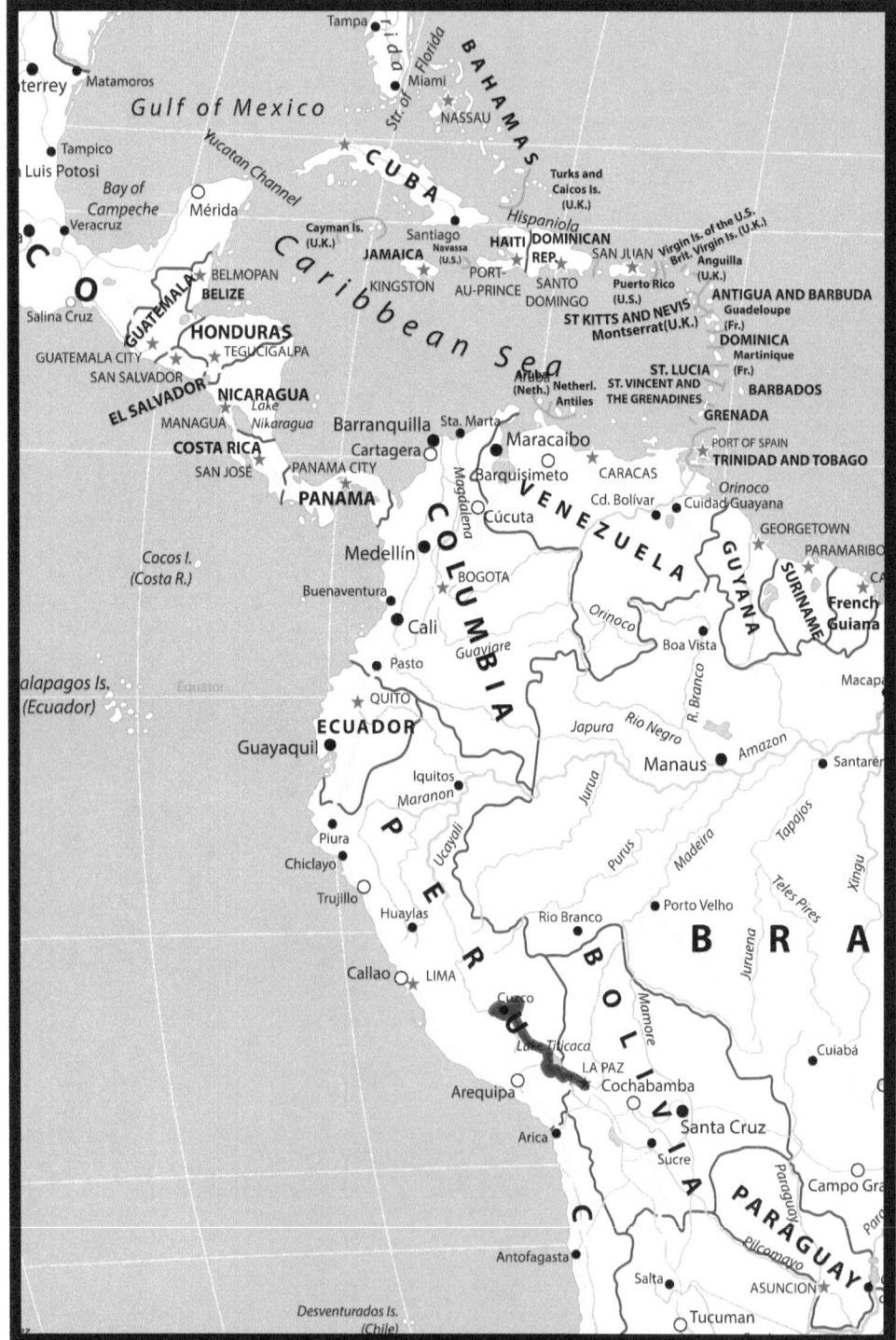

CHAPTER 10

MACHU PICCHU TO LA PAZ

There are two trains going down the valley to Machu Picchu. One is the early morning Indian train, and at a more reasonable hour, there is one for the tourists. There was never any question regarding which one we would go on. By the time it got to us at Ollantaytambo, it was pretty full by local standards and absolutely chocker by developed-world standards. With The Plastics, there are six of us and we more or less jam into the end of a carriage … but not quite … and we have a photo of a very pensive-looking Pete hanging on the outside of the train. He hung there for the two-hour journey, along with quite a few others … getting colder and colder. The conductor knows he only has to collect the newbies' money at each stop and they will only be at the ends of each carriage, between them … or on the roof. To traverse from carriage to carriage between stops, he makes his way along the roof like a Hollywood adventure hero, weaving his way through the travellers sitting up there, huddled down in ponchos. It must be cold on the roof, and we wonder if the roof-riders pay less. There are food vendors struggling through the solidly-packed throng. Once their platter is empty they get off. We've seen this on buses as well. There seems to be an informal protocol that these hawkers don't pay fares. Probably the drivers and conductors get well fed.

Machu Picchu is a complete citadel and remained intact during the era of conquest by the Spaniards because it was out of sight, 75 kms (and 3,000 ft) down the valley and not known to them. It was known to the locals and finally brought

Train down the valley to Machu Picchu with Plastic Pete clinging on

NO ONE SAID IT WOULD BE EASY

to International consciousness in 1911 by Hiram Bingham who is credited with its discovery ... although he found the name Agustín Lizárraga and the date 1902 written in charcoal on one of the walls. It seems that it was used as a Royal estate after its construction around 1450 – 1460 and was only used for about 80 years, possibly housing 750 subjects. One theory for its abandonment is that smallpox decimated the population. Once abandoned, the surrounding jungle overtook the site and it was unknown to all except immediate local Indians, who farmed some of the terraces. Yale University assisted Hiram Bingham's quest to uncover the site and many artefacts were removed 'for further study'. Bingham said it would only be for 18 months or so. Subsequently, Yale has always asserted that Peru lacked the wherewithal to look after them safely. Only in 2012 did they finally agree that Peru owns them and should be the guardians.

For us in 1977, the site was still manageable. The tens of thousands of tourists a day had yet to descend on the site. Upon arrival at Agua Calientes (Hot Water) in the valley below Machu Picchu, we were greeted by rangers offering rides up the zig-zag track to the site proper. Never ones to take the easy option ... especially if there is a cost, we decline and start out on the walk. Although it is only an hour and a half's trek, it is all uphill and by the time we reach the site itself, we are covered in a lather of sweat. Absolutely parched, we succumb to the vendors selling drinks. The saving by walking has been negated in a couple of gulps of Inca Cola. The site is substantial and magical with extensive terraces and walls. The views are stunning and we love how llamas and alpacas roam nonchalantly among us. We capture a lovely picture of Steph with a small llama ... what I suppose you would call a toddler ... too big to be a baby but not yet a youth.

We are really enjoying seeing the use of llamas in action. The Incas didn't have the wheel so used the largest of the South American camelid family to carry everything around for them. They were their trucks, and we have still encountered Indian families taking their wares off to markets loaded up on their herd of llamas. Sometimes we have seen them two or three days away from the village destinations ... resolutely strolling along. The smaller close-relative the alpaca is used for its fleece production and is shorn every year whereas the llama may not be shorn for two or three years ... it is primarily for carrying things and most farmers will have both. The alpaca wool is also finer and more valuable than the llama's, but even finer and rarer is the wool from the wild vicuña. We do struggle to pronounce the double-ll of llama as a y … even though we know it is correct and are happy to do so with tortilla (tor-tea-ya). Yama just sounds too alien for us and a tad pretentious. What do you call a laughing llama? … Yamaha!

Our day up on Machu Picchu is a trip highlight and thankfully there are good photos to show for it. There is just one sobering thought that tempers the satisfaction. The Australian Embassy has been distributing photos of a missing young woman solo-traveller who was last seen climbing the needle-like mountain Huayna Picchu which is across the river from Machu Picchu. It is 1,000 ft or so higher than Machu Picchu and is what you look at when you turn to the view over the valley. The Incas constructed a precarious zig-zag of steps to the top where there was a residence for the high-priest and local virgins. It is thought the young Aussie may have plummeted to her death from the incredibly steep climb, but her body had not been found. We hoped for the best and willed her to be safe and travelling on somewhere out of contact. It makes us think of our families at home who hear from us so infrequently. We wonder if they think about our trip and if they portray it as better or worse than it is. We all think it would be a wonderful, joyful, fabulous, great, marvellous trip if there was more food … but is still pretty damn good. We are still dreaming of delicacies from home and most nights there are culinary discussions which stimulate almost orgasmic recollections.

A convivial night follows down at the tiny village below with its hot springs. To wallow in hot, sulphurous water and chew the fat with your mates is pretty good, and that is what we did. We presumed that the Plastic Expedition would soon be off into the distance and of course there really is a possibility that we won't see them again despite Pete's dreams. They're writing for an Australian motorcycle magazine and we hope that we feature, at least just a little.

Disappointingly, the earlier delays in our ride mean that we won't catch up with a family friend who has been based at Puno on the Peruvian side of Lake Titicaca. He's been with a Kiwi QANGO (Quasi-Autonomous Non-Governmental Organisation) and I think he has been showing the locals how sheepdogs can be used to herd flocks etc. We have been fascinated to watch the Indians who often have quite large dogs but they are never used to round-up animals. That is usually done by the women who usually work as the shepherds. They will take the animals out of the village in the morning and walk them up onto the altiplano to graze. All control is done by the use of a sling-shot or by running around to head off and direct the

The needle-like peak of Huayna Picchu

MACHU PICCHU TO LA PAZ

Machu Picchu is a stunning experience, worth resting and enjoying

NO ONE SAID IT WOULD BE EASY

animals. Sometimes we see a diverse flock (herd?) of llamas, alpacas, goats, maybe a donkey or two and possibly a horse. These all seem to want to eat different matter in different places and the shepherd spends a lot of energy ensuring that her 'group' doesn't mix with her neighbour's. We can see that if they had herding sheepdogs then they could spend more of the day sitting down gossiping with their mates. As it is they are very busy, always on the go, usually while constantly throwing down a spinning-top yarn-maker. Talk about multi-tasking!

Dogs are also often a topic of our nocturnal revue of the day … or a comparison with The Plastics. Almost always as we pass through a small hamlet, a dog will slaveringly chase the motos … one at a time. Often these pursuits are a little scary but also sometimes amusing. There are occasions when we may be in a situation where we can't use the girls' speed to vanquish our canine attacker and they get a good go at us. Because we are usually a distance apart, some dogs will get three separate opportunities to chase us along, possibly enjoying the sight of us, with our legs in the air yelling obscenities. We have come to rate the dogs for aggression, perseverance and level of success. One day Steph and I had one that was going to score top marks for perseverance. It had run and run for many hundred metres just off to the side of us … all the while barking and snarling. We just couldn't seem to get enough speed to see it off, when wonderfully we passed over a culvert under the road and the dog which was fully-focused on us, ran off into fresh air at the side of the road. It was just like a *'Road-runner'* cartoon as for a split-second his legs kept running. His subsequent arcing descent to collide with the far bank left him fully-sprawled and unwilling to have a go at Samantha and Bessie. Dogs have always rated as one of the biggest dangers on the road. Never have we met one that you would pat … they just aren't those sorts of dogs.

At 12,507 ft, Lake Titicaca is the highest navigable piece of water in the world. It is also higher above sea level than any mountain in the United Kingdom, Australia or New Zealand. Here, two and a half miles above sea level is a huge lake not only with ocean steamers on it but also floating islands with people who it is rumoured never actually set foot on land. Both of these are intriguing. One of the steamers in use is the SS Ollanta. She is a 2,200-ton ship which was built in England in 1931 to augment another plying the Andean waters which was coming to the end of its economic life. The Ollanta was assembled first using nuts and bolts. Every component was marked and it was sent out to Puno as a giant puzzle. A launching slipway had to be built

Looking back over Copacabana to Lake Titicaca

and workers trained … but ultimately the 260 ft long vessel was riveted together and launched. Due to the narrow gauge of the railway from the coast where she had been delivered to, no part could be bigger than ten feet in breadth and eleven feet in height. The maximum weight of any 'chunk' was 12 tons. When launched the Ollanta had a capacity for 950 tons of freight, 66 first-class passengers on the upper deck of her deckhouse, and 20 second-class passengers in the forward part of the ship. She had a top speed of 14.5 knots and was the Peruvian Corporation's most luxurious steamer on the lake. The principal reason for the cross-lake service from Puno in Peru to Bolivian port of Guaqui was because the alternative route by land around the lake was so difficult. The road is still hardly worthy of the name.

Although there are guides who take tourists out to the floating reed islands of the Uru Indians, we feel we have neither the time nor the inclination. It is interesting to learn that they make their living from catching salmon in the lake … and by posing for photos. The Seventh Day Adventists have a school out on the lake among them, but we are still a bit off missionaries. At least in this instance, they are not just after their souls to record as a number in a ledger. It is on the lakeside that we have our last interface with The Plastic Expedition. It is a fitting site, on the edge of a stunning blue lake, overlooked by soaring mountains. We feel as though we are on the roof of the world. Mark Chin and Pete Willoughby ... you have enhanced our ride immeasurably ... go well, and go safely.

At the Peruvian border, we strike a different problem from any we have had before. This is nothing relating to getting into a country ... this time the problem is getting out. It seems we have slightly over-stayed our visas. Sensing an opportunity to get some hard cash the Peruvian officials decide we need to pay $100 to leave the country. Of course, this is like a red rag to a bull. "What are you going to do if we don't pay? ... kick us out?" They appear pretty adamant and inflexible. We withdraw and play cards indicating we will camp at the border-post. They think we are kidding, so after a few hours, we unpack and set up the tent. This is a game of dare. They want our money but I don't know if they want us still there when their opposing shift comes on. On the other hand, we're being big and brave ... but in reality, we need to get to La Paz because it isn't long until Steph's departure. She'd been in touch with London when passing through Cusco and we'd said we would be in La Paz in three days or so and she would be available to leave after that. We'd

Lake Titicaca is like an inland sea and some of it is crossed by ferry

MACHU PICCHU TO LA PAZ

One last joshing session with Plastic Pete

prefer to get there today as it is only about 120 kms away. A couple of interim offers are made and rejected. At one stage after lowering the offer, they up it again to $25. We finally capitulate for $6 and pass through to the Bolivians who give us no trouble.

We ride through a cold afternoon across the altiplano towards La Paz. We are a little bewildered because as the sun sets and onset of dusk makes things a bit murky, we still hadn't seen sight nor sound of La Paz. We knew we had to be fairly close, yet here it was getting dark and we can see no lights ahead. We find someone to ask and they seem equally bewildered. I could sense the person thinking "Are all gringos stupid?" He then indicated just ahead over to the side. We go to where he has indicated. Wow! We are at the edge of a rim and there below us are the twinkling lights of a substantial city. It is like the whole city is in a huge pair of cupped hands. There is nothing up on the plain, it is all in the curved valley below. It is a fascinating sight but not one we want to delay over. We get down into the city and find a suitably cheap hotel, stash the girls and go out exploring ... on the hunt for food.

La Paz is fascinating. It is the highest capital in the world ... just on 12,000 ft above sea level and is snuggled in its bowl-like surroundings, quite comfortably out of the chilling wind. The snow-clad mountain that majestically overlooks it (Illimani) has triple peaks and is 16,500 ft. The city is exotic. There are minimal flat areas with seemingly every street and lane inclined one way or the other. Street vendors abound, and now all the women have brown bowler hats topping off their squat forms. Their clothes are colourful and layered. Seemingly they wear numerous petticoats. In the cool air, no refrigeration is needed and hanging meat for sale is found everywhere, along with most other staples of life. Formal shops seem to be in a minority and the South American Handbook informs us that the Indians live mostly outside of the monetary system. The life expectancy for both men and women is 49 years of age. Whilst not overtly as attractive as the young mestizo women of Lima, the dark eyes and contrasting white teeth of La Paz's Indian young, light up their tan faces in quite a beguiling fashion. What is slightly off-putting for us is their habit of spitting. This is done indiscriminately … everywhere. A small group of girls will be walking towards you, arm-in-arm, looking a visual treat, when one will hoick out a big goobie, which will land splat, next to you in the plaza.

The other big thing about La Paz, is that it is where we saw the billboard

La Paz street scenes

La Paz street scenes

NO ONE SAID IT WOULD BE EASY

La Paz street scenes

proclaiming 'ELVIS ESTA MUERTO!'. Just like remembering where you were when you learnt of Kennedy's death, or man landing on the moon … some things go into your frontal lobe … and stick. You can't unremember them.

We soon establish a bit of a routine in La Paz. There are Banks to be visited (sans balaclava) in the hope we have some funds, the Poste Restante of course, for contact with the outside world, Steph's plane ticket to be found and uplifted. That sort of 'work' fills the days and in the evenings we go down a few hundred metres from the hotel to an alfresco eatery we have settled upon. Here we muse on what might be … and what has been. These are good nights, albeit pretty cold ones. After we finish our eating, we transfer to another street-hawker for coffee. As soon as her meal is down, Steph is off at the best jog-trot she can achieve at this altitude. She knows her food-triggered, 'Inca-two-step' can only be decorously managed if she is back at the hotel sitting on the facilities. We order her coffee and in no time she is back … with a roll of the eyes. The coffee is strong, black and with six sugars. Not something we would normally imbibe but here it seems appropriate and we all enjoy. Roly is also suffering from the lingering effects of a not-fully settled digestive system and one night has no hope of making the hotel and to his mortification has to make do in the darkness of a building site. These are minor prices to pay for the exotic nature of our adventure.

Steph's departure is a big one for us all. She has made us laugh, she has entertained us at times, particularly when passionately detailing her mum's baking. She has grafted away, turning out humble but always edible meals with the rudimentary ingredients we glean. She is also my South American Handbook back-up person. She is all-things-to-all-people. Her ability to openly interact with the communities we have travelled through has been masterful ... women and babies being her speciality. Her linguistic skills are still sitting at learner status, she still tells bemused locals that she doesn't have a shop (tienda) when she means she doesn't understand (entender). We all chuckle at her ability to fall asleep. She is like a life-size doll, with eyes that close when she is laid down. In the tent at night, she would start to tell us a wondrous thing she had spotted from the back of Penelope. *"Did you see those Indian women with their herd g..g.. going up the, the ... the ... zzzzzzzzzz"* We would sometimes wake her back up, to get the end of the sentence ... if we thought the tale was interesting. Otherwise, we'd let her drift away peacefully. She deserved her sleep. The ride on without her will be empty. I know we will feel like we are cheating, seeing things that she is not seeing, doing things she won't be doing. She has been on the back, through thick and thin, hot and cold, wet and dusty for six months. She's shared the euphoria and the disappointments and with only a few tweaks to the words of Kris Kristofferson,

'From the jungles of the Yucatan to the watery Andean sun, Stephy shared the secrets of my soul ... Standin' right beside me through everythin' I done. And every night she kept me from the cold'

Her pending departure is inspiring more than a sense of loss. The last couple of weeks has blunted the enthusiasm for relentless surging on and on and on to Valparaiso. It is like a final bridge too far. We are pretty spent. The deprivations are telling on us. There is no dissent. No one has said, "Why are we doing this?" But we are beginning to envy the 'Norms' back in our other lives ... the normal people, the ones with jobs and mundane lives. Lives where you sleep in the same comfortable bed each night after an evening of dull TV, fully replete from an evening meal of lamb chops and vegetables. Maybe we should cut short the adventure? There is consensus when this is suggested. Sometimes you do need to know when to cut and run. It is not something I have always been good at ... just one of the many things I am not good at. I know there are a lot of dreams being cut loose. We'll never see or experience Rio, nor the wondrous alpine lakes of Bariloche ... or Chile at all, and Tierra del Fuego is way too much of a dream. Mum's a wee bit right. Our cloth

Sweet repose ... or exhauseted collapse

isn't big enough, but it is a bit more than that. Our physical engines have run out of puff ... and our internal resolve is waning. It is hard not to think of our 'expedition' as just a tiny bit of a failure. It is not a 'death or glory'... 'Charge of the Light Brigade' failure but our success will always be muted by the truncation of the ride. Deep in our dreams, we probably do romanticise ourselves as Tennysonian figures.

'Boldly they rode and well,
Into the jaws of Death,
Into the mouth of hell
Rode the six hundred.'

Once rested up ... and re-funded ... we'll do one last charge across Bolivia, through Paraguay and Argentina, ending the ride in Buenos Aires. The struggle with funding is on-going and there has not been the cash injection we had hoped for in La Paz. A letter home relays disappointment about lack of expected money from a 'publisher'. Several motorcycle magazines used to serialise adventures like ours. I was rejected by my favourite publication for the earlier 'Ernie the ES2' saga ... but not this one.

We've still got a little money, but getting to Asuncion would be touch and go. There is definitely not enough to get to Buenos Aires. Lawrie and I come up with a desperate plan. Our rugby club does have a lot of well-heeled 'toffs' and we wonder about tapping into this as a temporary source of money. We go through various names and reluctantly reject them one after another. The problem is that our close friends are mainly not the monied ones. We settle on two possibles. One is the Kiwi ex-Club Captain who may not have the funds … but might have some ideas about where to get some from. He'd been wonderful to both of us in our early days at the club. The other is a bit of a real long-shot. A Brit who is a close friend, and again may not personally have the wherewithal to help but we think he'd be sympathetic. We give Steph these names and ways to track them down. She doesn't know either, but she knows our deprivation first-hand and will be doing her best to get something to us. Possibly we could hunker down until she gets her first pay.

We've decided that we need to look at Bessie as she seems to have lost some compression and consequently a lot of her urge. The South American Handbook has made me aware of Bolivia's low Yungas valley area. This is in the Oriente and is the heart of one of Bolivia's problems. The area is at a low altitude … warm and fertile. However, the Indian populace resists going to live there … they are altiplano people with altiplano animals, not lowland agriculturalists. We've seen evidence of Japanese settlements in this supposedly benign region. Trucks bringing produce up to the capital often have hiragana script on the sides. Getting there will be a bit of an effort as again we will be getting close to 16,000 ft when we cross the La Cumbre Pass, before plummeting into the warm. We'll temporarily grit our teeth once more, and do bike maintenance in a much better environment than in the cold of La Paz. We also hope to camp, so going back into minimum-spend mode.

But first, it is a sweet-sorrow moment seeing Steph away. She'll briefly stop in Rio before arriving in London on 14th July. She writes to her brother saying that she is excited about seeing sister Anne and London, but tearful about missing out on the rest of our 'fantastic' ride.

Unlike the altplano the Machu Picchu valley is green and shrub-covered

MACHU PICCHU TO LA PAZ

Every dreamer knows that it is entirely possible to be homesick for a place you've never been to, perhaps more homesick than for familiar ground.

JUDITH THURMAN (1949-)

CHAPTER 11

LA PAZ TO ASUNCIÓN

At a stop-over in Paris, Steph was able to change her London-leg flight to an earlier one, so she would arrive at Heathrow quite a few hours before scheduled. This had two benefits. Not only did it shorten the journey time, but it meant she would be able to avoid the 'pick-up' by the Sheik's driver. Although it was a well-intended action by the Saudi family, Steph felt she needed a bit of sprucing up before fronting as 'the nurse'. Even without recourse to a mirror, she knew that six months of living 'on the road' in the same clothes had left her a little grimy-looking. My mum would have lovingly described her as a tatterdemalion ... 'a person wearing ragged or tattered clothing; a ragamuffin'.

Sister Anne was strongly of the opinion that there was more than a little sprucing needed. If a water-blaster had been available, Steph would have got the full treatment. In the absence of one, a bath was run, yoghurt applied to her hair and all the tatty clothing taken away for disposal. After her hair was washed and rinsed, the matted bits were cut away and the whole yoghurt process repeated. Finally, she was pronounced fit to be in company, and dressed in her sibling's clothing. In little more than 24 hours Steph had transitioned from adventurer to city-girl. Even in her new persona though, her heart was back with us.

Steph's Saudi family were always appreciative of her work and never anything other than generous, however, they were not structured in the way they paid her.

Soiled adventurer to City Girl

NO ONE SAID IT WOULD BE EASY

Tarseal road out of La Paz ... it didn't last

Employment conditions were never formalised and remained a mystery. When she had been in Saudi Arabia they had given her numerous gold trinkets and flown her off to Mexico, yet she never knew what her earnings were until she left. Now back in London, again she didn't know what she was being paid … or when. She did know however that they were going to fly her home to New Zealand when she wanted to go later in the year. Whilst she didn't want to upset the apple-cart about work remuneration, she did feel confident enough to ask for an urgent clothing advance. Fifty Pounds was settled on and whilst a small portion was diverted to a suitable 'op-shop', the bulk was soon winging its way to a bank in La Paz. Steph would continue to wear her similar-sized sister's clothes. A good result … endeavour at its best.

Her interfaces with the rugby club boys were awkward and ultimately unsuccessful. The ex-Club Captain was a bit surprised to be urged into a meeting at a pub with a young woman he didn't know but who claimed to be Des's girlfriend … and who had something to ask. They had a nice enough night but no money flowed our way as a result. She rang a couple of other club members but while there was interest, there was no spare cash. We were on our own … and probably that was the way it should be. She'd given it a good go and would forward on some of her earnings when she got them.

Lawrie looking pretty mellow and pleased to be off the altiplano

Coming down off the altiplano

NO ONE SAID IT WOULD BE EASY

Back in Bolivia, we were fending for ourselves ok, and I wrote in Sloper:

'As an excursion from La Paz we headed north over a high pass to Bolivia's low Yunga valleys. We did this so we could look at Bessie's internals in the warmth, to try and cure her sudden loss of compression and smoking. Once again we climbed higher than any mountain peak in Europe, then slowly descended into the valley for 11,000 feet, from the treeless Altiplano through the forests down to the lush tropical low-lands. It was a great day's riding only spoilt by a puncture on the high cold mountainside. Camping once more was welcome after the hotels of late. The dear old Empire Star was found to have worn out her piston rings and somehow her spares had gone. But by switching the two wafer-thin compression rings, compression returned and cleaning out all the carbon from the oil ring stopped the smoking. The slow high-altitude running causes the engine to run very rich and consequently everything carbons up. Bessie has done exceptionally well for a forty-year-old and this has been the first attention she has received. After five days of relaxing, we headed back up the valley slap-bang into a snowstorm. Even La Paz set at 9,500 feet was warm by comparison and it was a relief to gain a hotel once more.

Finally, it was time to head for Paraguay. For three days we rode across the Altiplano with the roads flat, rough, dusty and deserted except the Indian farmers driving llama herds, laden down with goods for market. It wasn't until our fourth day of riding we fell below 11,500 ft and saw trees again. Then it was a gradual descent with the road beginning to twist and turn and the surface changing from thick dusk to sand which we found we could only ride over at speed, ignoring the snaking and sliding of the laden Panthers. At 50 miles an hour, a front wheel slide would sometimes last for 30 yards. But as we got braver, our falls got less. With Stephanie, our good luck charm, no longer with us, Penelope and I finally hit the dust. Thundering along at 50 miles an hour on a long straight we hit a dog with a suicide wish. The damn, dumb canine ran from left to right via our front wheel. This resulted in one dead dog and Penelope and I sliding along on our respective noses, with my gear disintegrating behind us. The resulting carnage was incredible which greatly impressed Roly and Lawrie who were following closely.

With everything straightened out and the lower altitude increasing our power greatly, we carried on. The 60 octane petrol that they use on the Altiplano was not very suitable and as we made our way to lower altitudes the engines protested heartily. The following afternoon (Dog Day Afternoon plus one) we stopped to adjust Penelope's

Lots of Bolivia is tree-less

rear brake because it had developed a strange symptom of losing free-play. We then discovered that she had broken a suspension top bolt, and whilst repairing that, we noticed she had broken her frame. This was a clean break about 9 inches from the large bottom bolt below the swinging-arm pivot. This bolt arrangement, which we'd never liked, had stripped its thread and was spreading from the bottom — so it's not only Hondas and BMWs that break their frames in South America. Needless to say, roads that break Panther frames are not doing us much good either.

The next day whilst en-route to the welder 200 kilometres on, Bessie got in on the act by breaking her girder fork main-spring in three places. So it was a multiple welding stop, and on towards the Paraguayan border ... and the Chaco. The Chaco is a scrub desert which is virtually waterless and has a reputation of being very mean. There is a direct Bolivia-Paraguay route and we decided to take it. This is a dry-season, occasional truck route with the main problem being a difficult 170 kilometres between border posts. The South American handbook suggest food and water for a week, a high axle vehicle, a winch and a good compass,

We reached Boyvide, the last Bolivian settlement and decided we had managed all roads so far, and that we could handle the next one, as it could be no worse than the

Not a perfect result but only the canine fatality resulted

Yet again the frailty of our pannier boxes is evident

LA PAZ TO ASUNCIÓN

ones that we had been on. It was then discovered that the welded frame had broken and nine inches of tubing has disappeared, along with the long through-bolt at the bottom. Also, the frame had broken under the seat, as had the top suspension bolt once more. The nearest welder was a hundred kilometres away, off our route. So we made a temporary repair with wire and stocked up for the trip through no-mans-land. We bought 12 oranges, some bread buns and two kilos of potatoes and then merrily set off into the Chaco with two gallons of water, figuring on 10 hours of riding to the Paraguayan Army Post at Fortin Garay.

Within half a mile. We discover that we hadn't handled deep narrow sand ruts before where you didn't have any room to go at speed. Simultaneously all three bikes bogged down and we realised it would take longer than we thought. It was late afternoon and we'd only struggled 10 kilometres before camping and eating some victuals. Next morning, we did some much-needed maintenance and mended yet another puncture before setting off. Cleaning air filters, plugs and points becomes necessary every two or three days because of the fine choking, dust which gets in everywhere. We struggled along in the hot, baking sun until one o'clock when another puncture needed fixing. We were exhausted already and we knew that progress had been bad. All afternoon we fought on but the bikes often bogged down, plugs fouled, things broke, our panniers fell apart and we fell often. But the worst of all was the sun's telling effect on us.

With us struggling in the thick sand with hulking great motorcycles using up all our energy, we were dehydrating fast and rapidly getting weaker. Our food, except for the potatoes was soon all gone and the water was soon very low, and when dusk fell so did we. We lay in the road exhausted for two hours. We lay without talking or moving. We were too exhausted to cook potatoes or put up the tent. Lawrie was too exhausted to take off his boots for an hour … and if you knew what our boots were like, you'd appreciate how we felt. All day we had thrashed the bikes through thick sand, sometimes paddling with our feet and slipping the clutch for a mile at a time. Every kilometre was a battle. Samantha was now smoking badly and getting through our oil rapidly. Penelope was scraping and rubbing and creaking and I worried desperately whether she'd get through, or not. All the bikes had become very difficult to start as they were pre-heating all the time because we are not making any cooling forward motion. Even the 120-degree heat of Central America had not done to the bikes.

We had now rationed our water and after six mouthfuls each, we finally had the

The lowland roads got softer and softer

The sand of The Chaco was very hard to ride. Bessie's crankcase often ploghed a furrow

LA PAZ TO ASUNCIÓN

Roly works to free Bessie's jammed carburettor while Lawrie rests in the only shade he can find

NO ONE SAID IT WOULD BE EASY

The last three feet of a boa constrictor

strength to pull out our sleeping bags, and ignoring thoughts of snakes and scorpions, bedded down, leaving us with two mouthfuls of water each for the next day. In the middle of the night, our saviour in the form of a truck struggled up to us. Very surprised at the sight of a great bearded gringo in his underpants waving a plastic container the driver gave us some water and told us we had 60 kilometres still to go to the border. In a day and a half, we'd only made 90 kilometres.

We got an early start the next day confident we'd soon have the remaining kilometres beaten and we'd soon be resting, eating and drinking. Just down the road from where we had slept I saw a four-inch log in my path and figured I could run over it when suddenly when I came close, it started moving. It was the last five feet of a boa constrictor. Fumbling badly, I managed to get the last three or four on film. Although it was impressive to look at, it was very slow moving and didn't frighten me as much as the smaller, wriggling snakes of Guatemala.

Progress was even worse than the previous day as we were getting weaker. Penelope broke her chain for the fourth time. and Roly put in our last split-link. Our spirits were falling as rapidly as our bikes were. The full-throttle, clutch-destroying, massive holes and bumps were destroying our bikes before our eyes. Penelope had both suspension top bolts broken and the whole back-end was sagging and swaying but I had to keep thrashing her on. Three times carbs had to be unjammed. After one fall it took Roly two hours to get the throttle slide to move. Samantha was now fouling her plug every half an hour.

We were literally clawing our way across the desert. By lunchtime, we'd reached the border where we rested, exhausted. The sun and lack of food had brought stomach cramps, headaches, nausea and weakness that cannot be described. We were beginning to suffer dangerously from heat exhaustion. We had only 15 kilometres to go to reach Fortin Garay. Our progress was now pitiful, as our arms and legs were almost totally dead. We had to keep going on although it seemed futile as we had no food and our water was low again.

Our clothes were ragged, dirty and torn and sand and dust mixed with sweat making us look like chimney sweeps but with red swollen eyes. It was now two days since we had eaten and as our physical condition deteriorated so our panic grew. Lawrie was now vomiting from heat exhaustion and lack of food and was delirious, with all his strength going completely. By dusk, we still hadn't made the 15 kilometres, and things were becoming very desperate.'

It is interesting reading our account decades later and recalling how I used to try and report back every month to share our ride with fellow club members. In the early 'episodes' there is little emotion ... not all that much of us. As the trip unfolded the reports became longer and more graphic ... more personal, such that I see no reason to rewrite the above. It is at times clumsy but has a currency and accuracy I still feel all these years later. Of course, writing in those days was a one-hit scribble. Unlike today, where we use our word-processors, to edit, cut, copy and paste etc, those were done on whatever paper I could find and there was only one go.

The Panther Owners' Club was a fledgling club at the time and we didn't know more than a hand-full of club members. We had met a few of the London area guys one night before we set off, but that was it. Sloper was going out to all of the world's members. I didn't know how big that was. I was also initially not at ease with sharing our souls ... we didn't want to seem like dorks or inept try-hards. We were all too aware of what naïve stumble-bums we were. We lacked the requisite professionalism, competence and resources that an ambitious ride like this needed ... but didn't want the world to know just how useless we were. I chuckle too at how the poor old editor then had to transcribe my scribbles into something he could type up.

The tin mines often spawn small supporting settlements

Many things were never explained in any detail, and often I couldn't remember what I had written the previous month. So it was all pretty random and hit and miss … very much like the rest of the ride. Some things should be explained and one of them is why the large number of punctures were experienced … and why did they always come at awful times.

I don't really know why the numerous punctures we experienced came at such inopportune moments, perhaps it was some sort of resilience test being regularly bestowed upon us by the 'One I don't believe in'. There is a possible reason for the frequency of the punctures though. When our man Russell sourced the Dunlop Trials Universal tyres for us, we were unaware that the ones he gave us were for competition use. They were two-ply, so as to be soft and flexible when crawling up and over rocks as trials riders do with low tyre-pressures. For our use, we would have been better off with four-ply options with the same chunky tread pattern. This would have given us better resistance to the stiff thorns that we've encountered in our riding. The desert thorns are everywhere and once a spike gets stuck in the rubber of the tyre it will be worked inwards by the relentless hammering the rough road gives it. It may take a couple of days for the spiny point to be pushed through the protective plies and into the tube … but sooner or later it bloody does. They are also very hard to see and remove. I am sure there were times when the same thorn wreaked its havoc on us more than once when we hadn't been able to find and remove it fully. Our worst day was four punctures, not one in a shady idyllic spot.

We often reflect about the Chaco … it really did nearly do for us. Bolivia and Paraguay fought a bitter war over it in the 1930s and we always joked that the loser was made to have it. In reality, it was the bloodiest military conflict fought in South America during the 20th century, between two of its poorest countries — both having previously lost territory to neighbours in 19th-century wars. It is also referred to as La Guerra de la Sed (Spanish for "The War of Thirst"). Were we taking this route for the right reasons? Were we being just a little too gung-ho? Were we still trying to impress The Plastics? There is no accurate answer to those questions. It must be said that there has always been a bit of wanting to have a 'point of difference' to our ride. But it was what it was, and we all came through to tell the tale.

The opening paragraph in Chapter One recorded my dramatic arrival at Fortin Garay. I was safe! Penelope had got me through even while falling apart. She was like a loyal but seriously wounded beast. I was so proud of her even though I doubted her ability to carry on much further.

But back to Fortin Garay … after a short time at the army outpost, when my thirst was quenched and a small snack partaken of, it was time to find the boys. I wasn't sure how big a deal to make of this, and with poor communication skills limiting my explanations and needs, I decide I don't have to involve the army … I'll go on foot. Taking some water, it was only 20 minutes or so before I found them. They were about a couple of kilometres back with Samantha stuck in the sand and leaning over drunkenly. Roly and Lawrie were too spent to get her fully upright or started. We sent Lawrie off on foot towards the outpost. He was in an exhausted state and stumbled away, while Roly and I applied ourselves to getting the bikes one at a time up the 'killer hill'. In a great joint-effort, we managed this, although it took us also to the point of exhaustion. It was now dark and we decided to abandon the bikes and walk in too. Earlier we'd found Lawrie prone on the ground 'resting' while we were struggling with Bessie. We'd got him up and sent him on his way with much encouragement. We again stumble upon him in the dark, all but falling over his slumberous form. Once more he has run out of oomph and lain down. Getting him to his feet, it is a long difficult struggle in the soft sand for the three of us but ultimately, we gain the safety of the garrison.

El Capitán knew exactly how to handle us. He was calm and measured in his approach. He only allows Lawrie small amounts of water and is not perturbed when he is not able to sit with us at a table. Lawrie rests, stretched out on the floor, and we manage to get a bit of wild pork into him, before Roly and I attack our plates in an almost manic fashion. We'd been surprised how quickly we had gone down when the effects of a hot sun, lack of water and food had been combined with extreme exertion. We suspect that Lawrie has had some sort of heat exhaustion or sun-stroke. Normally he would have been the strongest of us all. It is interesting that Roly's wiry frame seems to have seen him in good stead this day. As surprising as our rapid decline had been, our resurrection was pretty quick as well. Within an hour Lawrie was up and sitting at a chair, fully interacting with our hosts.

We are only too aware that we are still nearly 1,000 kms from the end of the desert and a sealed road ... and this is quite sobering. The 'Capitain' assures us it will be easier, the road won't be as soft or rutted. We cross our fingers and hope he is

Covered up to minimise effects of sun and sweat bees

LA PAZ TO ASUNCIÓN

Sweat bees swarm around Roly' while he works

NO ONE SAID IT WOULD BE EASY

Probably our finest moment. Penelope structurally sound again

right. We wonder what all the soldiers do way out here in the wilderness. I wonder also if they 'clip the ticket' of smugglers going through to Bolivia. We don't have the energy or will to put up the tent, just laying it out as a groundsheet on the dusty quadrangle. One soldier comes over and makes wriggling, snake moves with his arms, indicating we need to be up off the ground. We can't take action on his suggestion and indicate that we will take our chances. In a flash, the night is over. Lawrie is looking much better but we confine him to camp and just after dawn a small army truck takes Roly and I back out to the girls. We ride back into camp and resume our rest and recovery.

Later when we looked at the almost-broken bikes we could only salute them. There was no reason at all for them to get through such a ride. It would be tough no matter what bike you rode because of how the dual-wheel truck tracks left the soft sand in a rut with no flat part to ride on. With no width to use, you were left with no option but to 'prod' and 'pedal'.

By lunchtime, we are feeling pretty good. We've been fed well and rehydrated. Lawrie had bounced back amazingly and in the early afternoon, we feel ready to do battle again. There is one slightly distasteful episode which unfolds when we come to leave. A wild puppy has attached itself to the garrison and they have decided that we will take it away. With ropes, they have crudely tied it to the back of Bessie. Our Spanish is not good enough to express our disapproval. We are completely indebted to them. The help and hospitality we have received cannot be dismissed. The tightly trussed puppy is clearly distressed. We are too, but can't really show it. We make our farewell and struggle away on the sandy road. It is wider but not much better than before. Our progress is pitiful and we gauge that it takes two hours to get 10kms. We untied the puppy after about five kilometres with some trepidation. Could it survive out in the desert, or could it make it back to the outpost? We were all happier though once the knots were slipped.

By mid-afternoon, Penelope's broken frame finally could take no more and started jamming against the back wheel. Because the roads were such a struggle, we've always looked at 100m won as being 100m won … and we're not going back. A yard closer to the end is a yard closer to the end. So, when Penelope and I ground to a final halt the others had mistakenly carried on before realising our predicament. No way was either Roly or Lawrie going to ride back to us. It ultimately meant that Samantha was 400m down the way and Bessie another 400m in front of her. Penelope was going to need some serious magic. The boys left the other bikes where they were and came back, Roly bringing some tools. The frame member going down to near the swinging arm was missing the full 9" piece from where we'd had it welded and our temporary repair had not held. There was nothing to hold the back of the bike up. The rail going back under the seat was broken again and once more the suspension top bolt had sheared off. This was going to need a roadside-fix of miraculous ingenuity.

Roly and I looked and looked, cogitating on how much we needed to be able to solve this. Where we had stopped was by far the worst location of the trip simply because of swarming sweat bees. These sickly-sweet-smelling 'spawn of the devil' just loved our sweaty bodies and dark orifices. They climbed in ears, up our nostrils and randomly stung us. Even working with tee-shirts over our heads we suffered, counting 12 stings between us that afternoon. In the cool of the evening, Lawrie was to reflect that it hadn't been a fair hand to be dealt … the worst afternoon of his life following immediately after the worst day. But back to the job in hand.

I think Roly and I jointly came up with the solution, with Lawrie on the wood-saw of Victorinox's finest. Firstly, we abandoned all of the unnecessary weight attached to the rear half of the frame … so the panniers went. Roly had a 'drift' which is a 5" long steel rod he uses to punch things with. This was inserted in the severed top rail of the frame and the tubing pounded and squeezed oval a bit to stop any movement. That made for a spliced top rail but there was nothing keeping everything up. We needed to stop the 'sag'. We saw that if we had a strong, springy timber branch with a fork in it, which we could use to locate itself on a top-rail bracket ... and then if it was the right length to cross over the top of the gearbox and wedge against the back of the engine ... we'd be in with half a chance. Go Lawrie go! We still had spare control cables that we could rob the inners from, and the pack on Samantha had a couple of turnbuckles. And so it was, that the new timber frame member pushed up the back of the bike and the turnbuckles pulled the cable-inner in the opposite direction, tightening the whole assembly. A new bolt for the top of the shock absorber completed the afternoon. Unbelievably this made her completely rigid and we fitted the seat back on, holding it by the front only. There was now no back mudguard or backlight and number plate ... nor panniers ... but man-oh-man we were back from the brink ... again!

We rose early next morning to beat the sweat bees. We didn't want to waste time with a cooked breakfast, but I knew from our recent experiences that food was a necessary fuel. I select three equal-sized potatoes and tell the boys to eat them. Knowing very little about these things, I was aware that the skins contained a lot of nutritional goodness. And so it was that we each struggled through a raw spud before setting off. The dryness of the skin made them awful but we were very loath to waste water sluicing them down. Not our best repast. There was a time when I was known as a fussy eater. We gather up some of our detritus and set off, hopeful of a big push.

I wrote for Sloper, detailing our crossing the rest of The Chaco.

'... Luck had it though that not too far on was an army work-camp and they supplied us with two helpings of good grub and coffee made from milk. Once again good luck equalled our bad luck as the chief drew us a map of the rest of the Trans-Chaco Highway marking army camps where we could expect free food and somewhere to sleep. This valuable document he signed and we set off confident that we'd beaten the Chaco Desert. Four punctures later that afternoon we weren't so sure. Luckily where we came to rest that night was only a hundred yards from a water-drilling camp and the two occupants came out to greet us. They guided us back to the camp and shared their supper with us, later giving us a bed. Vehicles still weren't averaging one a day, so

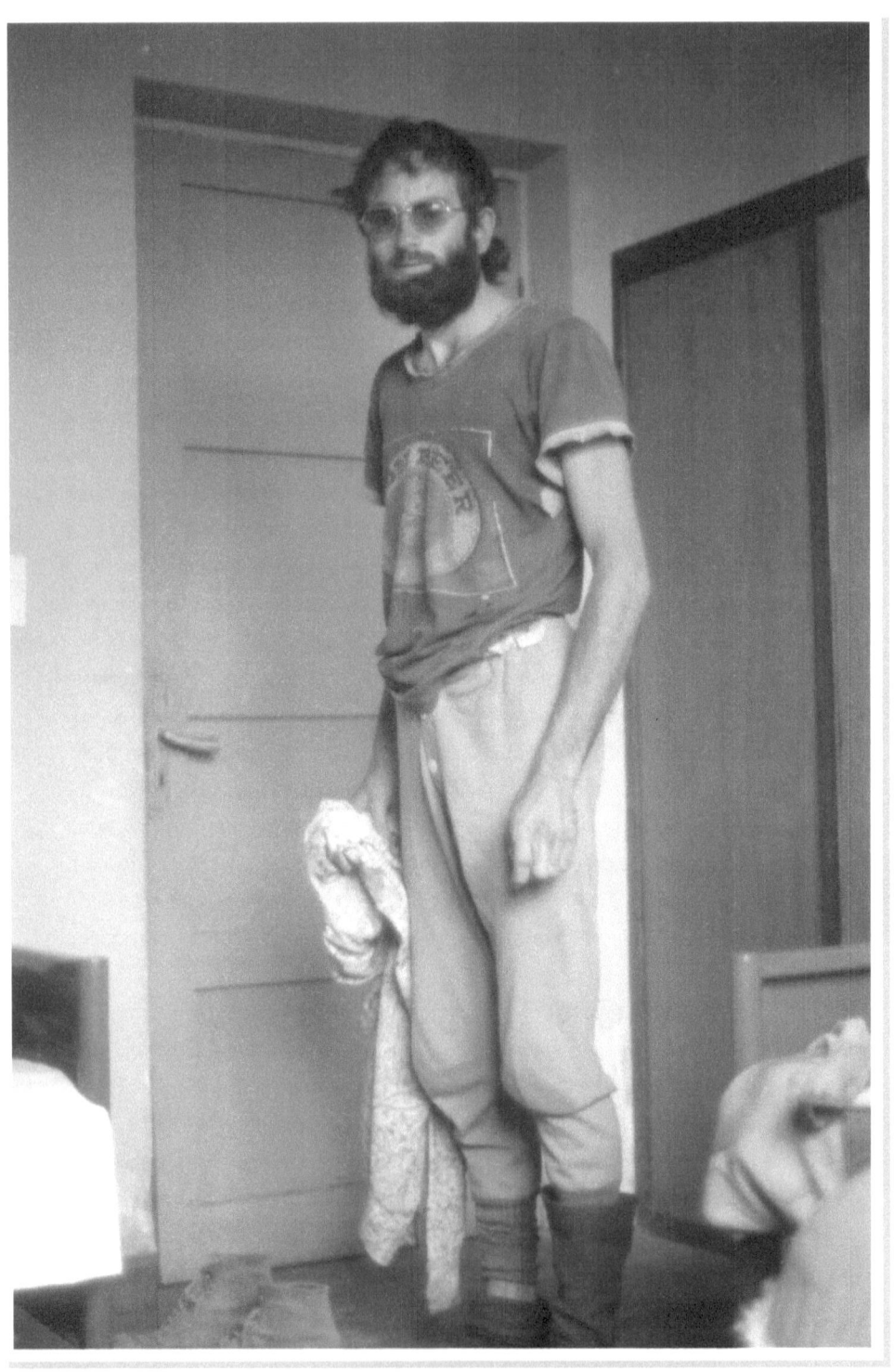

Satorial elegance was not always Roly's strong point

NO ONE SAID IT WOULD BE EASY

it must have been a great novelty to have three guests for supper and breakfast. Next day progress went well and by midday, we'd reached Kilometre 589 from Asunción on the Trans-Chaco highway (Fortin Garay had been at 750). Here in the middle of nowhere was a hotel/restaurant. We'd been told of welding gear to weld up Bessie's fork spring which had broken again, leaving her with about one inch of ground clearance, but that was found to be out of action. We turned this stop into a rest afternoon because staying at the hotel were four Americans studying the wildlife of the Chaco Desert, and after they had told us there was venison for lunch we just couldn't go on. We stayed all afternoon, enjoying the company and the rest. They told us we had had indeed been very lucky as at times no vehicles passed for seven days. They also told us of the abundance of reptiles.

The next day we set off early and then had our usual puncture. 10 kilometres out of Mariscal, an army town and checkpoint (Km 510) Bessie finally called it quits. We towed into Mariscal and waited for our passports to be stamped. We waited five hours, and it was dark before we left town. The next morning, we towed her another 70 kilometres to another military checkpoint on our map of eating places. They fed us and told us we could stay while we repaired the BSA but that afternoon they received a phone call warning them of a visit by a high-ranking officer and we had to leave. By this stage, we had ascertained that the piston needed welding and that new rings had to be found.

Luckily we'd made it to within 15 kilometres of Philadelphia (sic Filadelfia), a Mennonite community of about a thousand people. We shifted towards town and camped in a farmer's field. In Philadelphia we had the piston welded and turned down and second-hand rings were fitted. Rings were also found for Samantha to cure her insatiable thirst for oil. The total cost of the repair ... three dollars. The Chaco is not going to stop us.

We now had enough money for three days riding if we ate potatoes and rocks — small hard, dried bread objects they eat with coffee in the Chaco. With only 450 kilometres to go and the roads improving all the time, we figured we could do it. On the first day, the Chaco threw in two punctures to see how we coped. They slowed us right down and on the last day, we still had 270 kilometres to do. Suddenly, remembering the ferry crossing of the Rio Paraguay, we found we only had 40 cents between us. This we spent on rocks and we sped along, not going to be beaten. The Chaco managed another two punctures and some mysterious non-existent Panther ailments. Although *progress slowed again, we carried on and counter-attacked with tar-seal roads for the last 50 kilometres to the ferry. Too late the Chaco threw in a rainstorm ... because on tar nothing would stop us. At 4.15 we pulled up at the ferry landing with two hours of daylight left, and only 27 kilometres to Asunción. We had it beat!*

Too soon had we smiled, because there was no ferry until 6 pm and once more we were faced with darkness, but now with only one light between the three of us. The Chaco even tried one last desperate fare increase on the ferry. Tough luck Chaco! Five minutes earlier a friendly Paraguayan had given us a hundred Guaranies (80 cents) which took care of the extra fare.

And so in the dark and in the wet, we followed our new friend's car into Asunción and camped in the city park. We were as hungry as hell, but we were glad we'd finally made it. Crossing the Chaco had taken 13 days in which time we'd had six proper meals. The Plastic Expedition can't claim a victory now, even if they do make the tip of South America, as they took the easy route through Argentina. The Cast Iron Expedition had, as usual, blundered through the hard way and at best, we will award them a draw if they get to Tierra del Fuego.

The next day, with the bikes and us looking like refugees from the arches at Charing Cross, we took downtown Asunción by storm. People whistled, hooted, jeered, then broke up with laughter ... but we were beyond caring and finally, at 2.30 we sat down to eat. How we ate. It was one of the trip's highlights to see Lawrie, one of the world's great gluttons ... and tippler to boot, unable to finish his apple strudel or his wine, as he had eaten to the point of vomiting and had to retire to the footpath to lie down. How we suffer from excesses. Now the bikes only have to carry us on tar-seal roads for the next few weeks to Buenos Aries where we will call it quits and somehow make it back to England.

In Asunción, we received some Panther Owners' mags. Great! We even enjoyed reading of our earlier adventures. They almost sound fun. Roly had wanted every bike that had been advertised in Sloper and we can't wait to get back and start Panthering with you all again.'

There's just a few memories I would like to add to the Chaco saga. At one of the army outposts in the Chaco, sitting in an open-fronted crate, on a chain had been a sizable jungle cat. Sadly, not a Panther but it still impressed the hell out of us. It was more or less the same colour and size as a large tabby Labrador. There was also a frightening snake encounter that happened while I was towing Roly on Bessie. At

Easy going across the lowlands

the last minute, I saw a snake on my left side, raised up in the air with its tongue out ... wiggling fit to bust (strike?). In a reaction born from fear, I wrapped my feet around my head, hopeful that Roly did the same ... in time. A subsequent stop informed me that Roly never saw the snake but wondered about my impressive gyrations. The reason for our 'infamy' in Asunción was because of the rigidity of Dictator Stroessner's rule. At the time he had already had been in power for 25 years and whilst he had been happy to shelter Nazi war-criminals, he had no truck with 'ruck-sack' travellers. We'd come in the back door, across The Chaco. We'd never have been allowed in otherwise. The Americans staying at the eatery in the wops were primarily studying the Chacoan peccary which is a close relative to a pig. 'The Chacoan peccary has the unusual distinction of having been first described in 1930 based on fossils and was originally thought to be an extinct species. In 1971, the animal was discovered to still be alive in the Chaco region'

Another mystery of the Chaco took 40 years to solve. Early one warm dry evening, whilst resting in a farmer's field near Filadelfia, we were treated to the strange phenomenon of seeing lightning jumping from cloud to cloud without hearing any thunder. Of course we felt that was not possible, as lightning creates thunder and we all know that you count the seconds to ascertain how far away the lightning is. This baffled us somewhat, but was good entertainment at the time. Decades later I was working with a well-travelled American and somehow this odd occurrence came up. "Oh, you've seen summer lightning!" he told me. Google has expanded on this for me and I am now a bit of an expert on the topic. It is also known as silent lightning or dry lightning or even heat lightning. It doesn't happen when it is raining, which is why it is unusual for us. It seems that the clouds are further away than they appear and there really is thunder but it goes to ground without you hearing it.

Our dealings with the British Embassy were also notable, although not for the right reasons. Perhaps I didn't want to upset the predominantly British club members when I wrote for Sloper and made no mention of our interaction with them. The British Embassy acts on behalf of the NZ Embassy in places where we don't have them, like Paraguay. The NZ Government allowed for Embassies to assist travellers in dire need. They are willing to give an advance … and of course extract it from you later. I had a work colleague in Wellington who whilst in the UK had gone on a real bender in France and found himself with no money. In that instance, he allowed himself to be repatriated directly home and was having money taken from his wages years later. However, normally the Embassy advanced NZ$100 without much comment or rigmarole. When we awoke in the park after our arrival in Asunción, the first thing we did was do the rounds of the banks because we knew there should be funds waiting for us. When we could locate nothing and bearing in mind our hungered state, we threw ourselves on the mercy of the British Embassy, telling them to give us the $100. "Bollocks!" was more or less their response. It was Friday and we knew we would be in an even worse state by Monday when the banks would open again. Begrudgingly they let us cash a cheque for $15 and said they would 'look into matters pertaining to our request." The Ambassador (or Consul?) was a bit of a pompous git. It was that $15 that we gorged on. We were frugal over the weekend and after locating the funds we were waiting for … we returned to the Embassy … and this time the pompous git would not come out of his room to deal with us. He made an underling explain that … yes, we were right and they should have advanced $100 … however, telexes and calls to Peru and NZ (They even rang mum and dad) to find this out had cost $40 which we had to pay. He even had the gall to admit that the Kiwi staff in Lima had told them to 'Look in the Procedures Manual.' So borrowing $15 had cost $40. Bloody Poms!

But all is well that ends well and we're now back in meat-country and finding things quite cheap. Steak is 50c/lb, wine is 50c/bottle and fruit is almost free. Postage is expensive and a letter home costs two bottles of wine. It is nearly six weeks since Steph left us and we are a bit embarrassed to be scoffing al fresco BBQs each night without her. We hope she is feasting similarly with her Arab family. I know she was great pals with Umsaffwa the cook, so probably was.

Roly thanks mum for looking after his financial affairs *"It's very strange to be walking penniless through the streets of a very civilised city, as Asunción is, for half a day and then in the afternoon to have $1250 in one's pocket."*

"Come to the edge," he said.
They said, "We are afraid."
"Come to the edge," he said.
They came.
He pushed them ...
And they flew.

GUILLAUME APOLLINAIRE (1880-1918)

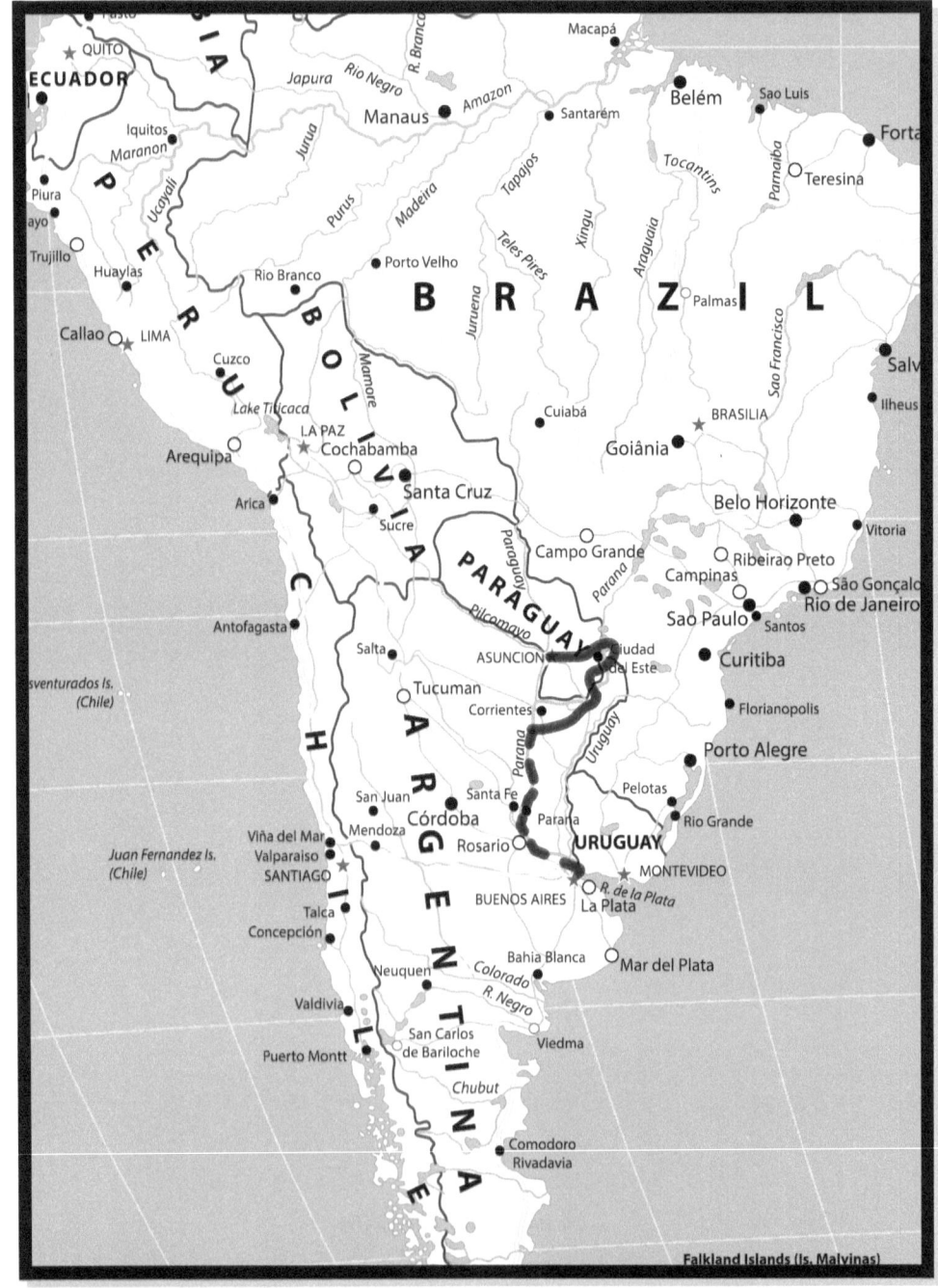

CHAPTER 12

ASUNCIÓN TO BUENOS AIRES

Asunción had finally seen us receive enough money to finish the ride without further deprivation. We weren't rolling in it ... but there was enough to get by with. Asunción wasn't too bad as far as big cities go. It is one of the oldest in South America, being founded in 1537 by the Jesuits as a base from where they would endeavour to convert the local Guaranie Indians to Catholicism. It gained real importance when the Indians destroyed Buenos Aires in 1542 and the Spaniards fled upriver to Asunción. It sits on The Paraguay River and it is interesting that on the eastern side of the river, the surrounding land is fertile and pretty lush, with green pasture. On the western side is the Chaco Desert and you couldn't find bigger contrasts. The country itself is not wealthy and in 1977 is still ruled by a right-wing military Dictator. The Paraguay River is the trade line to the outside world as Paraguay like Bolivia is land-locked. It is 1,200 kms down the navigable river to Buenos Aires and the ocean. The dry season was about to end and we found the mosquitos to be a real problem at night in our cheap and cheerful hotel. We're fascinated by the fleet of vintage trucks that wait outside the railway station each day for loading. There is nothing to keep us and now that our decision to end the ride in Buenos Aires has been taken, we are quite excited. We now can see the end of the rainbow .... It is only a few weeks away, not off in the unseeable distance. I wrote at the time:

After resting awhile and enjoying the fruits of civilization in Paraguay's capital, we hit the road again on the last leg. Unfortunately, that last phrase describes the condition of Samantha. Since our ordeal in the Chaco, a worsening big-end knock had been apparent but we had decided to press on regardless. Asunción had been full of BMW 250s and 600s which we would have loved to have swapped for our tired steeds, but we knew that was impossible, and so happily headed off towards the Iguazú Falls. The roads were interesting and the countryside fabulous. Being back on tarseal roads was a welcome change, even if it did mean you heard far more mechanical noises i.e. Penelope's rear wheel bearings. These were great days with nice warm weather.

One day sticks in our minds particularly and that was the day on which we arrived at the Falls. On that day we rode about 170 kilometres to the Brazilian border and with only a few hassles, crossed over despite Lawrie not having a visa. We then rode for an hour or so to the Argentine border where the Brazilian officials initially wouldn't let us cross the river because we didn't have any permits for the bikes in Argentina. Finally, they decided it was no skin off their noses to let us pay five dollars to cross the river, to try to get through the Argentinean frontier. Once across we only had a few problems getting all the paperwork processed and soon we were in Puerto Iguazú buying food for the night meal. The ride from Puerto Iguazú to the camp at the falls is one that I will always remember. We each had a bottle of red wine in our pockets (18c/litre), we had cheese, we had eggs, we had tomatoes, we had a huge tin of peaches and in my crash helmet, which was hanging over my arm as a basket, we had three pounds of the best tenderloin steak (about 25 to 30p an lb). The sun was shining, we'd just crossed two borders and we even had the currency of the country we were in. As we rode, we sang at the top of our voices, such was the happiness and relief of finally getting to South America's most striking scenic attraction. This was really living.

I could never really hope to describe the Iguazú Falls and will only say that in six years of travelling through 45 countries, they are the greatest natural wonder I've seen. Their setting, in a lush jungle, is magnificent and everywhere are strikingly-coloured birds and butterflies in their thousands. We saw one butterfly as big as the telephone. The night sounds in the jungle are really quite impressive and overall the effect is tremendous. The numerous falls, which stretch one and a half times wider than Niagara and fall a greater distance, are a sight to be seen. Apparently, there are many members of the cat family lurking in the jungles nearby but they all seemed to know not to come around the more powerful cast iron Panthers. We met some great people at Iguazú and sitting around our campfire each night we swapped stories and experiences. Each morning

A balanced diet of red wine, steak, eggs, and fruit

we would consider leaving but the company of fellow travellers would always persuade us to stay another day. Finally, after a great week of drinking cheap good wine and feasting on steak and fruit each day, we finally dragged ourselves away.

On our second day away from the falls, Samantha suddenly belched out a great cloud of smoke, and so it was out with the tools again. The rings were all broken and the piston unusable, so we fished out all our spares and sorted out some rings for the very-used spare piston we had. To even get a reasonable side-clearance on the top ring, Roly had to pean the top of the piston with our hammer, then clean the ring land with a small file. This repair took most of the day and we were just packing up to leave when a gaily-painted old jeep pulled up and a very plump woman leapt out, saying how she loved motorcycles "mucho, mucho, mucho!". We then followed her and her husband to their small dwelling. Unkind people would say they were eccentric alcoholics. Maybe so, but as that's our kind of people, we got along great and laughed and drank our way through a day and a half, before we reluctantly dragged ourselves on again. It was very sad to leave these great people and their crazy house with all its trinkets and knick-knacks. They were probably in their 60s, yet had an old jeep which was painted yellow, blue, red and purple with three chromed bonnet emblems, a rabbit, a horse and a bull, all sitting up one behind the other - beautiful.

Enough is enough! Samantha's piston calls it quits

Perhaps nearly nine months of meeting every challenge head-on had taken its toll because we decided that we could not risk Samantha the last thousand kilometres, and so headed on towards Posadas - a railhead. Camped out 90 kilometres short of Posadas in what we knew was our last night in the tent, we were awakened in the middle of the night by shouts of "Arriba, Arriba!" which by now we knew meant 'Up, Up!'. Lawrie opened his eyes to see a machine gun stuck inside the tent entrance, and got out of the tent very quickly indeed. Roly and I fumbled for our glasses, but soon we were all outside, answering questions at gunpoint. Argentinean Spanish is a lot different to the Spanish spoken elsewhere so we had difficulty coming up with the right answers. We were getting very tired of everyone waving guns around the place. Finally, the police or military or whoever they were let us go back to bed and they left taking the fruit breakfast we set-out ready for an early start.

It was a sad moment when we loaded all three bikes on the train. It just didn't seem right. However, it was quicker cheaper and safer ... and we still got to ride into Buenos Aries as the train station was on the outskirts of town. We'll never know how far Samantha would have got. Perhaps she would have made it.

As always my missive back to the editor of *Sloper* was a short overview dictated by energy-levels and paper availablity. There is a lot more to be shared. Our time out at Iguazú was quite a social one and every night around the fire there would be tales aplenty. We were a group of like-minded souls. We were all 'tenters', there were no 'insiders' among us … a pretty hard bunch. I don't think anyone was trying to one-up over anyone else, we were just a group of young folk sharing our adventures with our peers. It was always light-hearted collegial reflections. One of our group's cautionary tale should be told. Actually, it related to a couple of our age, one Kiwi and one Aussie. They'd wandered southwards for months, doing a 'hippie' trail. They admitted that they'd smoked dope, everywhere they went, just because they could and it was so readily available. They never found 'scoring' too hard. They never crossed borders with any but were always happy to puff up a storm within each country. This had been their way of travel for many months. It was cheap and they were cheerful. They'd just reached an obscure provincial town in Paraguay when they felt the need to get mellow once more. They asked some young guys where they could get some marijuana. They were given a name and an address. Duly they found the house and knocked on the door. A hard-looking man opened the door and asked what they wanted.

"We're looking for Pedro Cruz."

"Why do you want him?"

"We have heard he enjoys the company of travellers … and may allow us to sleep the night"

And with no mention of drugs at all, the couple were taken off to gaol. The 'Pedro Cruz' had been busted that day and our couple had just happened along after the event. They were separated and incarcerated in different gaols of pretty squalid standards, having to pay for their keep. They were not charged with any offence, nor given any knowledge of the other's whereabouts. For them the scariest thing was that no one knew they were in gaol, there was no indication given if they would be charged with anything. They each felt they might rot there for months or even years. Their families were unaware of their whereabouts. Like our families … they would have only the wildest of ideas regarding current location … could be any of three or four countries. As luck would have it, after a week a local guy was being released. Fortunately, he had become quite pally with the Aussie guy. The released local agreed to take a message out and find a British representative. as mentioned

Wider and bigger than Niagara

NO ONE SAID IT WOULD BE EASY

Des looks out over the extensive Iguazu Falls

Lawrie and the power of nature

earlier it is one of the advantages of being from British Commonwealth countries, that Britain represents us in parts of the globe that our home countries don't. They also often have minor officials out in the provincial towns. So it was that a few days later both of the couple were sprung by a British Embassy representative. There was no apology or explanation. The couple were pretty philosophical about the whole experience as they were aware it could have been a whole lot worse being as they'd played a risky game for many months. We all drank to their good luck.

Of course, our experience of paying $40 to borrow $15 came up ... and a bit like the Monty Python sketch "lived in shoe-box! ... hah, we dreamed of living in shoe-box!" ... an American girl told of her experience of losing her money, seeking more from home, and like all of us there ... not being able to find which bank it had gone to etc. She toughed it out for quite a few days, doing the rounds of the banks every day. She realised it was Friday and she felt she couldn't face being foodless for a minimum of another two days. In desperation, she went to the US Embassy in Montevideo to see if she could get a $10 advance for the weekend. Ironically it was not even an American who gave her the news, it was a local Uruguayan.

"Miss ... this embassy has been here for two hundred years. During that time, we have not given out $1 ... and we will not be starting today!" There was no succour or sympathy, just hard-nosed rejection. She said she'd willingly have paid $40 for a $15 advance that day. Touché!

Another escapade not mentioned, was our quest to see the 'moon-bow' sometimes seen at the falls on the night of a full moon. It made sense to us that with all the misty spray thrown up, surely there would be such a phenomenon. Of course, this would need some nocturnal jungle bravery, maybe a torch or two, and seeing as I can't remember if we succeeded in seeing it ... possibly we failed, or 'bloused out' at the first chesty cough of a real panther. I always reckon the strong and important memories will stay with you ... but increasingly I am doubting my own blathering.

And our eccentric couple with the multi-coloured, multi-emblemed Jeep deserve a few more words. They liked us so much that when we left they gave us a gift. It was a couple of pre-revolution Tsarist Russian banknotes. An ancestor had fled the revolution to Argentina taking their fortune with them in paper money. Unfortunately for them, the success of the Bolsheviks and ultimate formation of the Soviet Union meant that the money immediately had no value what so ever. In case

Russian bank notes

things changed and with the hope that the "white" Russians might one day regain power, the money had been kept safe for 60 years. Later, thinking we might have some priceless part of history we asked for a valuation from a philatelist in Bueno Aires. He pronounced them worthless. Lawrie still has those 1909 Ten Ruble notes and I note with some disappointment that they are still more or less valueless … $1.50 to $20 for a mint one. The value, however, is in the giving and at the time we were all quite emotional and hopefully, not all of that was from the alcohol. As 'real' wine drinkers they had introduced us to putting ice and soda water in red wine in the heat of the day. Quite a nice drink.

    Recording our incident with the machine gun in so few lines almost trivialises a very scary incident. I cannot think of another with the potential to go so badly wrong. Lawrie's imploring calls for us to get up were not polite or genteel. He was facing the machine gun and Roly and I were sleepily telling everyone to go away. Of course, once our glasses were on and we were all outside at gunpoint things were not going well. Standing there in our undies seemed to add to our vulnerability. Randomly the 'soldiers' decided to pick on Roly and the subsequent interrogation was primarily aimed at him. None of us had what could be described as even basic Spanish, but Roly's lagged a little behind Lawrie's and mine. The different pronunciation of the Argentinian Spanish and the rapidity in which it was being shouted, appeared to confuse Roly. He didn't seem to know where we were going, or where we were from. He was struggling even with who he was. Each time Lawrie or I would butt-in with the answer and this was annoying our gun-holder. We gathered someone had been up to no good in the area and our inquisitors seemed to be a mix of military and police. Possibly they were confused as to why 'tourists' would be hidden away out of sight and not luxuriating in a hotel. Ultimately they decided that we weren't who they were after … even though they were sure we weren't up to any good either. I don't think we slept much after that, with every noise putting us on edge.

And Buenos Aires? In 1977 I covered it in a paragraph.

What a city! Buenos Aries' nightlife makes London's West End look like a cemetery. The movies don't even go in until 11 pm and after the people come out at 1 am, they sit down to dine. They really are incredible. Needless to say, we took the place by storm as we celebrated Lawrie's birthday, our first in nine months on the road. Buenos Aries' was in some ways a sad place for us as it meant that finally, we had reached the end of the long road. Every night as we supped from our bottles of red wine, we would reflect on what had been and what might have been if we had more money. However, even though we would have liked going on, we all did feel it was time for a rest and we are all looking forward to enjoying a pint in England. And so our great trek ended in a Buenos Aries, Argentina nine months and about 30,000 kilometres after leaving New Orleans.

Of course, arranging an exit was not quite as simple as finding a travel agent and asking for tickets to England. Endlessly we did the rounds of shipping companies, who interesting all seemed to have names like Hodder, Braithwaite and Simons Ltd. We'd be attended to by a be-suited gentleman who to us could only be an ex-pat serving a spell in Argentina … but no they would invariably be local-born of third generation or more British stock. Britain had held great sway in Argentina in the early part of the Twentieth Century. They'd built and owned most of the railways and traffic even drove on the left-hand side of the road until 1945. Argentina has the biggest British population outside of the Commonwealth. It was great being able to deal with fluent English speakers, even though getting what we wanted was proving

Penelope and Saamantha are severly disassembled for freighting

to be a little difficult. It was not going to be cheap getting the bikes back to England and early in the piece we found they couldn't go loose as they had to America. We'd have to cram them into a shipping crate. To this end, we measured out Bessie because she would stay fully intact and disassembled as much of Penelope and Samantha as we could. We managed a 3m x 1m x 1m crate ... and a lot of left-over bits.

We were in BA for most of a month. We were settled into a cheap hotel and had a daily-regime. Now we were in a country with such a history of beef production, we were carnivorous to the highest degree. It was cheap protein. We couldn't believe the tenderness of the meat and it was whilst camping earlier that I had discovered the beauty of rare meat. It was probably initially because of our impatience, but just waving a great slab of meat, which was impaled upon a green stick, over a fire for even a minute or so produced a succulent feast. Subsequently discussing this with a Kiwi butcher cousin-in-law Charlie, he told me it wasn't freshness that was giving this tenderness ... it was the opposite and our legislation in NZ precludes butchers hanging meat for as long as the Argentines allow. Whatever ... the steaks in Argentina are lip-smackingly tender and flavoursome.

One Saturday Lawrie and I decide that we should go out to the local rugby club and see if we could get a game. Roly tagged along as we more or less are the Three Musketeers. We convinced ourselves that even if we don't get a game, they will shower us with beers and hospitality. Argentina had only recently been accepted into the fold of first tier rugby nations and a second-string All Black team had toured a year earlier to great and popular fan-fare. (In 1976 the main All Blacks toured South Africa, so a young side went to Argentina). I remembered the wonderful welcoming in 1972 when us young Kiwis had fronted up to Centaurs in London. Kiwis are seen as coming from the home of rugby and we always seem to be graciously met abroad by the cognoscenti. The club was a long way from our hotel and now we didn't have wheels, it meant a tiresome walk. As we walked we built up our expectations more and more. As with most dreams … the bigger and brighter … the more likely they are to come tumbling down around you. So it was with our rugby club fantasy. It turned out that all teams were playing an away fixture and there was no one at the club to treat us at all. The walk home seemed even longer and harder as we didn't have anything to anticipate.

We'd run a very lucky race, with on balance, way more good experiences than bad ones. Our reflections have always seen us as revelling in how good it has been, what an amazing adventure. Interestingly this is in complete contrast to the two young Kiwis I had met in London who'd dropped off in Panama and ridden north to the US before getting to the UK. Of course, I was excited to meet them and asked them how was it … expecting an effusive response … one that would reinforce my plans. No, it turns out they had had a shit time, primarily because they felt they could never leave the bike … so one was always on guard while they took turns to see the market or whatever. They were newbies who had never travelled prior to attempting this pretty hard and ambitious undertaking. The ride had worn them down and turned it into a gruelling nightmare. In contrast, whenever we rumbled into a town, we looked for the street-vendor selling bananas etc and bought something from him and asked him to look after the bikes. Or sometimes, we'd spot the street-kids running to engage, and we'd pick out the leader and ask him to be 'the man' for us. Always worked a treat and the only things we have lost have been minor and quite trivial … although Steph didn't think losing her bikini bottom was a minor matter. We said she could do without, but she showed a complete lack of enthusiasm for our suggestion.

One morning we are walking towards the centre of town after our usual coffee and pastry. We were going to the bank to get some money as we were out of cash. Suddenly a police car stops and we are bundled into it. It wasn't too aggressive but there was no real enquiry about who we were, or what we were doing … or even where we were going. Could we have refused … probably not as they were the ones with the guns … besides we hadn't done anything wrong … everything would come out right in the end. We were only too aware that Argentina had reasonably recently over-thrown the Peronists and was now a military dictatorship aligned with the suppressionist ones of Paraguay and Chile. Whispers were abounding of the large numbers of people disappearing under Pinochet in Chile. But we've been enjoying our time in BA, so don't take an alarmist view of the potential for things to go wrong for us. It was a little concerning to find that on the floor with us in the back were hand grenades and seriously big guns … almost rocket-launcher-sized stuff. It was odd that we were in the back with this arsenal … couldn't we pick something up and threaten them? Maybe in the movies, but we sure-as-hell weren't going to start WW3 in the back of a locally-assembled Ford Falcon with stuff we didn't know how to use. So we ended up in a police station of a sort. We weren't thrown in a cell with bars or anything as dramatic as that. We were just 'detained'. We'd had to give out the name and address of where we were staying and that didn't concern us at all … but we were still very confused as to why they had kept us. Initially, we'd been grabbed because we looked disreputable. Our scraggy old clothes, even after a wash, made us stand out as looking like homeless hobos.

A few hours passed by and then there was great excitement. It was seemingly clear to them, that somehow we were CIA. Now that really confused the hell out of us, but they had to hand, Lawrie's US Treasury Sheriff's badge … and the hand-drawn map of Paraguayan military settlements, purportedly signed by the 'Sub-Chief of the Chaco Desert'. So they'd turned over our hotel room and thought they'd hit 'pay-dirt'. Trying to explain a 'hidden' US Sheriff's badge and a military document to people who didn't understand English and wouldn't get a translator, was a task beyond us. Of course, they couldn't work it out either … 'What the hell was the CIA doing? What were they up to … using these operatives … one with an Australian passport and two with British ones, who say they are from NZ … and they all claim to speak no Spanish? … and what is the map for? The Chaco? They've already had a war over that, and there weren't any minerals.'

Of course, as the day stretched into the night we were as hungry as back in the bad old days. There was never any thought that they might feed us. Maybe they thought hunger would see us confess. There was never any physical threat ... maybe that was still to come. Sometime after midnight they got bored with the whole puzzle and kicked us out. This still left us ravenous with all the banks shut, and a long walk back to the done-over hotel room. We supposed the manager wouldn't be very impressed by the Police raid.

The BA stay was mainly sheer-luxury. We were indoors at night and ate sophisticatedly when hungry. With not a lot to do and with an abundance of English-language movies on offer ... that is where we went almost every night. We'd not ever been to a city as classy, although Lawrie reckoned New York would run it close. Possibly he was just big-noting as neither Roly or I had been there. Ultimately we found what we wanted. The girls were crated-up and dispatched to the rugby club, and Roly and Lawrie were booked on a freighter to Genoa in Italy. I was to wait behind until some more money arrived from home, and I would fly back to London and Steph's welcoming arms. I would then borrow a vehicle somehow and meet them in Genoa.

One quirky thing about BA was their approach to parking in the central city areas. The CPD is flat and it seems that the accepted practice is to park up against the car in front of you and leave your hand-brake off. No gaps are left between the cars and sometimes we'd be walking along a foot-path when we'd notice driverless cars being inched along, pushed by a 'parker' six or seven cars away. We couldn't really work out how this would be managed, because surely sometimes the line of cars would push the front one out into the road ... or maybe the front car has its hand-brake on. That has a certain logic to it. It also seems to rely upon cars all having bumper bars at the same height ... and of course cars having said item. At the time, they did.

And so it was that I found myself on the docks at the port of Buenos Aires emotionally farewelling those who had been loyally and uncomplainingly at my side for all those months, through thick and some very thin (when throwing out the tape measure in the Chaco, I saw I was a svelte 28" around the middle). I was filled with a little trepidation when I realised I was waving down to them on the ship. When I had left from Auckland ... and even from Tilbury ... we waved down to those on the docks. I wished them Godspeed and watched them motor off into the distance. She looked a small vessel to be going off to battle both the Southern and Northern Atlantic Oceans.

Within a few days, I was boarding a British Airways flight to the UK. It was my first big International flight. I'd flown on a small propeller plane in New Zealand and I had done a charter to Italy and a flight to the Channel Isles on a rugby trip, but nothing like this. My inexperience showed up. There were only 9 passengers on this enormous plane. There were almost as many crew, but I lacked the confidence to speak to anyone … or do anything. I sat there like a pudding for the 15 or 16-hour flight. Probably we refuelled in Rio … I can't remember. I didn't know the protocols but toughed it out telling myself it was way easier than lots of what I had been through in the last year … and I was going to soon be with my Stephy, so didn't need to have discourse with the professionally-friendly 'hosties'. The adventure was nearly over. What a ride!

Here I am, safely returned over those peaks from a journey far more beautiful and strange than anything I hoped for or imagined. How is it that this safe return brings such regret?

PETER MATTHIESSEN (1927-2014)

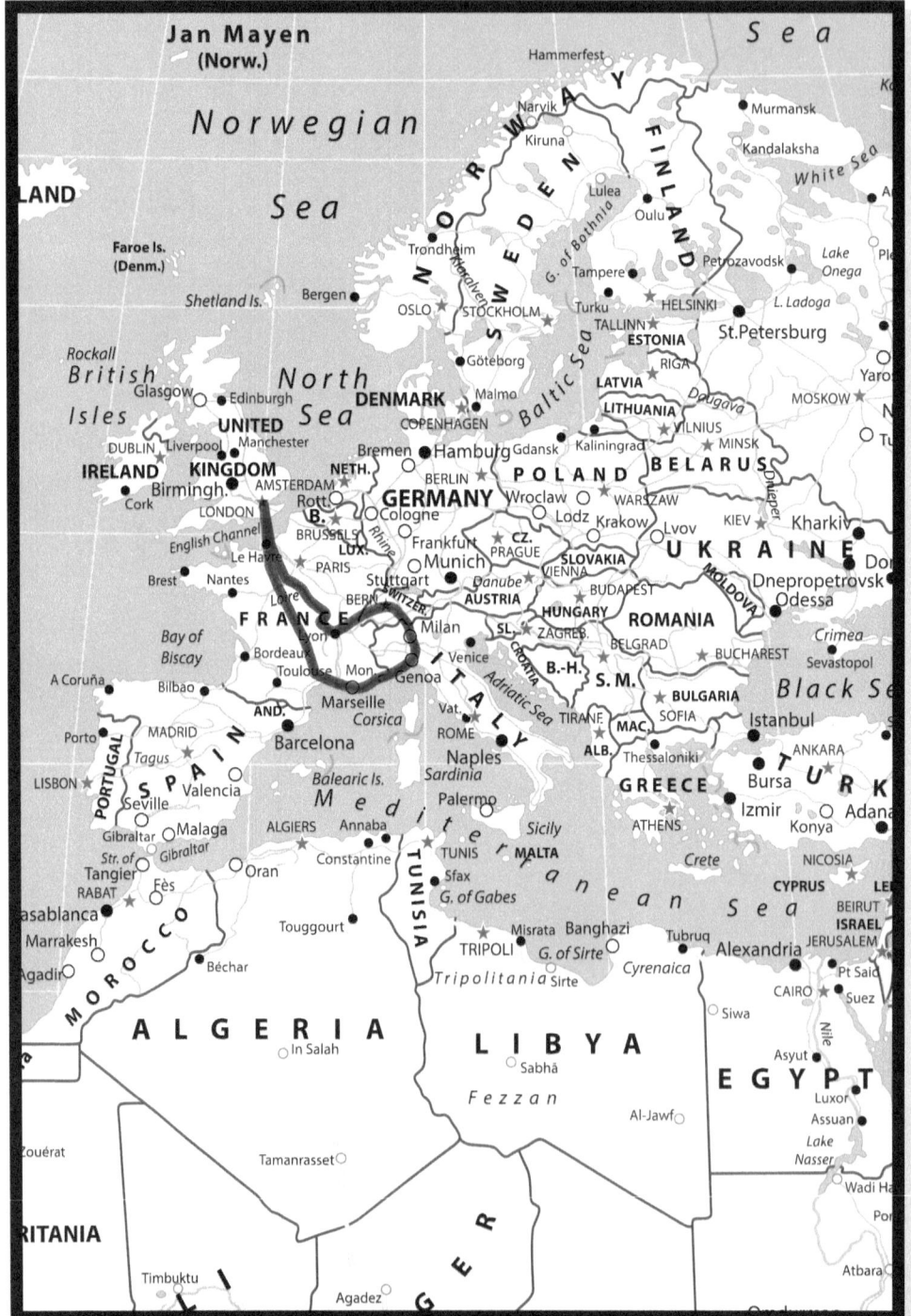

CHAPTER 13

OPERATION RESCUE

It is a bloody long haul from Buenos Aires to London and I arrived shattered. Steph was there to greet me, looking radiantly clean and pampered. Our greetings are enthusiastic, our hugs crushing and we talk over each other in the urgency of wanting to tell the tales of the last two and a half months. Our excitement slowly subsides and it is time to go back to the sumptuous and spacious love-nest she has ready. No more will we share a tiny tent with the boys. The contrast could not be more graphic. The Saudis have left for home and Steph can stay in their rented accommodation until the end of the month when the lease runs out. This is in Knightsbridge, the poshest of all London's suburbs. To say I am excited is the understatement of the month. We have four days of un-interrupted luxury ahead. I am ravenous for some opulence and whatever else is on offer.

But first, we need to get there. There is a delightful old New Zealand pioneers' recipe for Weka Pie which starts with the immortal line 'First find your weka'. Well on 27th September 1977 the first line to our 'pending delight' was 'First find your car!' Steph is not a big one for cars and in her heightened state of delirious anticipation, she has not taken note of which car park building she has parked in, nor the level on which the car was left. Adding to the slight problem was the fact that she couldn't tell me the make, model or colour of the car. "It's Mo's new one!" was all she could tell me ... so the Triumph Toledo was no more and this could be anything ... parked anywhere. The key gave no clue and those days, way before beeping car-locating devices, the task ahead of us was gargantuan. I did what any sleep-deprived person would do, I went back into the terminal and lay down to sleep while Steph went off with an enthusiastic young boy. It was his first day of work and he found this to be very exciting and he took on the task with relish. Probably the spotty youth was just happy to be in tow with an attractive grown-up woman who had been positively pulsating with happiness. Ultimately after several hours, they do return with good news and wake me.

I've told this tale many times over the last 40 years, possibly exaggerating the level of Steph's blind thrall and the number and height of the carpark buildings. I was sure there were five buildings and they were seven storeys high … or were there seven buildings, five storeys … well, you know what I mean … Heathrow is huge!!! One of the largest airports in the world! I've cautioned myself (and others) over the years not to be too adamant when relying on your memory. The fact-checking for this yarn, saw me fishing out the old British Passport and there clearly stamped is the approval for me to enter the UK courtesy of Immigration Officer (45) at … Gatwick! I am still amazed that British Airways flew from BA into London's second airport … it is not even really near London.

It was ten months to the day since Roly and I boarded the Stefan Batory. I'd seen myself in a lift mirror in Buenos Aires and even I'd been a bit startled. My beard was enormous and my hair hadn't been cut since Belize, so was a bit rampant as well. My old army-surplus combat trousers had seen us through some tough and rugged times but it was truly time to let them go … into an incinerator. Re-united with the car, we eagerly made our way to Knightsbridge where the Saudis' apartment waited. Steph acknowledged the doorman with a smile and a familiar greeting. I sensed him stiffen slightly. It didn't take a clairvoyant to know what he was thinking. This was a seriously-posh apartment he was 'guarding'. Of course, he was familiar with Steph, she had been staying there with the Sheik's entourage for 10 weeks … but she was 'the help' even if she was chatty and nice … and from the colonies. He didn't quite sniff at my entry … he just oozed disapproval.

The apartment wasn't huge, although there was room for the Sheik and his wife, their three children, a nanny, a cook, Steph and a maid. It was of course in my eyes … sumptuous. Steph was very keen that we just perched in one small area, as it was all very clean … and I could not be trusted to not impart some of my natural grime. I had never been in surroundings like this before and was astonished to find that there were three toilets, one of which deserves further description. Unbelievably, one of the 'thrones' was an actual throne. It was in a full-size bathroom and sat on a raised dais or plinth. It had a rattan back and 'arms' on each side. It really was a regal-looking throne. Despite Steph's concerns, I couldn't resist being 'Royalty' for 15 minutes. The first focus was getting me clean, tidy and presentable. To this end, I was scrubbed and trimmed, outfitted in new clothes enabling me to meet the critical eye of the doorman with a nod. I also went off to the Hospital of Tropical Diseases. The mosquito bites I had received in Paraguay had taken on a life of their own and at Steph's insistence, I sought professional advice and help. They were quite interested (and impressed!) with my lesions and ultimately some pills and unguents were prescribed. This was a bit of a relief as I had a few small concerns that I would be impounded and put in quarantine somewhere.

Being in Knightsbridge was such a contrast from our recent lives and I loved exploring posh suburbia as well as the 'High' street. I explored neighbouring Mayfair and Belgravia, often looking in at the long-established Sothebys (1764) and marvelling at their wondrous items coming up for auction. Steph had taken a live-in barmaid's job at a hotel quite close to the apartment. It had been her local when she was Faisal's charge. She showed me the rubber tyre marks on a white block wall where she had turned Faisal's buggy a bit early for the corner. She was running back from a quick illicit lunch-time tipple … and perhaps this had impaired her judgement a little. Of course, our four days of being 'toffs' in a Knightsbridge apartment went all too quickly, but what a time was had. The words indulgent frolic spring to mind.

It was an interesting time as now I was committed to going home after six years and was excited about it. In my time in London, I had seen many friends off home and had never once been envious. I was always quietly 'superior' in the knowledge that they were going too soon … there was still fun to be had, places to explore, adventures to be embarked upon. Finally, I was ready, my time was up and I was welcoming the thoughts of re-establishing contact with my mates, firing up the old BSA which still remained in the garage and hopefully showing Steph some of the South Island. To this end I did the rounds of travel agents, looking for the cheap score home. It was just at the end of the £10 Pom immigration schemes for Aussie and NZ. It was always a bone-of-contention among the impoverished expat ANZAC community in London that we often couldn't afford to go home, yet our respective governments were funding Brits to go in our place. I knew Roly was also pretty keen to get back, as his mates had moved on to, and in a letter home he'd said how much he was looking forward to seeing the brass numbers of 83 Stanley St and smelling mum's wonderful cooking as he walked in the door.

Soon I had odd-jobs with friends and of course, was having to answer the invariable "How was the trip?" questions. What to say? Do I just glibly say it was great ... or do I pin them to the spot with a blow-by-blow account? Usually, it was more the former than the latter. It just seemed too hard to give a reasonable recollection. Some people were truly interested but most people were just paying lip-service. When I would duly ask what they'd been up to, it would invariably be "Not much, been to a few parties ... but not much really." It was like they were treading water with their lives and mainly they were happy with that. So few could understand what we'd seen in the ten months, or even understand why we'd put ourselves through the difficulties that we did for the results attained. I am sure most thought that a subscription to National Geographic magazine would have been a better use of our money.

'Operation Rescue' had to be planned. I'd promised the boys that I would be there in Genoa, on the wharf waiting. Their fare was all-inclusive so only the bare minimum of funds went with them. They were expected on Wednesday 12th October. Rather than borrow a car we bought a Morris Minor 1000 for £65 and named her Minerva. She was splendid and sped up my journeys all over London. I was now back at Mo's place in Twickenham and Steph was mainly in residence at the pub in Knightsbridge. I figured on driving non-stop across France and through the night so I would be in Genoa in not much more than 24hrs. So I went out through Dover on the 11th on a hovercraft. I had a few deadlines I didn't want to miss ... Steph was turning 25 on the 18th Oct which was the Tuesday after the pick-up, and I had told the rugby club to select both Lawrie and I for a game on 22nd Oct. It was interesting that in those days of English rugby, they did not allow substitutions, not even to replace injured players. What this led to, was that once the team was selected, none of the non-selected team ever turned up. It was therefore very important to be back by the 22nd or the team would be short. Of course, this should be no sweat. I also understood Steph's 25th to also be a milestone I should at all costs attend, and this also shouldn't be a stretch either.

Minerva, our mighty Morris Minor and I droned across France, avoiding the toll roads. I had a map and I was filled with excitement. I was keen to find out how

Minerva the mighty Morrie Minor

the boys had got on since leaving BA. Of course, it got dark and we still droned on relentlessly ... it's what Morrie's do ... they drone. I had confidence in my stamina ... I'd done longer and harder. It wasn't much more than 1,200 kms if I short-cutted under the Alps. The road was taking me through darkened villages and sometimes a bright sign would jump out to tell me I was speeding, which of course could only happen in the urban areas. The first time it happened I nearly crashed in surprise. Sometime in the night, I realised that my resilience was ebbing, I was starting to nod off, even with the window wide open and me trying to sing my way along. Fortunately, I found an all-night service centre to refuel, top up on coffee and get a big stash of sweets. Chewing on some caramels seems to awaken me and focus my attention. I read somewhere that chewing does keep you awake due to something in the production of the additional saliva. So onward through the night we continued and by dawn, we were through the Mt Blanc Tunnel and in Italy. It was less than 300 kms to Genoa and I reckoned on 4hrs ... and I'd be peering out into 'The Med', scanning the horizon for the boys' vessel.

Mid-morning Genoa brought the first disappointment of 'Operation Rescue'. I could see many freighters in the proximity of the port. Which was the boys'?

NO ONE SAID IT WOULD BE EASY

"No, non è qui, vai a Savona!"

OK, so I will go to Savona, it could be on the way home. Apparently, the ship is running a bit late and will dock in Savona first. The coastal drive back towards France along the Italian Riviera is stunningly picturesque but very stop-start and tiny sea-side villages and resort towns are passed through. Above I can see an autostrada with cars speeding along, ducking in and out of tunnels, travelling at speeds I can only dream of ... but I know that they are tolled and I have to ration my money, as I don't expect Roly and Lawrie to come ashore with much if any left. After a struggle, I find the port authorities in Savona.

"No, non è qui, vai a Imperia!"

So where the bloody hell is Imperia and more importantly where are the boys and their toy-boat?

Sadly, there was no Thursday pick-up in Imperia and Friday's news made no sense to me. The shipping agent I was now dealing with was also saying no to today and no to tomorrow. Oh dear! On Saturday I get further bad news, the ship is partially disabled and making very pedestrian progress.

"Eet will be seex more giorni!" A handful of fingers ... plus one, goes up.

"SIX MORE DAYS! THAT IS NOT POSSIBLE! I MUST BE BACK IN LONDON ON 18th."

Shit, if the ship doesn't come in until the 21st, I will have missed Steph's birthday and will be touch and go for rugby ... and I will be out of money! This is a Triple-whammy. Not even my legendary loose planning doesn't usually turn up The Perfect Storm.

I send a postcard home to mum and dad, noting all these disappointments, but also with the slightly belated news that I have found the fares home to be £50 cheaper if booked in London rather than in New Zealand. Mum and dad have come through with funding to get us back to New Zealand. Our family background is one of humble working-class strugglers. There has never been a spare penny and we grow up knowing that you pay your own way. When as kids we reached the age of being able to do a paper-run, we all have them. We are about 9 or 10 when this happens. For years the going rate was 11/6 (11 shillings and sixpence) per week. Of that mum took 6/6 (six shillings and sixpence) as board and we got to keep 5 shillings ... and any tips. Similarly, when we finally morphed into working as semi-adults, we always paid more 'board' than our peers. Never was a penny borrowed. There were no hand-outs, there was no spare money. Now that dad has retired he has seen the fruits of his decades of contributing to the Hospital Board's superannuation scheme. Added to their pensions, and the end of paying off the mortgage, suddenly they are able to show the largesse that they couldn't in years gone by. They've loved our travels and never have I been under pressure to come home. For six years they have been content to share my life through letters. I have been thrilled though to have several of my returning friends to make themselves known and some of them have even been short-term boarders.

I couldn't tell Steph I wouldn't be making it back for her birthday and I felt very frustrated about that. In an ideal world, I would have rung her or sent a telegraph … but my world isn't always one which enables these things to happen. Sometimes situations seem to conspire against me. Meanwhile, I found a camp and settled in for the six-day wait. Luck had it that I fetched up next to an older Italian couple who didn't really have any English but they wanted to share red wine with me every day. My resistance was low and I would accept their generosity with a bow. In the evenings I would go with the gentleman to outside a flash casino on the hill above the town. There my new friend would get out his chalks and do some pavement art. I've seen pavement art in London, and it can be fabulous. Unfortunately, my mate seemed to be talentless … or so avant-garde that mere mortals could not appreciate it. We would stay till the wee hours, and get a few generous punters on their way out. It wasn't lucrative, but his work wasn't inspiring either. Great, generous people though, who I would have been lost without. They shared their meals and they shared their plonk. We shared many laughs … a commonality of language was never needed.

Steph's birthday passed and I felt contrite but helpless.

Finally, on Friday 21st Oct, the boys arrived. They were penniless but well-fed. Roly had put on weight and for the first time in his life had a covering of flesh on his bones. It suited him. The Italian food had been plentiful. We had to get underway immediately and I was happy to drive while they talked. It seemed that at some stage in the voyage they had to heave-to and do a major engine repair. Something had failed, so a complete, piston and con-rod had to be removed. Subsequent to that they were only creeping along at a few knots per hour.

The wee grey Morrie was soon speeding (as much as a Morris Minor can speed) her way across the Riviera with the boys chattering away, telling me all about their voyage and the short stop in the Canary Islands. In turn, I got them up to date with all the London news. Lawrie was thrilled that we'd be straight onto the field at Hounslow when we got back. There was very little money left, so food was put on the back-burner ... we'd concentrate on our petrol needs. I tell Roly about the news that we'll fly home as soon as it suits. Flights into NZ are twice a week and all go through Auckland. Coming through Auckland will give me the occasion to meet Steph's mum and dad. This'll be a biggie, as it is known that they'd always hoped she would fall in love and marry a local boy from their church. When she spilt the beans that she was going off with a man on the back of a motorbike ... to South America, there had been considerable consternation. Steph's mum had asked for a photo of 'the man' who seemed to have turned her daughter's head. After receiving it, her comment back was 'he looks like he has fine eyebrows'. I wonder if they know I am in for the long-haul ... will I do better in the flesh?

We follow the Mediterranean coast until we hit Marseilles and then we go straight up the middle of France. It doesn't quite look like the shortest way, but it looks the easiest and probably the quickest. Maybe we should have wiggled our way up through the hills closer to Grenoble, but we were happy thrumming along with Minerva well wound up at 55 mph (90 kph). Somewhere, fairly early in our northwards leg after a refuelling, calculations are done and the answer tells us that it looks like we don't have enough money for the required petrol to get home ... almost, but not quite. The long-division is checked and another strategy adopted. We amend our cruising speed to 45 mph (72 kph) and fret for the whole tank-load. Now it looks like we may be in danger of not getting to Calais early enough to meet the hovercraft we want first thing on Saturday morning. 200 miles (320kms) later, we check our calculations with another tank of petrol. Our slower speed has upped the economy enough that we now reckon there is enough money left to get us home. The fill-up confirms this and we're a much happier little crew. All we now have to worry about is getting there on time.

Day turns into night and we drone on at our now-modest speed. It is still a road-trip though, and lots of jollity is present. It is another 'Boys' Own' adventure. Our lack of eating is just another minor price to pay ... and not a Morris one! The earnest little 948cc engine keeps up its relentless drone right up the length of France and before dawn, we are in Calais. 1,300 kms had been drop-kicked into touch in way less than 24 hours in a tiny little Morrie ... Minerva the Magnificent. I was pretty spent as I had done all the driving but a quick snooze on the hovercraft restored the energy levels enough for the final push of 'Operation Rescue'. Ramsgate to Knightsbridge is about 100 miles, but they drag by, partly because they are miles not kilometres ... we love kilometres, they snick by so regularly. The journey is also long because we are now very hungry and I must admit to a little trepidation. Deep down I am sure Steph will be thrilled to see me ... but I did let her down ... I had promised her I would be back for her birthday.

Steph's face lights up from behind the bar when we come in. She can't help but be pleased to see us all safe and sound. She is less than happy when I ask can she lend us £20 and arrange some food ... Lawrie and I need to scoff and go!

I feel bad, even writing that last sentence, but all is well that ends well. Forty years, four kids, and five grandkids later she still shares the secrets of my soul, she still stands beside me and still keeps me from the cold. She is the hero of the story. I salute her with all my heart.

Blashers

Des and Lawrie make it onto the Rugby Field

Everything will be alright in the end so if it is not alright it is not the end.

DEBORAH MOGGACH (1948 -)

THE CAST

DES MOLLOY

Dreamer and schemer … my adventures sometimes fall short of the euphoric anticipation envisaged, but not this one. Every day was a challenge and every day an excitement. A real *Boys' Own* outing with the best of mates. The challenge of writing this account was another experience I came to relish. Each morning I would run to my writing cave and revel in the recollections, almost delirious with the enjoyment of bringing it back to the frontal lobe.

STEPH MOLLOY

It was the best of trips and the worst of trips. It seemed like a good idea at the time. I liked being on motorbikes, I had not been to Central and South America and I liked Des ... so why not? The route was filled with stunning geographical features and riding through them on the back of a bike must be the best way of experiencing them.

Even today whenever anyone talks about the Americas, I can still access the vistas and the views from my memory banks ... and almost smell them. As I did not have to concentrate on riding ... just staying on the back ... I could see in front, either side, and could even twist around to have another look at what we were passing through. I always felt incredibly privileged to be traversing our beautiful planet and sometimes being part of the indigenous people's days.

There were the times when I wondered how we could ever survive the heat, cold, lack of food, dirty clothes, dirty hair etc., and wished myself anywhere other than on the back of Penelope, whom I often felt more affection for, than towards Des ... and then we would sweep, or creep around another corner, and there would be another delicious mountain, lake, village, alpaca/lama, and if populated, there'd be loveable babies and infants whose smiles and fat waving hands were to die for.

ROLY MOLLOY

So Des finally deciding to air this tale to the wider audience has opened a Pandora's box of memories for me (not in a negative way). I am faced with somewhat of a task to portray what I have taken from the whole experience. I admit to some emotions being stirred by this.

A few enduring memories have surfaced from that time in London relating to our motorcycling venture. My first ride out on Bessie the 1937 500cc BSA Empire Star looms large in those. What an absolute delight that bike was/still is. I remember being aware of the girder front fork with the huge, big, proud Lucas 8-inch headlamp plunging up and down in the forefront of my vision, and the machine's very willing performance (in contrast to the heavier later models I was used to). I recall a ride to a nearby village green and back, and just parking up at that green, standing back and admiring a freshly rebuilt machine … and just saying 'wow' to myself.

Our time in the Chaco Desert is for me the biggest of the trip highlights. So difficult, and yet liberating for me, as I endured that time very well. When the going became really tough, I found a sort of inner strength, surprising for me at the time. Probably so close to complete exhaustion and ultimate collapse as I am hopefully ever going to experience. I will never forget that feeling of rolling into Asuncion, Paraguay, feeling ten feet tall … disheveled to hell, but not caring, and being proud … oh so, so proud.

LAWRIE SALTER

Des and I had been mates in London in the early/mid-seventies. Little did I know that when he tracked me down in America a year or so later I would be embarking on the greatest adventure of my life.

Des had three motorcycles shipped to New Orleans for what he described to me as a bit of a bike ride. He had conceived of and planned the journey, albeit none too meticulously, and then put his plan into action. "Blashers" was our leader and rightly so.

Steph joined us in Mexico and rode gamely with us to La Paz. She was good company, never complained and a dab hand at one pot specials.

Roly was Des's brother, fairly quiet but when the going got hard he was as tough as old boots. He could also take a bike apart and put it back together, sitting in the dust on the side of some dirt track, armed with little more than a shifter spanner and a screwdriver. It was through his skill and determination that we got as far as we did. Fuck knows why I was there.

For nearly a year we endured hardship that only the young and foolish could endure, saw many wonderful places and discovered the real meaning of camaraderie. We were also the recipients of great generosity and human kindness, often from people not best placed to be so kind. It was a privilege to be along for the ride.

PENELOPE

After an extensive rest, Penelope arose again, was fettled and successfully carried me (Des) across from Beijing to Arnhem in 2005 in an epic adventure titled The Last Hurrah. This ride spawned a book and a DVD of the same name. Since 2016 she has been chunking her way around Australia in a ride called The Big Sit. As of August 2019 she is 22,500kms in and resting in McLaren Flat, South Australia awaiting my return to continue on with that saga. We've done the full lap and 'down and up the middle'. There is still Tasmania to do.

SAMANTHA

In 1978 Samantha was gifted to Dick Huurdeman (Last Hurrah co-adventurer) in return for him funding the repatriation of the three bikes from the UK to NZ. Subsequently she was on-sold then later re-sold back to Roly. Currently she resides in many pieces in Roly's garage beneath his house.

BESSIE

In some ways Bessie has been the most active of the girls, in that she was quite quickly returned to service, and has been thumping her way up and down NZ for the last 40 years. Many a wonderful adventure has been had, often with Steph perched on the small pillion pad. There are not many parts of NZ she has not seen. She has many admirers as she shows every scar and scape of her many adventures. Patina is gold in my eyes.

THE CAST

www.ingramcontent.com/pod-product-compliance
Lightning Source LLC
Chambersburg PA
CBHW021058080526
44587CB00010B/298